"In a world where 'distributed' is the new watchword, this book fits the bill. It examines mobile-based distributed education in a wide variety of settings, ranging from the polar, temporal, and tropical regions as well as among people who are itinerant or homeless. Further, there is the analysis of the spectrum of learning situations, including disadvantaged learners, learners in traditional cultures, and adult learners. We owe the authors a debt of gratitude for this broad and comprehensive canvas."

—**Rich Ling**, Shaw Foundation Professor of Media Technology in the Wee Kim Wee School of Communication and Information at Nanyang Technological University, Singapore

"Helen Crompton and John Traxler are to be congratulated for bringing together such an unusual and interesting collection of essays around the use of mobile digital technologies for learning in some of the world's most marginalised and fragile contexts. This is not the normal eulogistic account of 'mobile learning,' but rather a volume of thoughtful contributions from diverse parts of the world that seek to challenge and fragment existing understandings. Their conclusions outline an agenda for the future use of mobile technologies in learning that is more nuanced and problematised, intent on empowering some of the world's most marginalised people and communities."

—**Tim Unwin**, UNESCO Chair in ICT4D and Emeritus Professor of Geography at Royal Holloway, University of London, UK

"This is a powerful, impressive, and challenging book. Whilst most discussion of digital, and particularly mobile, technology starts from either an exploration of the possibilities and challenges raised by the technology or by thinking about the educator's task in designing learning programmes using digital tools, the huge strength of these essays is that they start with learners' cultures, needs, and experiences. As a result, the examples offered of work with Indigenous people in Alaska, Wolof women in Senegal, refugees arriving in England, and people both materially and digitally marginalised in the Global North offer fresh insights and critical challenges to educators.

How can media which are overwhelmingly dominated by English and the languages of the Global North be adapted effectively so that speakers of languages marginal in their own countries can use them successfully? How effectively can material and learning programmes be co-created with people using mobile technology when access to wi-fi infrastructure is so uneven? How far can education strategies for critical engagement with on-line information and disinformation be adapted for very different cultural circumstances? What works in one context may not transfer to another – but the role of listening as a springboard to dialogue is common to the different experiences captured.

This collection will stimulate readers to think hard about how to most effectively use technology with and on behalf of disadvantaged and marginalised communities to enable them to engage on their own terms and for their own purposes."

—**Sir Alan Tuckett**, OBE, Professor of Education at the University of Wolverhampton, UK

CRITICAL MOBILE PEDAGOGY

Critical Mobile Pedagogy is an exploration of mobile technologies for designing and delivering equitable and empowering education around the globe. Synthesizing a diverse range of projects and conceptual frameworks, this case-based collection addresses the ambitions, assumptions, and impacts of interventions in under-researched, often disadvantaged communities.

The editors and authors provide a nuanced and culturally responsive approach to showcasing:

- indigenous, nomadic, refugee, rural, and other marginalized communities
- emerging pedagogies such as curation, open resources, massive open online courses (MOOCs), and self-directed learning
- contextual factors, including pedagogy, ethics, scaling, research methodology and culture, and consequences of innocuous or harmful implementation and deployment
- the nature of participation by global capital, multinationals, education systems, international agencies, national governments, and telecoms companies.

Scholars, academics, policymakers, and program managers are increasingly using mobile technologies to support disadvantaged or disempowered communities in learning more effectively and appropriately. This book's diverse research precedents will help these and other stakeholders meet the challenges and opportunities of our complex, increasingly connected world and work with greater cultural and ethical sensitivity at the intersection of education, research, and technology.

John Traxler is Professor of Digital Learning in the Education Observatory at the University of Wolverhampton, UK. He has been invited to establish a UNESCO Chair in Innovative Informal Digital Learning in Disadvantaged and Development Contexts.

Helen Crompton is Associate Professor of Instructional Technology in the Department of Teaching and Learning at Old Dominion University in Norfolk, Virginia, USA. She is part of the UNESCO Chair in Innovative Informal Digital Learning in Disadvantaged and Development Contexts.

CRITICAL MOBILE PEDAGOGY

Cases of Digital Technologies and Learners at the Margins

Edited by John Traxler and Helen Crompton

NEW YORK AND LONDON

First published 2021
by Routledge
52 Vanderbilt Avenue, New York, NY 10017

and by Routledge
2 Park Square, Milton Park, Abingdon, Oxon OX14 4RN

Routledge is an imprint of the Taylor & Francis Group, an informa business

© 2021 Taylor & Francis

The right of John Traxler and Helen Crompton to be identified as the authors of the editorial material, and of the authors for their individual chapters, has been asserted in accordance with sections 77 and 78 of the Copyright, Designs and Patents Act 1988.

All rights reserved. No part of this book may be reprinted or reproduced or utilised in any form or by any electronic, mechanical, or other means, now known or hereafter invented, including photocopying and recording, or in any information storage or retrieval system, without permission in writing from the publishers.

Trademark notice: Product or corporate names may be trademarks or registered trademarks, and are used only for identification and explanation without intent to infringe.

Library of Congress Cataloging-in-Publication Data
A catalog record for this title has been requested

ISBN: 978-0-367-20455-6 (hbk)
ISBN: 978-0-367-20457-0 (pbk)
ISBN: 978-0-429-26157-2 (ebk)

Typeset in Bembo
by Taylor & Francis Books

CONTENTS

Introduction 1
John Traxler and Helen Crompton

1 The Ju|'hoan of Nyae Nyae: A Case of Exclusion and Ka Jan 11
 Candi Miller

2 Combining Robust Technology and Gamified Learning to Democratize Access to Growth Mindset 22
 Aape Pohjavirta, Miemo Penttinen and Saila Kokkonen

3 Our Town: Towards Creative Mobile Learning in Community Focused Place-Based Education 39
 Angela Gerrard

4 Digital Inequities in Rural Alaska 50
 Jonathan T. Bartels and Matthew Bennice

5 Mobile Device Literacy: Status and Needs of Women in Senegal 63
 Christelle Scharff

6 Supported Mobile Learning in the "Third Spaces" Between Non-Formal and Formal Education for Displaced People 76
 Gabi Witthaus and Gill Ryan

viii Contents

7 Towards Participatory MOOCs 89
 Amit Pariyar, Narayanan Kulathuramaiyer and Poline Bala

8 Mobile Information Literacy and Public Access in the Era of Post-Truth: Reflections from Community Curricular Experiences in Latin America 110
 Sara Vannini and Isabella Rega

9 Awakening Sleeping Languages in Saskatchewan with Culturally Appropriate Curricula and Technology 123
 Cheryle Herman, Belinda Daniels, Kevin Lewis and Marguerite Koole

10 Empathy-Driven Mobile App Development (MAD) without Coding: A Case of Citizen Developers 136
 Dick Ng'ambi

11 Technology-Enhanced Higher Education for Refugees 151
 Meaghan Brugha, David Hollow and Catherine Gladwell

12 Disadvantaged Learners and the Digital Contractor: A Critical Perspective on Mobile Learning in the Global South with Reference to Paolo Freire 162
 Stephen Haggard

13 Mobile Learning Project Reports: A Contractor Delivery Review of Three Services for Disadvantaged and Marginalised Global South Learners 174
 Elena Deleyto La Cruz

14 Post-Critical Mobile Pedagogy in Aboriginal and Torres Strait Islander Contexts 186
 Greg Williams and Ruth Wallace

15 Mobile Assisted Third Space (MATS) in the Margins: A Tool for Social Justice and Democracy 197
 Rebecca Kelly

Conclusion: Breaking Hegemonic Structures and Conventions in Looking Towards a Critical Mobile Pedagogy 212
John Traxler and Helen Crompton

List of Contributors 227

Index 232

INTRODUCTION

John Traxler and Helen Crompton

Welcome

Welcome to our latest book. This book was led with vision and a purpose that was captured in the original book proposal we sent to invited authors. We moved beyond traditional approaches, formats, and voices around educational technology, mobile or otherwise, beyond the case-studies of successful and subsidised small-scale innovations. We wanted to open up to more critical accounts at the intersections of digital technologies and to people often marginalised culturally, linguistically, educationally, ethnically or economically. These people on the margins might include gypsies, circus folk and travellers; native, nomadic, indigenous and marginal communities; people with physiological or cognitive difficulties; women and girls in traditional or conservative cultures; adult literacy learners and non-traditional students entering higher education; refugees, displaced persons and the homeless; people in townships and informal settlements or in rural and subsistence communities. We felt that these populations were largely under-researched, under-documented and un-heard groups. The intention was specifically to question any assumptions that programmes and projects based on education and technology were always unconditionally benign or even necessarily neutral; to get beyond whether they *do no harm* and have nevertheless *unintended consequences* and to ask *whose interests are being served* by these projects and programmes. We hoped that policy, professional and practical directions would emerge that in future would enable learning with mobiles to contribute to authentic and meaningful well-being amongst very different and disparate communities.

The book is significant for activists, academics and researchers interested in the interactions between mobile technology enhanced learning and exclusion, disempowerment, disenfranchisement and disadvantage. However, the book is also significant for policymakers, programme managers, public officials, institutional funders, corporate social responsibility (CSR) departments and charitable foundations interested in seeing a more rigorous and nuanced account of interventions, initiatives and programmes. The book will create a bridge amongst the various research and professional bodies, both domestic and global, that work with these various communities, but who sometimes have only simplistic, generalised or perhaps naïve notions of education and learning with mobiles.

Development of an edited book is always bounded by practical concerns. We have nevertheless encouraged our authors to read widely across each other's contributions, conducted informal conversations on points of interest, and run an informal online Delphi process around key points, discussed later.

The Context and Critique

Clearly no-one creates a book if they think it does not answer a need, says nothing new and serves no purpose. In creating this book, whilst there was the motivation to create something unique and useful, there was also considerable discontent and disillusionment with what was already published; there was an implied critique. This was a critique of 'mobile learning' (quote/unquote) as it has become defined and understood, of its achievements, direction, impact, literature and history, especially in relation to disadvantaged and development contexts. It is difficult or disingenuous to avoid seeing the current book as anything other than an implicit critique of the established thinking and practices of what has come to be called 'mobile learning'. It is worthwhile outlining this critique, as it may not be universally shared and but deserves an audience. We can develop it in two ways:

- In its own terms, asking, has 'mobile learning' as a research community been intellectually and logically coherent and convincing?
- In the terms of the people and communities represented in this book, asking the question, did 'mobile learning' do them any good?

First, was 'mobile learning' coherent and convincing? Elsewhere (Traxler et al., 2019b; Traxler, 2018a, 2012) we have explored whether 'mobile learning' has run its course as a paradigm, perhaps using 'paradigm' in a less grandiose sense than the canonical version (Kuhn, 1970) and more akin to how software engineers would use it (Rajlich, 2006; Wernick & Hall, 2004, Petre, 1994). Of course, it was never an explicitly articulated paradigm as such and we have to infer its axioms, adherents, research questions and foundational texts from the evidence, both formal and informal. Nor was it ever completely coherent, consistent and homogeneous. The ongoing disputes around definitions underline this, whilst they also strive to embrace and replace all their predecessors, never however freeing themselves of their e-learning parentage or of education predicated on the work of educators (for example, Peng, Su, Chou, & Tsai, 2009). Furthermore, definitions do not happen in isolation, but rather attempt to show how a paradigm is different and distinct from its 'parents', 'siblings' and rivals, in this case from 'tethered' e-learning (Traxler, 2018c). There is also always likely to be a difference between the espoused definition and the one enacted.

We can, however, see it emerging out of the e-learning communities of the global North at the turn of the century and inheriting some of the e-learning visions, theories and personalities (Kukulska-Hulme, Sharples, Milrad, Arnedillo-Sánchez, & Vavoula, 2011). It bought into the prevailing ethos of small-scale and state-subsidised, curiosity-driven, trickle-down innovation in research-active universities in a handful of 'mobile learning' *hot-spots*, mostly western Europe, Asia Pacific and some more widely dispersed individual institutions (Boekholt, 2010). This was an understandable response to the pressures and opportunities of the time and saw 'mobile learning' seeming to deliver on the promise of 'learning anytime anywhere' that had eluded the tethered e-learning community. The 'mobile learning' community did not, however, move with the times as mobiles transitioned from being fragile, scarce, difficult, complex and expensive to being cheap, easy, robust and universal, nor did it respond to the withering of state enthusiasm and state resources as we entered the second decade of the twenty-first century. Perhaps also in a looser sense, the community did not make the transition from the web1.0 world, where the majority consumed what the minority produced, to the web2.0 world, where the majority consumed what anyone and everyone produced. Either way, the apparent benefits of 'mobile learning' did not trickle down from the global North to the global South in spite of the mobile's intrusive ubiquity in most of the communities of the South (Dunkerly-Bean, Crompton, & Moffit, 2018; Dunkerly-Bean & Crompton, 2015). It may be an over-statement but the 'mobile learning' research community seemed to stagnate, becoming inward-looking, backward-looking and self-referential, just at the time when the near-universal connectedness and mobility challenged it to look outwards and forwards and make links across the disciplines. Perhaps 'mobile learning' research was at first fortune's favourite then history's victim, surfing on the state-funded innovation paradigm but then caught by rip tides of retrenchment.

There were some inherent contradictions in the first decade of the twenty-first century and perhaps that was part of the explanation of the failure to move forward. The most trustworthy evidence came from research that used the same platform, that is the same mobile device, provided across the whole population of research subjects, that is the learners, and this eliminated the devices as a confounding variable. This was, however, the least realistic scenario, since scaling and sustaining would depend on learners using their own diverse and ever-changing platforms. The contradiction here was that the best evidence was the least useful. Another contradiction was that the positivist mindset of the researchers was progressively less useful as the post-positivist world leaked into the classroom and the lecture theatre from the outside world. So, at the risk of parody, the positivist researchers were increasingly enclosed in a post-positivist world, whilst psychological perspectives were failing to keep up with sociological realities. This change was transforming learners with no mobile experience or expectations to enough mobile experience and expectations to overwhelm the pre/post empirical setting with a dedicated app (e.g. Basoglu & Akdemir, 2010). Research with mobiles could no longer rest on the assumption that learning with mobiles was somehow disconnected from the outside world.

In the first decade of 'mobile learning', alongside the small-scale research projects, there were also larger-scale programmes using mobiles to reach some of the types of learners represented in this book. The nature of their funding meant they were less committed to rigorous evaluation or to widespread publication and they too were probably hit by the global economic downturn post-2008.

Secondly, did 'mobile learning' serve the people and communities represented in this book? This requires an examination of the political, economic, policy and structural contexts though which 'mobile learning' has operated. There are various historical accounts of the development of 'mobile learning' and they make clear the extent to which 'mobile learning' was a product of a specific historical period. We have already described the loose assumptions that 'mobile learning' could provide demonstrable learning gains and that innovation would ensure that these 'trickled down' to become established practice. These assumptions were probably most applicable to the institutions and communities that represented the mainstream of their societies.

The year 2008 marked a transition. On the one hand, the global economic downturn and shifts in government thinking in many countries led to a dramatic reduction in the public money going into 'mobile learning' innovation and research in the global North. On the other hand, global agencies and international development ministries finally noticed mobile technologies as a way to deliver their humanitarian and educational missions. This led to a shift in focus to the global South. But the pressures for scale and sustainability, on and from these agencies and ministries, reinforced traditional didactic teaching based on the school sector and on content, but largely ignored lifelong, adult or informal learning, also marginal, peripheral or indigenous communities and their languages.

We can look at 'mobile learning' from a variety of angles, for example, we could focus on its pedagogies, its content, its user interfaces, its fonts, its languages and its technologies; we can look at their impact on mother tongues, indigenous cultures and nomadic peoples; or even just those countries, communities and individuals away from the large, the norm and the mainstream, and we can then conclude that 'mobile learning' is skewed away from these countries, communities and individuals, and instead is usually skewed in favour of Anglophone American interests or perhaps the global North more generally (Dunkerly-Bean et al., 2018; Traxler, 2017).

This links to our discussion later about the epistemicidal nature and epistemic hegemony of European research publication (Bennett, 2015), of Western universities (Grosfoguel, 2013) and, by inference, to the global knowledge economy (Morley, Alexiadou, Garaz, González-Monteagudo, & Taba, 2018).

We can also look at how 'mobile learning' research is funded, how it interacts with the policymakers and how policy is formulated; how in fact policy and research feed off each other (Traxler, 2016). We see more trends that have skewed 'mobile learning' away from the marginal and the peripheral. These include the appetite for projects reported as successful case-studies with simple outcomes, for American English as the medium for publication (and its relationship to global league tables for universities), for conference presentations from researchers with travel budgets and for university systems that recognised the value of research alongside teaching.

We can also look at the demographics and bibliometrics of the published 'mobile learning' research community and these too are sometimes worrying, with authors, speakers, reviewers, editors, publishers and readers from the global South not well represented in the journals and conferences actually devoted to their own region, and their region not being thought about in the ways that they themselves think about it.

We could add the extent to which early 'mobile learning' theorising has been dominated by European names, though we should also recognise contributions from the highly sophisticated Pacific Rim (viz. Ally, 2005; Keskin & Metcalf, 2011; Sharples, Taylor, & Vavoula, 2005). This was, as we noted earlier, a consequence of the 'mobile learning' hot-spots and the funding and political environments which nurtured them. An antidote to these is the decolonising movement (Heleta, 2016; Langdon, 2013) but it is not clear whether this has yet reached a position where individual cultures and communities have explored the interaction between mobile digital technology and local and indigenous knowledge systems. This would, however, certainly be valuable because there is an argument in the case of fragile, peripheral and indigenous communities, cultures and languages, that pervasive mobile technologies and everything that comes with them represents the next decolonisation of knowledge and the next epistemicide (Traxler, 2018; Hall & Tandon, 2017; Hall, 2015).

These are not necessarily widely accepted positions and are, to some extent, expounded as a way of promoting uncertainty and debate. Hopefully, this book will contribute to that debate, but the chapter authors each have something to say independent of other chapters and publication in this book does not connote that chapter authors subscribe to this or any other overarching ideological or theoretical position.

Digital Literacy

Several of the chapters refer directly or indirectly to digital literacy and in one case to mobile digital literacy. This is an important concept because of its potential role in learning with mobiles. It has been loosely defined in terms of the skills, attitudes, knowledge and access needed to survive, prosper and flourish in an increasingly digital world (Beetham, 2010; Belshaw, 2011) but more precise definitions are rooted in specific cultural, economic and political contexts, namely those of the global North (Bawden, 2008). Even in these contexts, they show a bias towards skills for mainstream employment and mainstream digital consumption and away from the creative, the subversive, the critical and the expressive. Whilst this is problematic and partial in the global North, it is even more so elsewhere when concepts from the global North are pasted uncritically onto systems in societies elsewhere and then impact on the disadvantaged and disenfranchised at the margins of those societies. Other societies and cultures may have more diverse livelihoods or economic systems, compared to the norms of the global North and have a different balance of mobile infrastructure and systems than desktop infrastructure and systems. They may also have a different balance of physical space, physical identity and physical community compared to their digital equivalents, namely digital space, digital identity and digital community, a different balance of individualism and collectivism, of authority and consensus and other significant differences from the assumed norms of the global North. So whilst we could assume loosely that digital literacy, mobile or otherwise, is the prerequisite to digital learning, 'mobile learning' or some kinds of learning with mobiles, we should be careful how these definitions and ideas play out in different cultures and countries. These arguments have been developed in specific instances (Traxler et al., 2019a) making the point that Eurocentric understandings of digital literacy cannot be rolled out globally, least of all, over those at the margins.

The Chapters and Contributors

We, the editors, have struggled with how to organise and sequence the contributions in this book. We were determined to keep near to the individual experiences and individual accounts and avoid seeming to theorise or generalise. We were conscious that different groups sprang easily to the surface, for example, the various accounts from indigenous peoples, or various sequences, for example from the first-hand narratives to the more scholarly. This was what we wanted to avoid, partly because there were probably multiple dimensions of commonality and difference that we could identify plus a few more that different readers would see. So, we opted for starting with the most easily accessible and then moving unevenly towards the more scholarly. The same was true of those summaries of authors and their chapters that traditionally appear at the end of the introductory chapter and do, in effect, do some of the readers' reading for them. With that in mind we must let the authors speak for themselves at this point and merely acknowledge our gratitude to their commitment and talent. Feel free to start in the middle of the book.

The development of this book involved a Delphi process to discuss, develop and expose some consensus, or perhaps some views, on criticality, policy making, exclusion, cultural fragility and learning. The chapter authors should collectively take credit for any of the following anonymised quotes and reflections.

The most obvious clue to our aims and ambitions was the emphasis on *critical*, something that probably explicitly separates our work from most others in the field of digital learning, certainly of mobile learning. This term was not, however, always understood in the same way by all our contributors. Some of their ideas were quite diverse, ranging from seeing it as an attribute of methodological rigour, for example, something about "a broader picture".

With "deep approach or method to understanding", or, methodologically, in a different sense, with criticality meaning "in a timely state, [it] puts pressure on a person because we're on a timeline. There's an urgency". Then to more political stances, ones that ask about power and exclusion, such as, "perceiving people, their knowledge, and basic needs as a circumstance constrained by various degrees of exclusion at the development front and identify[ing] the call for action" and "structures of power, gender or class may be shaping the outcomes".

This variety of interpretations is quite significant and informs how authors see the world and their work. The process gave the authors the chance to reflect on all the other contributions and subsequent remarks made. Whatever the perceptions of criticality, they would be merely academic without engagement with the policymakers and programme managers who decided priorities and managed resources. There was unfortunately a prejudice that these communities, in their interactions with researchers and activists needed simple, clear findings untroubled by contingency, failure, mess and multi-causality. Some of our authors thought that researchers should "make friends with policy makers, add them to the research table" and include "data on issues that matter to policymakers (delivery, cost, reach, sustainability)", alongside "managing funder expectation via promising fewer specific and more generic outcomes". The latter brought about the critique, "we seem to always see complexities and need to account for them. I think that we, as a collective, could address this by trying to prioritize the interests of the most marginalized" and "The voices of the unheard should reach to the office of policy makers".

In considering the meaning of education and learning, one author notes, "I think the definition of education depends on the context ... mainstream education comes to mind and teaching the western approach to subject matter. Learning, lifelong learning, takes a different route where it is perhaps more meaningful, involving growth and evolving to be a better human being. Indigenous languages teaches this ... lifelong learning, observation, appreciation, meaningful dialogue, inner knowledge". Defining and understanding mobile learning should be easier. We do not make assumptions based on simplistic technological distinctions but rather a pragmatic judgement that 'mobile' is what most of the world uses, especially the least privileged parts of it. Mobile has, however, led to an important new distinction, the Fourth World (Donner, 2008, p. 29) being added to the First, Second and Third. It represents those communities, mostly indigenous or nomadic, previously uncontacted and specifically referred to as being at the edges of the Third World. In the context of this book, however, it could almost also represent those communities on the edge of the First World, cut off from the mainstream. This is something we come back to briefly when we make the argument that Heeks' (2008) concept of an ICT4D 2.0 for the 'poor' of the global South should equally apply to the 'poor' of the global North, and that in the current context, the same is true of any critical mobile pedagogy.

A significant ambition was for the messages in this book to reach policymakers and officials, who seem to need simple clear outcomes and priorities. Our discussions suggested that we, researchers and activists, needed to deliver these ideas in spite of causality and evidence seeming so messy and contingent. This was a difficult task, but one that could be accomplished if we focused on "delivery, cost, reach, sustainability" and "prioritizing the interests of the most marginalized. Policy makers usually simplify, by prioritizing one group only, which is usually either the majority or the upper medium class. We could also simplify by producing guidelines that would work for the last mile".

Next, we asked the authors to think about fragile communities at the margins of mainstream society, about their need to engage with global resources and opportunities but their desire to preserve their culture, language and livelihoods. So, there are problems, tension, threats or compromise in our work. One view was that "There is a tendency among developing countries to adapt to this changing world by pushing global technology and knowledge resources from the global north to produce economic development in the global south. Certainly, there are many positive outcomes in terms of growth in socio-economic opportunities for marginalized communities. But there is also a greater risk of social and cultural disruption by promoting and imposing external beliefs and value systems to people who have been living a certain way for generations. The communities are marginal not by choice but by their situation." There was, however, an alternative position, expressed as, "Why do they need to engage in the 'global' – when really these fragile communities are doing their best just to survive?" This is at a least a consensus that cultures and communities are all different.

In this book we have moved outside the predictable success stories and case-studies from what has been called the 'edtech bubble', we have moved beyond an exclusively academic community of authors. In particular, two or three of our authors are active across programmes and projects and one or two others are entrepreneurs, driven to change the world by getting their products into it or making their programmes effective. There is consequently a range of voices and styles. Please enjoy.

References

Ally, M. (2005). Using learning theories to design instruction for mobile learning devices. In J. Attwell, & C. Saville-Smith (Eds.), *Mobile learning anytime everywhere: A book of papers from MLearn 2004* (pp. 5–8). London: Learning and Skills Development Agency.

Basoglu, E. B., & Akdemir, O. (2010). A comparison of undergraduate students' English vocabulary learning: Using mobile phones and flash cards. *Turkish Online Journal of Educational Technology*, 9(3), 1–7.

Bawden, D. (2008). Origins and concepts of digital literacy. In C. Lankshear & M. Knobel (Eds.), *Digital literacies: Concepts, policies and practices* (pp. 17–32). New York: Peter Lang.

Beetham, H. (2010) *Review and scoping study for a cross-JISC Learning and Digital Literacies Programme: Sept 2010.* Bristol: JISC.

Belshaw, D. (2011) What is 'digital literacy'? EdD thesis, University of Durham. Retrieved from http://dougbelshaw.com/thesis.

Bennett, K. (2015). Towards an epistemological monoculture: Mechanisms of epistemicide in European research publication. In R. P. Alastrue & C. Perez-Llantada (Eds.), *English as a scientific and research language: Debates and discourses* (pp. 9–36). Berlin: De Gruyter.

Boekholt, P. (2010). The evolution of innovation paradigms and their influence on research, technological development and innovation policy instruments. In R. E. Smits & S. Kuhlmann & P. Shapira (Eds.), *The theory and practice of innovation policy*. London: Edward Elgar Publishing.

Donner, J. (2008). Shrinking Fourth World? Mobiles, development, and inclusion. In J. E. Katz, *Handbook of mobile communication studies* (pp. 29–42). Cambridge, MA: MIT Press.

Dunkerly-Bean, J., & Crompton, H. (2015). The role of mobile learning in promoting global literacy and human rights for women and girls. In B. Guzzetti, & M. Lesley (Eds.), *Handbook of research on the societal impact of digital media* (pp. 581–608). Hershey, PA: IGI Global.

Dunkerly-Bean, J., Crompton, H., & Moffit, C. (2018). Tensions between the local in the global: A cosmopolitan view of mobile learning initiatives. In S. Arafeh, D. Herro, C. Holden, & R. Ling (Eds.), *Mobile technologies: Perspectives on policy and practice* (pp. 3–22). Charlotte, NC: Information Age Publishing.

Grosfoguel, R. (2013) The structure of knowledge in westernized universities: Epistemic racism/sexism and the four genocides/epistemicides of the long 16th century. *Human Architecture: Journal of the Sociology of Self-Knowledge*, XI(1), 73–90. Retrieved from https://scholarworks.umb.edu/humanarchitecture/vol11/iss1/8.

Hall, B. L. (2015). *Beyond epistemicide: Knowledge democracy and higher education*. Retrieved from https://dspace.library.uvic.ca/bitstream/handle/1828/6692/Hall_Budd_BeyondEpistemicide_2015.pdf?sequence=2.

Hall, B. L., & Tandon, R. (2017). Decolonization of knowledge, epistemicide, participatory research and higher education. *Research for All*, 1(1), 6–19.

Heeks, R. (2008) ICT4D 2.0: The next phase of applying ICT for international development, *Computer*, 41(6), 26–33.

Heleta, S. (2016) Decolonisation of higher education: Dismantling epistemic violence and Eurocentrism in South Africa. *Transformation in Higher Education*, 1(1), 1–8.

Keskin, N. O., & Metcalf, D. (2011). The current perspectives, theories and practices of mobile learning. *Turkish Online Journal of Educational Technology*, 10(2), 202–208.

Kuhn, T. S. (1970). *The structure of scientific revolutions.* Chicago: University of Chicago Press.

Kukulska-Hulme, A., Sharples, M., Milrad, M., Arnedillo-Sánchez, I., & Vavoula, G. (2011). The genesis and development of mobile learning in Europe. In D. Parsons, *Combining e-learning and m-learning: New applications of blended educational resources* (pp. 151–177). Hershey, PA: IGI Global.

Langdon, J. (2013). Decolonising development studies: Reflections on critical pedagogies in action. *Canadian Journal of Development Studies/Revue canadienne d'études du développement*, 34(3), 384–399.

Lomas, J. (2000). Connecting research and policy. *Canadian Journal of Policy Research*, 1(1), 140–144.

Morley, L., Alexiadou, N., Garaz, S., González-Monteagudo, J. & Taba, M. (2018). Internationalisation and migrant academics: The hidden narratives of mobility. *High Education*, 76, 537–554.

Peng, H., Su, Y. J., Chou, C., & Tsai, C. C. (2009). Ubiquitous knowledge construction: Mobile learning re-defined and a conceptual framework. *Innovations in Education and Teaching International*, 46(2), 171–183.

Petre, M. (1994). A paradigm, please—and heavy on the culture. In D. J. Gilmore, R. L. Winder, & F. Détienne (Eds.), *User-centred requirements for software engineering environments* (pp. 273–284). Berlin and Heidelberg: Springer.

Rajlich, V. (2006). Changing the paradigm of software engineering. *Communications of the ACM*, 49(8), 67–70.

Sharples, M., Taylor, J., & Vavoula, G. (2005, October). Towards a theory of mobile learning. *Proceedings of mLearn*, 1(1), 1–9.

Traxler, J. (2012) Mobile learning – the future already behind us. In *Proceedings of 2012 International Conference on Interactive Mobile and Computer Aided Learning (IMCL)* (pp. 7–9). New York, NY: IEEE.

Traxler, J. (2016) Mobile learning research: The focus for policy-makers. *Journal of Learning in Development*, 3(2), 7–25.

Traxler, J. (2017) Learning with mobiles in developing countries –technology, language and literacy. *International Journal of Mobile & Blended Learning*, 9(2), 1–15.

Traxler, J. (2018a) Learning with mobiles in the digital age. *Pedagogika, Special Monothematic Issue: Education Futures for the Digital Age: Theory and Practice*, 68(3), 293–310.

Traxler, J. (2018b) Learning with mobiles: The Global South. *Research in Comparative and International Education*, 13(1), 152–175.

Traxler, J. (2018c) Mobile learning: The philosophical challenges, problems and implications of defining and theorising. *South African Journal for Open and Distance Learning Practice*, 38(1), 17–33.

Traxler, J., Khlaif, Z., Nevill, A., Affouneh, S., Salha, S., Zuhd, A., & Trayek, F. (2019a). Living under occupation: Palestinian teachers' experiences and their digital responses. *Research in Learning Technology*, 27, 1–18.

Traxler, J., Read, T., Kukulska-Hulme, A., & Barcena, E. (2019b) Paradoxical paradigm proposal. *Argentinian Journal of Applied Linguistics*, 7(2), 89–109.

Wernick, P., & Hall, T. (2004). Can Thomas Kuhn's paradigms help us understand software engineering? *European Journal of Information Systems*, 13(3), 235–243.

1

THE JU|'HOAN OF NYAE NYAE

A Case of Exclusion and Ka Jan

Candi Miller

I'm a storyteller and writer who has worked with the San, often with the Ju|'hoansi in the Kalahari Desert in northern Namibia. This piece is based on personal experience and is consequently partial and subjective. The references I make come mostly from anthropological fields, though I'm not an anthropologist. By choosing to write novels about people with an ancient culture that is not my own (*Salt & Honey* and *Kalahari Passage*) I became an accidental ethnographer, taking my first research trip to visit a Ju|'hoan group in 1994.

Many would argue that novelists are, by definition, ethnographers and that Writing as Other is part of the job description. I therefore include a creative piece in this chapter, namely "The Season of the Researcher", where I imagine what it is like to be a research participant in one of the most "fully described people in all of anthropology" (Biesele & Hitchcock, 2011, p. vii). My other creative inclusion, "A Machine for Making Things Easier", takes the form of a folktale out of respect for the San, perhaps the world's oldest storytelling culture.

Scientific consensus suggests that today's San, a linguistic label for groups of click-language speakers in southern Africa, the Ju|'hoan being the largest are descendants of the people who remained in Africa when the rest of us decided to leave. "Contemporary Khoisan are now the only people who still carry some of the distinct sequences of DNA associated with … the first small group of anatomically modern people who bind all humankind together into one family" (Suzman, 2017, p. 28).

Because storytelling is "one of the oldest art forms in human history and until the invention of written language was the primary method by which wisdom, knowledge and information was passed from generation to generation …" (Czarnecki, 2009, p. 6) it's likely these ancestors sat around their camp fires telling tales. Today's Ju|'hoansi still do. This group preserved their language and culture exclusively orally until 1984 when the first Ju|'hoan orthography appeared.

Stories are "sturdy little packages of our ambivalence, our hopes, our fears" (Heckler 2016). They are useful for "our difficult conversations" (Heckler 2016), our moral dilemmas, such as

introducing potentially hegemonising technology into vulnerable communities. Gottschall (2013, p. 67) points out that "[f]iction is a powerful and ancient virtual reality technology that simulates the big dilemmas of human life". Ju|'hoan folktales, which can be seen as this culture's age-old way of making sense of the world, do not come pre-packaged in interpretation. Their meaning is open to debate. However, more tangible "[t]echnologies, and expectation about their use, privilege particular ways of encountering, organizing and making sense of the world, and these can conflict with the heritage that is lived … in different parts of the world" (Bidwell & Winschiers-Theophilus, 2012, p. 197).

Ka jan

Ka jan is the Ju|'hoan expression for 'good' as in 'okay', the term used to indicate a tolerable state of being. The Ju|'hoansii, now dispossessed of traditional land and lifeway and struggling with frequent and prolonged cycles of drought in their semi-desert homeland, say 'Ka jan' in response to 'How are you?'

In many measurable ways they are not okay: there is tremendous pressure on water resources in this arid land; Ju|'hoan bush food is being eaten by the livestock of invading pastoralists – legal claims against them are upheld but seldom enforced; the game traditionally hunted is now inaccessible in safari parks; the Ju|'hoan homeland, the Nyae Nyae Conservancy, has been whittled down to a third of its original size by the national government. They "participate only marginally in national politics and the cash economy … [and] are at the very bottom of the socio-economic hierarchy" (Hays, 2016, p. 4). Consequently, they have few employment and training prospects (Hays estimates 90% unemployment) and an educational system that fails them – about 1% of San students make it through secondary school (Hays, 2016, p. 118). Many Ju|'hoansi have drug-resistant tuberculosis and alcohol addiction blights lives. To escape, more than half of the 4 000 Ju|'hoan people now living in the Nyae Nyae have moved back to traditional villages in the Kalahari bush. They live in kinship groups in approximately 40 villages, many accessible only by foot or 4WD, scattered throughout an area of 9 000 square kilometres. No longer nomadic, they have swapped grass for mud huts, and live near boreholes fortified against thirsty elephants. They have neither electricity nor internet connectivity. Even in town (more hamlet, really) the connectivity is erratic, resulting in a non-dependable ATM –"a recently installed ATM that, as one Ju|'hoan explained to me, 'shits money if you know what numbers to tell it'"(Suzman, 2017: 80) – and fuel pump. Not a problem for most Ju|'hoansi who have neither cars nor bank accounts. But some do have phones, simple ones, and a 'credit' problem – insufficient funds to buy airtime or data bundles.

Consequently, people do what they've always done, talk to one another: face-to-face, sitting in the sand, legs often intertwined, shoulders touching. They cuddle their children, make ostrich eggshell beads, whittle a walking stick, coax a bow into shape, tell jokes, tease one another, create new words for new things – 'iguana fingers' for 'fork', is one that Megan Biesele reports (1993, p. 24). More recently, one Ju|'hoan wag referred to a project I'm currently working on using phones with the battery-draining features disabled, as "the phone is cooking" project – I suspect he meant 'half-baked phone'. Their children run, climb trees, jump off termite mounds, problem solve as they seek to construct playthings from local materials: cars out of wire, dolls out of grass, flying toys from seed pods. Children follow adults out on foraging walks or watch them set traps for game fowl; they learn about animal behaviour, bush food, plant medicine and how to read the landscape. They are fully literate in this environment.

Reading-writing literacy is a problem, even in their mother-tongue. Swift have designed a Ju|'hoan keyboard for androids, but the problem of download remains. Alan Tuckett (2017) says: "[technological] developments further marginalise the most rural communities outside of internet coverage, and those speakers of languages other than English or the other dominant languages of international exchange".

Those who can connect encounter further exclusion. Consider the Apple security questions shown in Figure 1.1, from the perspective of most Ju|'hoansi who live as previously described.

The Machine for Making Things Easier
This story takes place not in the Early Days, when people were animals and animals were people, but Now, when people are just people and the animals are gone from the land, fenced in so they no longer stream across the hunting grounds like water after the Big Rains.

Now is the time of Hunger, when the Questioners have returned to their remote homes. Now, people's bellies bite while their children fret at empty breasts. There is no Hoodia to hush hunger – all given to Big People from Somewhere Else for weight loss. Women go out foraging but come back with empty karosses – the bush food has all been eaten by livestock belonging to people from Elsewhere.

"We should kill their cattle, chop off their horns and turn them into weapons for when the owners come looking!" The people laugh at the young man whose intelligence has not yet come.

"We are not fighters; we are talkers. We will talk to the cowherds, explain it is illegal to drive cattle into our Conservancy. We will talk to the cattle owners, we will even talk to the police."

Security Questions

Select three security questions below. These questions will help us verify your identity should you forget your password.

Security Question	What was your childhood nickname? ▼
Answer	
Security Question	What was the name of your first pet? ▼
Answer	
Security Question	What is the name of the street where you grew u ▼
Answer	Please select
	What is the last name of your favorite elementary school teacher?
	Where did you go the first time you flew on a plane?
	What is the name of the street where you grew up?
	What is the name of the first beach you visited?
	What was the first album that you purchased?
	What is the name of your favorite sports team?

FIGURE 1.1 Apple security questions

"Uhn, the cattle may be confiscated; the farmers may get compensation; then they will buy more cattle."

"Eh-weh," people sigh, "so it is, now."

"And what about the school problem – how can our children remain in a school where they are beaten and bullied?"

"Uh-nh. But if they don't become paper people, how will they get jobs?"

People gather under the Upside-Down tree to talk-talk-talk, while the sun slams down, while the moon shines between the branches. Finally, finally, they all agree something – they need a machine to make their lives easier, even in a small way. It must be out there in the peripheral world. They must find it.

So, the people ask Young Bo, who learned to read and write among paper people in the peripheral world, to travel there and bring back such a machine.

Young Bo doesn't want to go. In the peripheral world he'd been shamed; told he was primitive, his people too stupid for school; people had mocked his clicking speech. It was better at home among his kin. But it was his duty; he did know something of the ways of the Peripherals. Still, he was nervous of the task. How would he know which thing would be the one to make his people's lives easier?

He asked Blind Bo, Owner of Other Sight, what the Machine would look like. "It might be small thing, but you'll know it when you see it."

He asked N!ai n!an'an, the Owner of Story. "It will be something light enough to carry with you, but when you open it, you will find the thing you need to know," she said.

He asked Xoan||'a the Loud, who seldom spoke. She murmured that it should be something to make it easy for people to talk to one another.

He asked Besa Blow, the Owner of Music, and he said: "You will know it when you hear it."

So Young Bo set off. He travelled for many dusty days and Kalahari-cold nights, walking and walking, sometimes lucky enough to get a lift, sometimes lucky enough to be given some food or a place to sleep. Sometimes people said "Stay and be our bushman. We'll give you skins to wear and porcupine quills for making arrows and we'll bring tourists who will pay to see you shake your buttocks and rub sticks together to make fire."

But Young Bo knew he had to keep going until he reached the Ivory Tower where the Woman Who Worked with Sky Things would help him choose the right machine for his people.

And finally, one day, he reached the tower. He stepped into the lift and was whooshed up and up and up, to the place of the Woman Who Worked with Sky Things. She sat at a desk with screens, before glass windows with a view of the sky and all the land that lay beneath it.

She was very interested in Young Bo's quest and via her screen showed him many fine machines designed to help people all over the world. But to Bo they seemed screen things, without smell or sound or weight. He tried to explain but had no words for these new things. He wished his people were with him. They were good at finding new words for new things.

The woman rose from behind her desk and took him to the window, from where she showed him clouds, bellyful of rain.

"Do you have a machine for making clouds rain?" he asked eagerly. The woman laughed, then explained she had machines for predicting when it would rain.

Bo was surprised that she couldn't see, couldn't hear when birds and insects told of rain.

"No-no, this machine can tell you to the minute, so you avoid getting wet."

Bo laughed. "The minute it rains in the Kalahari Desert we run outside. We splash and laugh and dance to its drumming, we let it soft-throat down our necks. Our dust pans become swimming holes, our brown earth turns green, and the smell, eh-wehh," he closed his eyes, "the smell is fresh, like possibility. It's ..." His yearning to be home stopped up his speech.

The woman turned screen-wise as Young Bo composed himself; he saw her fingers flick as if shooing flies as he tried to explain better what his community needed. And while he talked night fell like a black curtain over the big glass windows, and now they could see stars in the sky.

"I know just what you need!" The woman rapped on the window. "A machine to take you up among those. It will give you a better perspective; from top-down, an overview."

Countless nights he'd lain in the Kalahari sand and stared up at the sky. What would his world look like from up there? But as the Woman Who Worked with Sky Things explained further, he could tell it was not a small thing, this Overview. And he might lose sight of things from up there. Also, how would such a machine connect his people with one another any better than their legs now did, walking the pathways of the Nyae Nyae bush? Would the sound of this Overview machine be loud? Would it drown out talk?

Just then a small black box on the woman's desk began to dance. It moved across the glass surface in time to a tune that made Young Bo's feet want to tap in his too-tight shoes. When he saw the woman pick it up, talk into it and heard a voice reply from inside the black box, he wondered if this might be the machine for his people.

"It's a telephone, but also a library and a camera," the Woman who Worked with Sky Things explained. "You could use it to teach people, to reach people, to beseech people. Mmm …" She lifted the black box closer to her mouth. "Make a note: 'to teach people, reach people, beseech people' …"

"Okay, I created a note," said the black box.

The woman smiled. "Useful, isn't it? And small so you can carry it wherever you go. It will connect you not just with people in the next n|ore, but with people all over the world! It can teach you things, it can help you add up your earnings, erm … find a job, though, erm, that depends on …." She stood up and began putting on her coat. "The point is, it can connect without cables and wires. It's a mobile telephone."

Young Bo knew that this was the thing to help his people; he just knew it, as Blind Bo said he would. It would help people to talk to each other, as Xoan||'a had asked; it was light to carry but when you opened it up there was the thing you needed, as N!ai n!an'an had advised, and Besa Blow would love its song. In his mind he could see the teacher in the tent school using it to better teach the children, the people who harvested Devil's claw using it to spread the news that the crop was ready, trackers telling one another about animal spoor, people photographing the ear tags of illegal cattle and using the pictures as evidence in court. It was The Machine for Making Things Easier.

"Take it, take it," said the woman jiggling her keys in her coat pocket. "But," as she ushered him out the door, "it needs a transmission tower for signal and power so it can charge."

"We have those," Young Bo beamed. "We have a tower higher than the baobabs and a machine that catches power from the sun. It hardly ever rains in the Kalahari," he grinned. With the phone in his pocket he set off back to his people.

They crowded around the phone on his return. "It is not shiny." "It is so small." "How will we share it?"

"Don't think that because you have brought us a machine you are a big person now."

He expected that one, but still it hurt.

He took the machine to the teacher and showed him how he could use it. But all the lessons were about the Peripheral world and showed people from Somewhere Else with things from Somewhere Else. The children liked the games though – very much, so much that a fight broke out when one refused to share the phone with the others. "Take away this fight-thing," said the teacher, thrusting the phone at Bo.

Bo took the machine to the illegal grazing monitor and together they photographed the ear tags of the cows and took them to the police station. But the police couldn't print them off, nor open them in an email.

That night Bo lay on the ground and held the phone up to the sky and used the app the Woman Who Worked with Sky Things had shown him to name the constellations for the people. But they had their own names for them, and pointing to the much brighter stars above they said screen things were not the same as real things. They returned to their camp fires.

Xoan||'a the Loud picked up the phone. "I hear it can talk without speaking?" Bo was pleased to show how. But she didn't know the letters or the language. He showed her pictures for texting with, but she'd never seen people nor food nor animals like those. She scurried off to listen to Besa Blow playing a familiar tune on his homemade lyre.

Young Bo hung the phone up in a tree.

"Wipe that worry from your face, son," said N!ai n!an'an coming to stand beside him, "with that machine, you showed what we needed."

"With respect, Grandmother, I did not," Young Bo said. "The machine did not help with the cattle problem, nor could we use it in the school. It did not teach people anything they needed to know!"

"Uh-hn, I think it did," said N!ai.

Proposed San Projects, 2012–2018

In 2012, with a group of young writers, I explored the idea of creating an ebook of San folktales in several San languages as a mother-tongue educational resource. San involved in its creation would acquire transferable skills which we believed would improve job prospects. We were excited by the unique pan-San aspect of the idea – via a mobile device, users might learn something of one another's languages. However, when we calculated the cost involved in garnering consensus among geographically distant, linguistically distinct San communities with little to no access to the internet, the idea became unviable.

More achievable was generating a bank of Ju|'hoan children's stories, specifically with Nyae Nyae village school children. The idea was to transcribe the stories and upload into the African Storybook (ASB https://africanstorybook.org), as both an educational resource and cultural showcase. Storytelling collaboration techniques were trialled and resulted in some charming stories and illustrations done by the children. ASB created a Ju|'hoan platform on the website. But with a 100-km round trip for some children and no guarantee of seeing their work at the local library due to connectivity issues, there was no hope of obtaining follow-up funding.

I turned to the existing local radio station, !Ah, whose transmission reach was said to be 50 kms into the surrounding bush. The station owner, the Namibian Broadcasting Corporation (NBC), expressed delight at the prospect of generating local content while the people of Nyae Nyae were enthusiastic about recording their songs and stories, and especially about learning to create their own educational radio drama. Funding was identified and bids written. However, research funding bodies (rightly, in my opinion) insisted that potential projects be managed by local organisations. Despite bid-writing support, deadlines came and went as the beleaguered NBC tried to find the extra capacity to make this work.

On reflection, local capacity and access to information technology including the internet are significant hurdles for San projects. Additionally, exclusion from digital connectivity is an ongoing problem, currently. But, indigenous "minds [are] shaped by the flexible storage of knowledge in an oral tradition, [f]orged through intense community bonding … shaped by thousands of years of oral transmission of experience and knowledge …" and the Ju|'hoansi have "the problem-solving based thinking required to respond to an ever changing and challenging environment" (Heckler, 2018, p. 2). So while all ostensibly fragile communities are potentially vulnerable to hegemony of all kinds; many have and will make their own adjustments to this. In the interim, we researchers might do well to heed folk wisdom with its long tradition of inverting assumed hierarchies and undermining facile assumptions; it is we, after all, who are the Other. We pass and are gone within a season of the researcher.

The Season of the Researcher
Night after night she sat watching elephants storm into town, desperate to drink at the only watering hole. They were thirsty. Year after year the Season of Big Rains came and went without leaving gifts. On the hot, dry wind she heard people's voices: "We are hungry. Fruit trees have been destroyed by elephants; bush food has been eaten by cattle and goats."

Then she hears the people smile.

Now it's the Season of the Researcher and we will eat again. Researchers with shaded eyes in sand-coloured clothing will drive into our villages and set chairs under our trees, inviting us to talk with them. And we will, because afterwards, after lots of confusing or, if we are lucky, amusing questions, the village will get a bag of oranges to share or 10 kg of maize meal, biscuits for the children, perhaps some cooking oil and soy mince. Never any real meat – the trespassing cattle cannot be killed.

This researcher wants to talk about our TB, *that* one about why our children run away from the government school. Remember yesterday's who wanted a sample of our faeces?!

Tomorrow's will ask our children to spit into bottles, today's want to talk about mobile phones – do we have a smart phone like the shiny one she pulls from her pocket, the one she will use to take pictures of us? (Why do they always take pictures? What do they do with them? Some say they will bring the pictures back to us but most never return.)

On and on with questions about phones. We show the few simple ones we have, hanging in a tree to get them out of the sand, away from the sun – the Kalahari can eat phones. We show the researchers the tree we climb to get signal. (The tower is many hours walk from here, in the town where the researchers stay, in a lodge with a swimming pool and mosquito nets.) We explain that weak signal is not our biggest problem; the biggest problem, what researchers call "A Challenge", is credit. We don't have money to buy talk time and data. Some, a few, who get work, buy what they can, but soon run out of credit because there is always someone in the village who has a crisis – a death or an illness. Then calls must be made; none would refuse the use of their phone.

"What about charging the phones," says a researcher staring into our huts at the booster system we've rigged up from a solar panel. She marvels at our nest of cables.

We have solar panels – mostly small ones we buy from the Chinese shop. They don't last long. There are big ones at the borehole but we may not use those or we'll drain the power needed to run the water pump.

Today's researchers are promising a machine that will hold our voices. "*Not* a phone," they say — it doesn't need credit and we cannot use it to call a vehicle to take someone to the clinic.

"A half-baked phone," our Owner of Jokes quips.

Some of our old people aren't interested in talking to the researchers: "Paper people are always coming with a project and promising things but nothing ever changes." We feel embarrassed that the old ones say what is in most people's minds.

"Why can't they just give us phones?" ask the younger ones. "Or cars, so we don't have to walk to neighbouring villages for our machines to talk to each other?"

Then a very old woman, N!ai, the Owner of Beads, whose eyes have gone smoky and whose walk has left her legs, says she would like to have a machine such as these researchers are describing. She has not been able to visit her relatives in neighbouring villages since before the Big Rains stopped being reliable. People begin to talk about when that was.

"It was after the days of the Early Race," says the joker.

"It was before the missionaries came and told us to stop our healing dances because they were against God," says our shaman.

"After-after that, when the army that came to live in our place, gave us that poison flour."

"Uh-uhnn, many died. We remember that time …"

"Wasn't it before the season when the one with the sex questions came?" People smile behind their hands.

"But after the one who talked about shit." Now they laugh out loud.

"Uhn, those days it rained – researchers *and* water!" More people laugh, none louder than old N!ai. Wheezing, she reminds us of what funny tales our far-off relatives could tell. She longs to hear their voices.

As we take the food gifts from the researchers and pose for the never-never photo, we all hope these ones will be back with the promised machines.

References

Bidwell, N. & Winschiers-Theophilus, H. (2012) Extending connections between land and people digitally: Designing with rural Herero communities in Namibia. In E. Giaccardi (Ed.), *Heritage and social media: Understanding heritage in a participatory culture.* Abingdon and New York: Routledge.

Biesele, M. (1993) *Women like meat: The folklore and foraging ideology of the Kalahari Ju|'hoan.* Johannesburg: University of the Witwatersrand Press.

Biesele, M. & Hitchcock, R. K. (2011) *The Ju|'hoan San of Nyae Nyae and Namibian Independence: Development, democracy and indigenous voices in Southern Africa.* New York and Oxford: Berghahn Books.

Czarnecki, K. (2009). Chapter 1: Storytelling in context. *Library Technology Reports*, 45(7), 5–8.

Davis, W. (2009). *The wayfinders: Why ancient wisdom matters in the modern world.* Toronto: Anansi Press.

Gottschall, J. (2013). *The storytelling animal: How stories make us human.* New York: Mariner Books.

Hays, J. (2016). *Owners of learning: The Nyae Nyae village schools over twenty-five years.* Basel Namibia Study Series 16. Basel: Basler Afrika Bibliographien 2016.

Heckler, M. (2016, November 12). Personal correspondence. Subject: Ancient Wisdom words of comfort.

Heckler, M. (2018) The story mind: Education for democracy: Reflections on the Village Schools Project, 1990–2015. In R. Puckett, & K. Ikeya (Eds.), *Research and activism among the Kalahari San today: Ideals, challenges, and debates*, Senri Ethnological Studies 99. Osaka: National Museum of Ethnology.

Miller, C. (2006) *Salt & Honey.* London: Legend Press.

Miller, C. (2011) *Kalahari Passage*. Birmingham: Tindal Street Press.
Suzman, J. (2017) *Affluence without abundance: The disappearing world of the bushmen*. New York and London: Bloomsbury.
Tuckett, A. (2017) *Effective strategies to improve low-skilled adults' learning for professional development: A literature review*. Commissioned by UNESCO, unpublished.

2

COMBINING ROBUST TECHNOLOGY AND GAMIFIED LEARNING TO DEMOCRATIZE ACCESS TO GROWTH MINDSET

Aape Pohjavirta, Miemo Penttinen and Saila Kokkonen

Vision and Mission – a Global Approach to Learning

All problems stem from interconnectedness and interdependence. As stated by systems scientist Peter Senge (2014), "Our interdependence has grown whereas our awareness about our interdependence has diminished …. Our ability to extend our compassion makes us innate systems thinkers." So too, then, must solutions stem from interconnectedness: all humans must be equipped with the knowledge and the mindset to become a part of the solution through compassionate citizenship. Social cohesion increases once individuals can take care of their immediate needs economically: they also have more capacity to engage as well-rounded community members and citizens.

In 2014 a group of mobile industry veterans founded a social enterprise, *Funzilife Ltd*, to develop a mobile service that scales access to quality learning to everyone with a connected mobile device. This service is called *Funzi*, and it is based on a theory of change which supposes that access to quality learning acts as the toolkit for all individuals to build the life they want. The service has three goals: to give everyone access to skills that:

1. help them achieve a better livelihood,
2. enable them to lead healthier and happier lives,
3. support the resolution of conflict and creation of peaceful and sustainable communities.

According to the business model of the company, learning will be made available for free for the learners, if the targeted customers are third party organizations such as companies, NGOs, and public institutions which have an interest in sponsoring learning for certain target audiences. The commercial side is

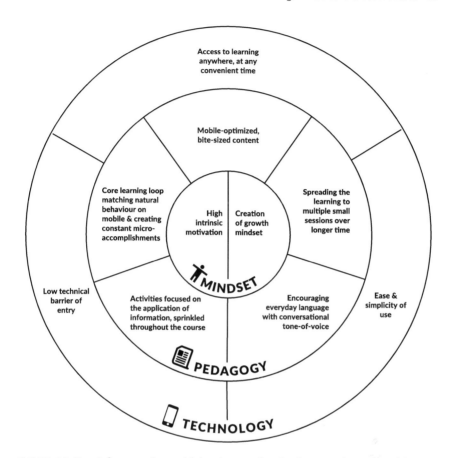

FIGURE 2.1 Funzi framework combining layers of technology, pedagogy, and learner mindset

beyond the scope of this chapter, which focuses on the development of a service and public courses that learners in large numbers can truly reach, use, and love.

In order to be truly accessible, the service has to work on all connected devices, not just new smartphones. And it needs to be scalable enough to serve the global population. In this chapter, we outline the growth of Funzi into a mobile service that combines a pedagogy proven to deliver great learning outcomes with a technology that runs on billions of mobile devices smoothly, even in slow networks. We also look at the lessons learned and the challenges that remain ahead.

Who We Do This For – the Funzi Audience

When designing a high-quality service, it's important to focus on a well-defined primary audience and shape the service around their lives, needs, and affordances. For Funzi that primary group of users was *literate, aspirational young adults in urban*

FIGURE 2.2 Selected screens from the mobile learning service Funzi
Source: http://funzi.mobi.

and peri-urban areas in emerging markets – during the evolution of the service, target audiences have extended to include also other user groups discussed in more detail in the case studies.

In emerging markets, the need for quality education is the greatest globally. These countries have predominantly young populations, and many of the young adults have been left without the education they need to get ahead in life. These individuals often have a high internal motivation to learn, they are literate in either English or their native language, have mobile devices, and live in or near cities with mobile networks. They are a group that is moderately easy to reach, with the potential for large social impact through providing non-formal and informal learning opportunities to bridge skills gaps.

To test the scalability of the service, courses have initially been made available in multiple major global or regional languages, including English, Arabic, and Swahili. Due to the web app format, translation of the user interface (UI) and course content into additional languages is quick, easy, and affordable – more so than would be the case with native apps, where each operating system (OS) in effect requires its own version. This initial targeting has led to over 7 million learners accessing Funzi in the first five years of operation, most of them from Africa, Asia, and the Middle East. In Europe, asylum seekers and migrants have been targeted. The publicly and freely available courses have gained a *50–50 ratio of female and male users*. The importance of reaching learners in their own mother tongue has been acknowledged, and therefore this initial reach illustrates the potential to expand the service to more minority local languages in the future.

How We Reach Our Audience – Robust Technology

The use of new technologies starts among groups of innovators. As the technologies evolve, they become more available, reach the mainstream, and finally extend their coverage also to the margins of less advantaged and less digitally savvy user groups. As an example of a technology moving towards the margins, mobile subscription rates are approaching 50% in Sub-Saharan Africa according to data by GSMA (2019) – an impressive figure considering it's a larger share of the population than those connected to the electrical grid (which was 44% in 2017, according to the World Bank (2019)).

However, there's always a gap between what is available at the forefronts of development vs. at the margins. This gap is clearly visible in the speeds of the mobile networks: data compiled by GSMA (2019) shows that 4G network penetration in Sub-Saharan Africa is currently at 7%, compared to 70% in the US (GSMA, 2018). Most of Sub-Saharan Africa mobile data usage still happens on 2G networks (GSMA, 2019). 2G speeds are not enough for pleasurable surfing on a modern website, let alone video streaming. Gaps like this are the reason why in order to reach people at the margins we need to look at what is well established and readily available – robust technologies.

Robust vs. Fragile Technologies

On the *Gartner technology hype cycle*, which describes how technologies evolve through five phases, robust technologies exist at the end of the curve on the *"plateau of productivity"*. Here the technology is already commonplace and widespread enough to also reach less advantaged and less digitally savvy users. In

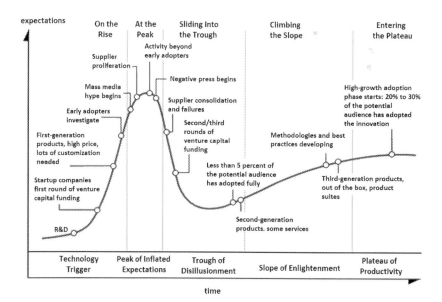

FIGURE 2.3 Gartner technology hype cycle
Source: Tarkovskiy (2013).

addition to wide accessibility, both in terms of availability and affordability, other characteristics of robust technologies include their ease to set up, utilize, and fix if something breaks down.

Unfortunately, robust technology is not getting much attention in the media or among investors. Instead, the attention falls on the first developmental phases of the Gartner technology hype cycle, "Technology Trigger" and "Peak of Inflated Expectations". According to Panetta (2019), technologies currently, in 2019, in those phases include for example AI, robotics, blockchain, augmented reality (AR), virtual reality (VR), 360° video, and voice-based interactions. These technologies are advanced and have great potential, but they come with a considerable fragility: they are the opposite of robust. Utilizing these technologies comes with a risk that they may vanish fast, before they become widely available. Even in developed regions services or hardware can cease to work, for example because the company providing a technology goes bankrupt.

Another type of fragility of technologies is that they rely on layers of other fragile technologies, making the whole system exponentially more fragile due to interconnectedness. For example, in order to have a state-of-the-art VR experience, you need not just a VR headset, but also a computer with massive amounts of processing power and memory, and if the content is streamed, an ultra-fast 5G network, too. If any of these components is not available, due to you not being able to afford them or your local infrastructure not being able to support streaming them, your VR experience will fail.

In the global north we encounter the fragility of advanced technologies only occasionally: as described by Nichols (2017), when Amazon's cloud infrastructure goes down, temporarily disabling many popular services from communication tools to security cameras – or when your smartphone is being repaired for a week and you need to replace it with your older phone, which doesn't have enough processing power or memory to run the latest apps. In the margins this kind of fragility is constantly present.

Mobile Web as the New AM/FM Radio: Robust Par Excellence

One historical example of a very robust technology is AM/FM radio. Its core technologies are a century old and it's used everywhere from the Antarctic to the Sahara. Local radio stations can be set up with little effort. A receiver can be either purchased with just a few dollars or even built from readily available components following simple instructions. Listening to the radio requires little power: the receiver can even be powered by hand crank if no batteries are available.

What is the current equivalent of AM/FM radio in terms of robustness – and the power to reach massive populations effortlessly? We suggest that the technology that is almost as ubiquitous and robust today is the mobile web. And while it's robust, it's also much more advanced as an information delivery mechanism than radio. Therefore, it has an even larger potential to deliver positive change to people's lives, especially in the margins.

What makes the mobile web so robust? First, it's really well established: the mobile web has progressed on the Gartner technology hype cycle for a couple of decades. It was in the first phase, the "Technology Trigger", around the turn of the millennia, with technologies like WAP, which made mobile browsing possible for the first time ever. The mobile web hit the "Slope of Enlightenment" with the introduction of the iPhone in 2007, making normal websites conveniently accessible on mobile for the first time. The "Plateau of Productivity" was reached around 2010 when Android surpassed iOS in the number of devices in use (as numbers on the 'Mobile operating system / Market share' Wikipedia (n.d.a) page shows) and extended the use of the mobile web also to devices at lower price points. Simultaneously, as shown on the 'Opera Mini' Wikipedia (n.d.b) page, it compacted the web both in terms of the UI and data amounts to something that was usable even on smaller screens and slower connections. The desktop-focused web had hit these phases already much earlier, in the 1990s.

Content delivery on the web is easy and inexpensive to set up: almost any old desktop computer that is connected to the internet (or a $25 deck-of-cards-sized Raspberry Pi) can function as web server hardware, and all the necessary software is available as well-documented open source without licensing costs. Another option is using a cloud service for just a few dollars per month. For content creation, existing open-source software can be utilized – or you can write the hypertext markup language (HTML) documents yourself. HTML, used for structure and content, and cascading style sheets (CSS), used for styling, are some of the easiest computer languages to learn.

Content consumption on the mobile web is even more robust: processing power requirements for displaying the content sent by the web server are so minimal that the cheapest feature phones and the oldest computers are all capable of browsing web content. There are also no requirements regarding what operating system to use, unlike with apps which are developed for the specific requirements of each operating system separately.

The infrastructure for content delivery from the server to the browser is readily available globally. While internet penetration in the global north is around 80 to 90% according to Meeker (2019), it is growing fast and steadily everywhere: in Sub-Saharan Africa the penetration is currently 23%, and projected to rise to 39% by 2025 according to data from GSMA (2019). Even the current 23% is already 238 million people in absolute numbers, calculated from the Sub-Saharan Africa 2018 population numbers on Wikipedia (n.d.c).

Access to Funzi public courses is free for everyone. However, mobile data cost will always affect the accessibility of the mobile web itself. In low to middle income countries (LMICs), the price of 1GB of mobile data represents around 5.5% of monthly income, a figure which, according to the Alliance for Affordable Internet (2018), is "a cost that remains out of reach for many of those in these

LMICs, and particularly for those earning less than the average income". This is where solutions like Facebook's Free Basics are an important extension of accessibility. Free Basics offers cost-free access to a subset of the standard internet in collaboration with local operators. Funzi has been available on Free Basics since 2015 in 15 countries, and this is a valuable method for reaching certain user groups.

Making the Web Truly Mobile and Accessible to All

So, what do we mean by the *mobile* web? Isn't it all just one web? While there are no separate technologies required to reach mobile devices, a lot of the web development focus has been on the desktop and laptop paradigm. And with enhancements for mobile, the focus has been on expensive, high-end smartphones. Not much thought has been given to low-end devices, if any. Together these pose a challenge for reaching more disadvantaged users in the margins.

The modern web puts more and more stress on the device and its browser software, because many modern websites are actually apps running inside the browser. This is a considerable shift from the traditional setup, where all logic resides on the server, with static pages sent to the browser. The static pages do not require any functionality to be processed by the browser, meaning it works on practically any device regardless of its age or price range. To function well, the contemporary approach of transferring major parts of the functionality from the server to the device and browser requires higher-end devices.

To achieve the true robustness of the mobile web, websites must be built in the traditional way: run all the logic and program code on the web server and send static pages to the browser. This is what we mean by a truly *mobile* web: something that reaches every device with a browser out there, including all mobile devices whether they're smartphones or feature phones, new or old, how much memory they have, and whether they're connected through 4G or 2G. With this approach we can reach the disadvantaged margins and have a real impact.

Innovating with established technology

Not much innovation happens in the field of the robust mobile web, where the product offering is quite limited, especially in the e-learning business. Many e-learning solutions target the higher end of the technology spectrum and utilize fragile technologies like VR or artificial intelligence (AI). This means that there's a major gap in what's available for the margins in the field of digital learning. Funzi bridges that gap with the use of robust technology.

Using established and robust technologies doesn't mean that they couldn't be used in novel ways. In fact, if you use a technology that is on the "Plateau of Productivity" of the technology adoption curve, according to Jump Associates

Democratizing Access to Growth Mindset 29

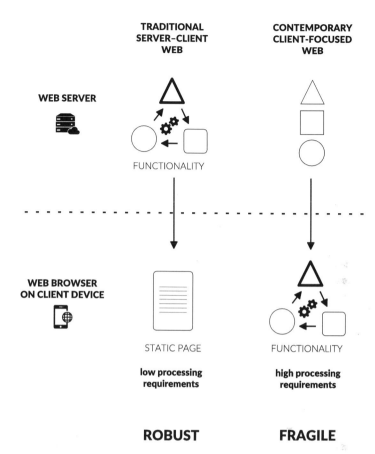

FIGURE 2.4 The difference between the robust web and the fragile web

(2016), you need to find new ways to add value by reinventing existing offerings. When the value doesn't come from the novelty of the technology, it has to come from a novel way of utilizing the technology: from the design of the solution. The design principles that work on higher-end devices can't be relied on to create something that feels natural and even pleasurable on a robust mobile device.

How We Teach Our Audience – Game-Inspired Behavioral Patterns for Pedagogy

To meet the goal of reaching the disadvantaged margins via the robust mobile web, we needed to choose a robust media: learning on Funzi is communicated primarily with text, supported by more visual components to a limited extent.

Visual communication is efficient, but it does come at a price when the images are transferred over slow networks. Text has an unparalleled *information per kilobyte ratio*: the full text of a 300-page book fits in the same number of kilobytes as one medium-resolution photo. Both take about 20 seconds to load over a 2G network. Text can be displayed on all devices without scaling issues, something that is problematic with images on small screens, when details disappear or become unrecognizable.

Images are of course used on Funzi to support the text and communicate certain aspects better suited for visual communication. However, the images are optimized for tiny screens and don't require much bandwidth: one learning topic, which is a day to a week of learning, with all the text and images on Funzi requires no more data than a few minutes of music streaming.

Structuring Course Content into Bite-Sized Learning Cards

While text is bandwidth- and device-friendly, long texts are not reader-friendly on a small screen. Funzi's solution for that is *bite-sizing* content into *learning cards*: compact units of learning consisting of around 200 words. A learning card can be read in just a few minutes. In addition to feeling natural on mobile devices, bite-sized content is great for producing effective learning results according to multiple studies, summarized, for example, by Gutierrez (2018) and Grovo (2016). It is also great for learning during small, idle moments of busy days.

The Core Learning Loop

At the heart of the Funzi pedagogy is the *core learning loop*, a game-like behavioral pattern modeled on the way people use mobiles. According to Opera Mediaworks data reported by Brandy (2016), sessions on a mobile are just a few minutes long. For learning results to be achieved, content must be structured to fit such usage.

Learning cards are grouped into *handfuls* of 5–10 learning cards. One handful takes 5–15 minutes to complete – a natural session length for mobile usage. Completing one handful unlocks the next one. This consumption plus unlocking is the core learning loop. It creates a meaningful, compelling structure for learning, providing motivation-boosting, game-like micro-achievements during the learning process. Taking breaks between handfuls gives learners time to digest and assimilate new information while building anticipation.

Positive and Human Tone of Voice

Funzi courses are written in encouraging and everyday language, allowing the learner to feel relatedness, as if the course is speaking directly to them. A conversational, unofficial tone of voice in the text keeps the barrier of entry low even for non-native speaking learners while also making the learning feel less like a chore and more like something that's actually fun to do.

FIGURE 2.5 The core learning loop consisting of a handful of learning cards

Growth Mindset and Learner Activation

According to Bawden (1999, 49), "A critical learning process must ... include discourse about the nature and influence of worldviews on the process of learning." Bawden (2010, 95–96) describes the importance of our mindsets and worldviews for our capacity to learn and live:

> It is our worldviews that act as the 'filters' to our understandings ... Given their significance, it is quite amazing that worldviews do not attract much attention by educators: Most of the time we are not even aware that our behaviour is a reflection of a particular set of essentially tacit assumptions ... They are thus the major determinants of the decisions and judgments that we make and the actions that we take. They play a major role in defining the goals that we set for ourselves ...

Influencing a shift in mindset and behavior change is difficult. As Sir Winston Churchill stated, "Personally, I am always ready to learn, although I do not always like being taught." Sensing someone trying to change us creates a threat response in our brains. Therefore, real change necessitates an individual themselves choosing to change. This changing of our brains is called *self-directed neuroplasticity*, as discussed by Rock (2009).

The learner feedback Funzi receives on its empowering and encouraging approach stresses the importance of a coaching tone of voice in courses: asking the learner questions activates their brain into a solution-finding mode (Rock, 2009), which is more useful and empowering than telling learners what to do. Asking questions has more impact because it helps learners find gaps in their own thinking *processes*, and working towards developing a growth mindset.

Engaging activities, a key ingredient in effective learning, are also sprinkled throughout the courses to encourage learners to practice lessons in their own life; to learn what actually works in their situation. The development of mindsets in an empowering direction therefore affects learners' lives more than individual hard skills, since a growth mindset builds general autonomy and confidence in one's own ability to navigate life. We would also like to argue that supporting the growth of learners' own agency is also a more ethical road than directly imposing black-and-white information and solutions on them.

What We Teach Our Audience – Supporting the Growth of Entrepreneurial Livelihoods

Earlier market research done by Nokia Life Tools has shown that consumers in emerging markets were interested in learning about livelihoods on their mobiles. This together with the fact that entrepreneurship is a globally relevant theme easily adapted to local contexts prompted Funzi to choose entrepreneurship as the theme for its flagship course.

Entrepreneurship is terrain where a growth mindset is important: with continuous problem-solving and innovative approaches required, one cannot succeed with hard skills alone. Campos et al. (2017) showed that the combination of *developing new skills and proactive mindsets is superior to solely focusing on building entrepreneurial hard skills* like budgeting or marketing.

A concrete example of the value of the growth mindset is the change reported by learners of the Funzi entrepreneurship course: even if their business didn't immediately succeed, they have learned how to problem-solve and keep learning. The fundamental change in how they see life and their role in it shows up in feedback:

> "The course boosted my confidence."
> "This course could be a means to alleviate poverty and change mindsets of many for self-reliance life style in Dzaleka." (Dzaleka is a refugee camp in Malawi)
> "Thanks Funzi … you've really made it possible for me to see my abilities in new light, don't really need a Degree to do something positive with my life, we can all start somewhere."
> "Funzi is a platform which empowers everyone to realise their potential."
> "Wow, this course has awakened the sleeping giant in me."
> "Am a 29 year old unemployed south african, learning on funzi has given me hope that I can still make it in life."
> "Thanks for making me eager to pursue my dreams."
> "It has motivated me to become the best version of myself."
> "funzi give me hope and trust, also motivated me about learning skills."
> "So encouraging, motivational and a life changer."

Such empowerment is especially important for disadvantaged target audiences, who might otherwise not have sufficient support to see opportunities to create change amidst difficult circumstances.

Cases of Empowering the Margins

The Funzi service has shown signs of being a culturally neutral learning platform: usage patterns of the same course were identical in Nigeria, Kenya, and the Philippines, as shown by testing large populations through social media campaigns. The local relevance of programs is built in through content partnerships with local experts, as the cases below illustrate.

Case 1: Informational and Upskilling Services for Refugees

- The *Program for Migrant Integration* was implemented from 2015 onwards with partners in government, the private sector, and academia.
- The basis for the program was a Refugee Journey Map based on the human-centered design method. The journey map was created to get a big picture view of the target audience, their actual challenges, needs, how the systems in their arrival countries communicated with them, and where access to information was lacking. The Refugee Journey Map proved invaluable and allowed Funzi to quickly move into actual content creation to bridge gaps in information by matching the identified real needs of refugees.
- The Refugee Journey Map was created and the first and most critical courses launched in just six days.
- Courses of the Program for Migrant Integration in Finland included:

  1) Migrant Information Services: About Finland
  2) Migrant Information Services: About Turku
  3) Business Lead "microMBA" for Migrants
  4) Food Safety for Migrants
  5) Sexual Health and Equality in Finland for Migrants.

- Courses in Finland reached over 20 000 users in total, with great retention.
- Publicity in international media was gained as Funzi became the first example of mobile technology as a solution to the migrant crisis (see, for example, Khalaf (2016), Bock (2016), and Griffith (2016)). One course in the program won the *Facebook Global Digital Challenge* in 2016 at the White House as part of its Challenging Extremism initiative.
- The program was extended to Syria to support *UNDP Syria* in increasing resource efficiency through training for local partner NGOs that were spread across the country, which were unable to travel to onsite training courses due to the crisis.
- Courses in Syria included:

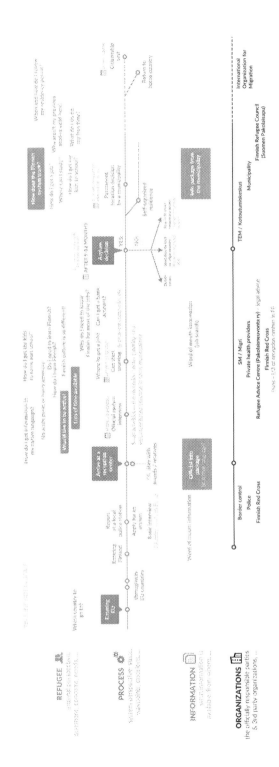

FIGURE 2.6 The Refugee Journey Map: a refugee's journey in Finland (aka the Penttinen-Remitz model), September 30, 2015. Source: Funzilife Ltd (2015).

1) Project Cycle Management
2) Monitoring and Evaluation
3) NGO Management in Crisis Times
4) Warehouse Management in NGOs.

- Course usage in UNDP Syria partner organizations consisted of over 400 individuals as of August 2018, with course topic completion rates of 80–100%.

Case 2: Supporting the Development of Hubs for Entrepreneurship in the Global South

Funzi has supported the spread of entrepreneurship through both mobile-only and blended learning solutions.

Mobile-Only: Spreading the Founder 101 Entrepreneurship Course in Iraq

Social media campaigns were run from June 2016 to August 2017 in Iraq, resulting in:

- 3 500 000 potential learners becoming aware of the Funzi Founder 101 course
- 350 000 visiting the Funzi service,
- 40 000 becoming active Funzi learners, of which 50% were female, 50% male.

Blended Learning: Mobile Complemented by On-Site Training in Entrepreneurship Hubs

In blended learning programs for entrepreneurship, the Funzi Founder 101 course is studied online, after which participants attend weekly on-site training sessions, to further develop their ideas or already existing businesses through facilitation and peer support – and help in growing a valuable network. Programs have been organised with, for example:

- *Westbury Youth Centre (Mashup Community Development)*, for youth at risk of marginalization in urban and rural locations in South Africa. In 2016, 230 participants, of which 51% were women and 49% men, created 32 new business concepts. Eleven of them were running as actual businesses at the end of the program.
- *International Trade Centre* and *Zimba Women*, for women entrepreneurs in Uganda. In 2018, 35 participants started the program, with a 71% completion rate. Seventy-four percent of respondents considered that the program definitely made them better equipped to start or grow their business, and 16% considered it likely.

Blended Learning: Mobile Complemented by Community Study Groups

Funzi Ambassadors are Funzi's most engaged learners, who have self-identified as wanting to spread Funzi in their communities on a volunteer basis. Ambassadors have hosted:

- Events to spread awareness of the opportunities to develop new skills via mobile learning. In 2016–2017 they reached nearly 400 people, primarily in Nigeria.
- Study groups around entrepreneurship, for example, in 2017 two groups of around 20 individuals facilitated in 2017 in Nigeria for low-income adults.
- Graduation ceremonies for community members completing Funzi courses in entrepreneurship and job-seeking skills, for example in 2019, 53 youth graduated in Dzaleka refugee camp in Malawi.

The value of the Funzi Ambassadors is that they are able to tweak locally relevant sessions around the core courses provided by Funzi, as well as to provide a more in-depth learner feedback loop through communication with Funzi staff.

Key Learnings and Looking Ahead

During the five years Funzi has been operational, it has established that its robust technology works: the service has been used by over 7 million learners from countries all over the globe apart from North Korea. Learners have accessed Funzi utilizing a vast range of devices, from feature phones to smart watches, without any insoluble technical hiccups. It has also established that its gamified pedagogy works: key performance indicators look better than industry benchmarks, for example, course completion on Funzi ranges from an average of 15% to over 35% in certain courses and locations, while Coursera's figure for unpaid learners is 4% according to Meeker (2019). Also, the constant stream of unsolicited feedback given by its learners illustrates the power of developing a growth mindset along with hard skills and therefore supporting a major shift towards the positive in the learners' worldview.

While the core of Funzi's service seems to be working well, there are interesting challenges ahead in, for example, scaling up its content library: in terms of the absolute numbers of courses offered, languages catered for as well as course themes broadened beyond the current livelihood-focused offering. Challenges will be faced in keeping the quality of the courses high and in ensuring local relevance in various locations, languages, and socio-economies. Also, the importance of growth mindset remains to be seen, once it moves beyond livelihood training, where it has proven to be essential. There's also the persistent question of power dynamics related to "who gets to teach what" and with what motives: evaluation of mission alignment and ethics will be needed continually with content partners in especially culturally sensitive themes like sexual and reproductive health. Funzi will also need to further attempt to verify the deeper impact that learning on Funzi has on learners, and to further encourage them to apply new skills in real life. We've taken initial steps of impact verification in certain courses with the Kirkpatrick model (see Sulaiman (2019)), but the layers of *behavior* and *result* in the model need further attention. And finally, we will need to start addressing the one key component of good pedagogy that is missing completely currently from the service itself: the social aspect of learning. Getting that done right, especially in a mobile context, is something that no-one in the industry has really figured out yet. But it's a challenge worth solving in order to really digitalize learning.

References

Alliance for Affordable Internet (2018). New data: What's the price of 1GB of mobile broadband across LMICs? Retrieved September 28, 2019, from https://a4ai.org/new-mobile-broadband-pricing-data-2018.

Bawden, Richard (1999). The community challenge: The learning response. In Chris Blackmore (Ed.) (2010), *Social learning systems and communities of practice* (pp. 39–56). London: The Open University, in association with Springer-Verlag.

Bawden, Richard (2010). Messy issues, worldviews and systemic competencies. In Chris Blackmore (Ed.), *Social learning systems and communities of practice* (pp. 89–101). London: The Open University, in association with Springer-Verlag.

Bock, Pauline (2016, February 29). The 12 startups using tech to tackle Europe's refugee crisis. *Wired*. Retrieved September 28, 2019, from https://www.wired.co.uk/article/tech-startups-refugee-crisis.

Campos, Francisco Moraes Leitao, Frese, Michael, Goldstein, Markus P., Iacovone, Leonardo, Johnson, Hillary C., Mckenzie, David J., & Mensmann, Mona (2017). *Teaching personal initiative beats traditional training in boosting small business in West Africa*. Washington, DC: World Bank Group. Retrieved August 1, 2019, from http://documents.worldbank.org/curated/en/865931506094667006/Teaching-personal-initiative-beats-traditional-training-in-boosting-small-business-in-West-Africa.

Griffith, Erin (2016, March 16). Refugee crisis? There's an app for that. *Fortune*. Retrieved September 28, 2019, from https://fortune.com/2016/03/16/business-apps-refugee-relief.

Grovo (2016). Why microlearning drives over 20% more information retention than long-form training. Retrieved September 28, 2019, from http://blog.grovo.com/microlearning-22-percent-more-retention/.

GSM Association (GSMA) (2018). The mobile economy, North America 2018. Retrieved September 28, 2019, from https://www.gsma.com/r/mobileeconomy/northamerica.

GSM Association (GSMA) (2019). The mobile economy, Sub-Saharan Africa 2019. Retrieved September 28, 2019, from https://www.gsma.com/r/mobileeconomy/sub-saharan-africa.

Gutierrez, Karla (2018, September 27). *Numbers don't lie: Why microlearning is better for your learners (and you too)*. Retrieved September 28, 2019, from https://www.shiftelearning.com/blog/numbers-dont-lie-why-bite-sized-learning-is-better-for-your-learners-and-you-too.

Jump Associates (2016, August 9). Design strategies for technology adoption. Retrieved September 28, 2019, from www.itsaboutgrowth.com/aj/learning-posts/design-strategies-technology-adoption.

Khalaf, Roula (2016, February 24). Technology comes to the rescue in migrant crisis. *Financial Times*. Retrieved September 28, 2019, from https://www.ft.com/content/a731a50a-da29-11e5-a72f-1e7744c66818.

Meeker, Mary (2019, June 11). *Internet trends 2019*. Retrieved September 28, 2019, from https://www.bondcap.com/report/itr19/#view/256.

Nichols, Shaun (2017, March 1). AWS's S3 outage was so bad Amazon couldn't get into its own dashboard to warn the world. *The Register*. Retrieved September 28, 2019, from https://www.theregister.co.uk/2017/03/01/aws_s3_outage.

Panetta, Kasey (2019, August 16). 5 trends emerge in the Gartner Hype Cycle for Emerging Technologies, 2018. Retrieved September 28, 2019, from https://www.gartner.com/smarterwithgartner/5-trends-emerge-in-gartner-hype-cycle-for-emerging-technologies-2018/.

Rock, David (2009). *Your brain at work*. New York, NY: Harper Collins.

Senge, Peter (2014). Systems thinking for a better world. *Aalto Systems Forum 2014*. Retrieved August 1, 2019, from https://www.youtube.com/watch?v=0QtQqZ6Q5-o.

Shaul, Brandy (2016, November 22) Report: Average app session length is around 5 minutes. *Adweek*. Retrieved September 28, 2019, from https://www.adweek.com/digital/report-average-app-session-length-is-around-5-minutes.

Sulaiman, N. (2019). *Impact of mobile learning on NGO staff: Evidence from Syria*. Unpublished Master's thesis, Hanken University, Helsinki.

Tarkovskiy, Olga (2013). Gartner technology hype cycle. *Wikipedia*. CC BY-SA 3.0 license. Retrieved September 28, 2019, from https://en.wikipedia.org/wiki/Hype_cycle.

Wikipedia. (n.d.a). Mobile operating system / Market share / By operating system. Retrieved September 28, 2019, from https://en.wikipedia.org/wiki/Mobile_operating_system#By_operating_system.

Wikipedia. (n.d.b). Opera Mini. Retrieved September 28, 2019, from https://en.wikipedia.org/wiki/Opera_Mini.

Wikipedia. (n.d.c). Sub-Saharan Africa / Demographics / Population 2018. Retrieved August 14, 2020, from https://en.wikipedia.org/wiki/Sub-Saharan_Africa#Population.

World Bank (2019). *Access to electricity (% of population) – Sub-Saharan Africa*. Retrieved September 28, 2019, from https://data.worldbank.org/indicator/EG.ELC.ACCS.ZS?locations=ZG.

3

OUR TOWN

Towards Creative Mobile Learning in Community Focused Place-Based Education

Angela Gerrard

Introduction

The use of quick response (QR) codes to provide information at tourist destinations and sites of historical interest is a well-established practice in towns and cities, as is the practice of businesses using them to display advertisements (Pillai, Prakash, Al-Marhoobi, & Shrivastava, 2017, Traxler & Kukulska-Hulme 2015). Similar codes are also used by some tech-savvy teachers: QR codes linked to photos and videos of work are printed and attached to pupils' workbooks, QR codes on classroom doors lead to the book of the week or a short video about the current topic. The codes provide an easy bridge between the physical and digital worlds, "connecting real world experiences with virtual ones" (Kossey et al., 2015).

Our Town is an attempt to utilize mobile learning in combination with place-based learning to either augment the existing educational features within a town or to create new geographically linked learning resources by adding challenges and showcases of content accessed via mobile devices. However, far from being an academically driven project with standard text multiple choice questions written by education professionals, the project obtains its challenges and content from sources such as local schools, local community groups, arts projects, a ramblers' association and a handful of independent businesses. Inevitably some of these engagements have not always gone to plan and the following chapters detail both the successes and the pitfalls of the work so far. The high levels of interest and engagement by local stakeholders in the project combined with the accessibility and the ease of use is seen as a positive indicator for not only the longevity of the project but also the educational value of it to the communities who implement the model.

In our local park in Pontypridd, Wales, a code at the bandstand links to a video of a brass band playing and a collection of stories from local residents recounting the music they have played or listened to in that place. Another code links to a series of ever-changing challenges associated with the bandstand; musical composition, an exercise in hypothetical event planning, the mathematics of the circular structure and paths leading to it, the history of public entertainment in parks, the science of acoustics. Over at the playpark, primary school classes are challenged to see how many people can fit on a giant see-saw; then taken to the trees, to collect and sort sticks and leaves of varying sizes into sets; and on to the war memorial to reflect on the reasons for war and poppies and to see the photos and hear the stories told by their grandparents; and finally to the historic Old Bridge, a collection of artwork and poems written by schoolchildren.

Dysgu Ponty

The idea was conceived around an old Welsh kitchen table, over tea (one bag each of black tea and Earl Grey in the same pot) and Welsh-cakes (freshly made on the Aga stove-top). The discussion was focused on how parental involvement can affect a child's education and the pros and cons of homework for undersevens. I had recently created a maths and science resource, overlaying questions about the local park onto a Google map of the town, and Jenny Hughes, my late colleague, was in overdrive about making it a physical mobile learning activity. Our company, Pontydysgu, (named after both the town and the Welsh words *dysgu* – to teach, to learn – and *pont* – a bridge) operates from remote offices, which is the professional way of saying we work from home at our dining tables. Pontydysgu is a small business, working this way allows us to keep the overheads down, it also means we can work with anyone with a laptop and an internet connection no matter where they are based and so we have staff in Germany, Valencia and Wales. The kitchen table discussion back in 2014, prompted an unfunded action research project involving a local primary school and a small cast of interested volunteers and interns who were tasked with taking photographs, sharing stories of local history and checking out the connectivity black spots around Pontypridd town centre. The project was named Dysgu Ponty after the file name I had jokingly given to my interactive map.

Six years on and an updated version of the Dysgu Ponty model is finally being implemented in four European towns with the help of funding through the Erasmus+ Our Town project. The consortium consists of partners in Evora, Portugal; Bucharest, Romania; Xylagani, Northern Greece and Pontypridd, Wales. The towns all have a different geography, climate, culture and language but share many of the common features of European towns; a river, a bridge, a town square, a market, a park, a museum and a library. Also, migrant communities, high levels of poverty and a disconnect between education and the local community.

The idea is simple – to flood a community with QR codes leading to learning challenges for children and young people. The codes can be put everywhere – on buildings, trees, flower beds, shop windows, pavements, walls, street furniture, rubbish bins, lamp-posts – even manhole covers! This last one, suggested by children themselves, turned out to be one of the most popular in the pilot because children were curious to know what happened 'underneath' the cover. The challenge was to find out and the code led to photographs, cross-sections of the services under roadways and a 30-second interview with a road-worker who explained how he kept them all in working order and what happened if he did not!

Early Observations and the Need for Community-Oriented Learning

The project originated as a response to the long-term damaging impact of low parental involvement in their children's education.

> From the early years to high school [this] remains among the key factors contributing to a child's success in school and life. It is widely associated with better learning outcomes, school improvement and lower risk of early school leaving and greater educational aspirations.
>
> *(NESET, 2016)*

There are many reasons why parents do not engage: time, money or they simply do not know how to. One of the several stimuli for the pilot was watching parents walking along the street, with their children, whilst talking on their mobile phones and not interacting with the children. The impact of the Dysgu Ponty pilot was immediate – suddenly children were spotting the codes and asking to borrow their parent's phone to scan it. Most significantly, the parents were curious to know what the learning challenge behind the code was and in almost every observed case it prompted a spontaneous dialogue between parents and children. The feedback from parents showed that the majority said they were then likely to become actively involved in supporting their children to complete the challenge.

The second observation was that younger teenagers, not accompanied by their parents, also scanned the codes with their own smart phones. Although some challenges were clearly more suitable for younger or older ages, it was not difficult to create challenges that were attractive to a wide age range. The pilot showed that young people just ignored the ones that were too easy or too hard. The feedback showed that young people perceived the trails as 'a sort of game' – which was 'cool' – rather than informal learning – which is 'not cool'.

In addition, some demographics have specific needs that can be met through mobile learning.

There is an observed tendency that single-parents, families with low socio-economic status or low educational background tend to be less involved in their children's education process and do not always understand what role they might have in their child's learning. Also, low proficiency in the state language/language of instruction may hinder communication between parents from a minority and/or migrant background.

(European Commission, 2014)

From Concept to Reality or, How We Convinced the Funders

Over the years following our initial pilot with laminated cardboard codes we revisited and improved the idea with collaboration from business partners and community stakeholders. We wanted to show that the project could work anywhere and so the title changed to Erasmus+ Our Town. We also wanted to show that the project could be adapted to different contexts so in addition to encouraging parental involvement and independent engagement with informal learning, Erasmus+ Our Town also looks at the additional needs of particular demographic groups. The challenges can be grouped around themes so the 'careers trail' will be targeted at older teenagers. There will be trails for minority language speakers who are disadvantaged in terms of learning opportunities. In towns where there is a significant number of refugees, the trails could present challenges related to finding out about the neighbourhood, the community and the culture they live in.

The use of QR codes to provide information about the local environment is well established (e.g. at tourist attractions, museums and historic buildings). However, this project is not just about giving information. The codes lead to interactive learning challenges involving a variety of technologies, incorporating content created by local people, local groups and local businesses, using the physical environment as a resource for developing a whole range of core skills and knowledge. Some codes may relate directly to an artefact or building but many will use the environment just as a stimulus for learning about maths or exploring scientific concepts or making music. In addition, much of the content is being created by young people showcasing what they can do in order to promote a greater integration of generations and different demographic groups.

A significant difference between Erasmus+ Our Town and other QR code projects is that the main aim is one of inclusivity – including everyone in the town or neighbourhood in providing educational opportunities, including excluded or disadvantaged groups and individuals in a new way of engaging with education and hopefully creating a community which takes some responsibility for its own learning. Schools, educators, adults in local community groups, civic organisations and businesses are all engaged with creating content which is both relevant to them and which also provides a learning challenge for children and young people.

Before we delve into the real-life experiences in testing out the model, it is worth exploring the challenges in funding such a project. It was clear from our initial pilots that further technical development was needed, in particular developing a dedicated app and a proper database of challenges. Furthermore we wanted to experiment with different kinds of trails and to produce a package allowing others to take up the project. At the same time we were committed to open source technologies, ruling out private-investment funding. This left us the choice of trying to crowd fund the project or applying for project funding. We chose the latter path and made an initial application through the Nominet trust. The application made it to the final phase but was ultimately rejected by the final decision panel. We made some adjustments and submitted the project for Erasmus+ funding, it was refused again. In both instances the rejections were related to the funders being unsure about the sustainability of the project. They assumed that the success of the pilots locally was intrinsic to the Pontypridd community and the interactions with us as researchers and facilitators, and that without key personalities, the project would stagnate. They also believed that the project could not be successfully replicated in other situations. Above all they could not see a business plan behind our development proposals. This is a common problem for those wishing to open access through open education. In our third and successful proposal, once more through Erasmus+ we put forward a premium model with the software and support manual remaining open source, but with the option of a hosted version of the software application and for consultancy in developing new uses of Our Town for different organisations.

Lessons Learned from the Pilot

Much of the groundwork in the early days was carried out by Pontydysgu staff taking a stroll around town with a camera, a notebook and a smart phone. Occasionally, as can be seen in the original Dysgu Ponty promo video, we would drag our children along too. We mapped out areas with free Wi-Fi and costed the cheapest pay as you go smart phones on the market with a view to creating a low-cost school kit. Using a basic WordPress blog, each post became the destination for a single QR code, scanning a code led to a webpage with photos, videos, text, information and ideas for activities. We translated the posts into Welsh meaning there were two codes needed for each place, one for each language version. We reached around 50 challenges meaning we had over 100 WordPress posts each with a unique QR code printed on card and laminated. Looking back through the shared Dropbox today I can see that our workflow was somewhat haphazard, I have a folder full of 500 helpfully named photographs of town, '004.jpeg' and 'old bricks', a separate file of pre-generated QR codes numbered to match the blogs and three different spreadsheets attempting to catalogue which photos match which codes and activities. We knew that the concept worked, scanning the codes linked the user to the website, but there needed to be a better way of working if we were to make it scalable and sustainable.

We arranged our laminated QR code cards around the town, tying them to lamp-posts, displaying them in shop windows, the museum notice board, the library and the subway tunnel. Local businesses were happy to be on board, some even offered incentives; free coffee for scanning the codes or completing certain challenges.

The next step was to take a group of primary schoolchildren to test it out. We assembled a set of 3G enabled iPads and a couple of smart phones, enough for one device between three, and set off on foot. As the old adage tells us, you should never work with children or animals, particularly when trying to prove a concept which is meant to work with children. Leading to the centre of town is a small subway decorated with beautiful mosaics depicting famous local characters. We had a code prepared for each picture; video of a Welsh male voice choir, footage of Tom Jones in his prime, a request for the group to sing some of their own songs. Unfortunately, in a tunnel there is no 3G.

The next few challenges were more successful except that we had placed many of them at adult eye height and not child eye height, so some were missed or had to be revisited. And the final challenge came when the group decided that racing to find all of the codes was a far more interesting activity than stopping to read the content or complete the activities.

It is interesting to note that six years on, many of those codes from the pilot project remain in the shop windows, the content they link to has also remained unchanged in that time.

Incidentally, in relation to languages, the early pilots were done with a Welsh language primary school with questions in Welsh and the tour done in Wenglish, an informal mix of Welsh and English. The early work with the Erasmus+ Our Town project was done with a different Welsh language primary school and a Welsh speaking teacher lead the activities, so it was a mother tongue experience. It has never actually been tested with kids in English! The second school has rearranged their teaching for the next term so that they can fit in a trip to town and have created some new content for us so that is a positive reaction. It's also being done in Greek and Romanian, referred to later, but it's hard to draw anything other than preliminary conclusions.

New Name, New Codes, Same Old Problems

Around 30% of the population in Wales are able to speak Welsh (StatsWales, 2019) and the language is supposed to be given equal status with English in the public sector. However, when it comes to education, resources in English are ubiquitous. A key challenge for the project is to make sure that the challenges are accessible to everyone, including the local Welsh language schools and families. There is funding available in the Erasmus+ project to translate all of the English materials into Welsh and vice versa, indeed this is the aim before the end of the project.

One of the themes used by the local education authority to teach at Foundation level is 'Above my head, below my feet'. This gives schools the opportunity to explore the local area and take a class trip into town. We worked together with the class teachers from the Welsh medium primary school YGG Pont Sion Norton, Pontypridd, to devise a series of challenges, written in Welsh, and based in the local park. Questions in the cafe asked to determine the price of a cup of tea and a slice of cake, challenged pupils to create their own menu, required them to count the keys on the communal piano and to sing a song they had learned in class. At the playpark they were asked to estimate the number of pupils who would fit on the oversized swing and see-saw before finding out the answer for themselves. At the bandstand they worked out how many of them were needed to form a chain, holding hands, around the perimeter (Figure 3.1). Photos of the outcome were then shared on the school Twitter page.

As activities they were all successful in that the pupils were engaged in estimating and testing their predictions and also having fun. As a QR code linked learning trail we failed at the first hurdle. In an attempt to customise the activity for the school I had printed out red and green coloured codes with the school logo in the middle, which I tested at my desk with a good internet connection and artificial lighting. It was an unusually sunny day for Wales; bright blue sky, not a cloud in sight. The school had brought a set of iPads which could not

FIGURE 3.1 Pupils of Ysgol Gynradd Gymraeg Pontsiônnorton completing a challenge

connect to the public Wi-Fi at the cafe, so we used my mobile phone and those of a couple of teaching staff.

No one could scan the codes. Five different devices, five different code reader apps, not one could read my fancy red and green squares. So, I reverted to old technology and wrote the challenges out on paper during the lunch break.

This example begs the question of why we are using mobiles at all if the same outcome is possible without them. The answer is that with the involvement of other schools and other local community actors, there won't just be the handful of activities created by the one school, there will be many activities created by many groups covering different topics, different angles and different ideas. To write everything out on pieces of paper makes no sense, to collate and add all of the ideas to a database which can be searched and filtered for relevant challenges makes for a rich and useful resource.

Xylagani Folklore Museum

In early 1923 around 1.6 million people were forcibly denaturalised from their homelands on grounds of their identified religion; indigenous Greek Muslim families were expelled to Turkey and 'exchanged' for Orthodox Christians native to Turkey.

In the grounds of an old converted mill in Xylagani, Northern Greece, is a community sourced museum of the history of the inhabitants who were subject to the migrant exchange. What started as a one-woman campaign to preserve her family history and culture spread to include donated items, photographs and accounts of the events from all over the village. Eventually a building was donated to the cause and finally, enough funding was secured to carry out the work required to set up and run the museum.

Working closely with the museum and members of the community, teachers from the local primary school, a partner in the Erasmus+ Our Town project, have created and tested a bank of over 150 challenges to date, linking aspects of the museum to aspects of the school curriculum, and augmenting the learning experience within the museum for all who visit.

In this example we can see how the history and culture of a once forcibly disadvantaged group can be kept alive through community involvement and kept relevant through technology. In future there will be multimedia content produced by schoolchildren, adding their own stories, pictures and ideas to the collection. Some of this content (Figure 3.2) will be exchanged, via the codes, with schoolchildren in Wales.

Inclusion

The project is complementary to the idea of Learning Regions and Learning Cities, but focused more intensely on communities, building on high levels of

FIGURE 3.2 Example challenge

social engagement and capitalising on community identity. This it is not a project about educational professionals creating structured learning opportunities for local people to 'consume' but about working with people in the community so that they can create learning opportunities for others in their community. Working directly with community groups means we have input from both mainstream and marginalised sectors of the community in the form of older people, minority language speakers, young people and low-income families, which helps to bridge the disconnect between community and school education projects.

> As the agenda for public education is increasingly determined by state and national education policies, a growing schism between schools and local communities has resulted. Mandated national curriculum frameworks with prescribed outcomes and standardised testing regimes are far less accommodating of local contexts, school-based curricula and community-oriented approaches to learning.
>
> (McInerney et al., 2011)

However we are still missing those groups without access to technology or who do not perceive that the project is for them, for example, the homeless community. Work also needs to be done to ensure accessibility for those with disabilities.

Why Mobile Learning isn't Used in Community Groups

All of the groups we have worked with have been clear that static text and encyclopaedic information sheets do not interest them, nor do they want endless quizzes with correct answers which become redundant once solved. If the content behind a code remains unchanged there is little to no point in scanning it for a second time. Another bugbear is the need to download yet another app or at least a specific app in order to access content. The same usability rules apply to mobile devices as to websites, only with the added time pressure that people scanning codes on their phones are often doing so whilst on a journey.

Many people, researchers, local stakeholders and potential end users have enquired about the popularity of QR codes. It is true that the technology is no longer new or exciting. For a while I wondered whether groups of people would stop to scan an area, would walk around looking for the next part of the trail, would access material through their mobile devices or would make an event of it, but then I passed a crowd of people playing Ingress, the precursor to Pokémon Go, in the local park. People do behave in this way. Erasmus+ Our Town needs to find a way to hold people's attention, to make them want to come back and scan again. As we further develop the system, we intend to add games and rewards, but these will be developed alongside the community groups and end users. When I began writing this chapter, I wanted to take the emphasis off the use of QR and focus on the idea and methodology of augmenting a town with educational challenges. It soon became apparent that it was impossible to tell the story of the project without the QR aspect featuring prominently.

At this point in time QR is the most efficient technology we have with which to do the job, in future new ways to access the challenges may become apparent but the concept and the underlying pedagogy will still remain.

Conclusion

The project is ongoing at the time of writing, mid-2020, and has been received positively by all who have taken part so far. The enthusiasm and commitment from outside actors indicate that the project and offshoots born from the original idea will continue to work and remain active into the future. As previously mentioned, the schools directly involved with the Erasmus+ Our Town project have begun working together on a way to use QR codes to exchange content with each other. A classroom in Greece will display one single code on its wall, this code acts as a portal to a classroom in Wales. The class in Wales will upload photographs of their artwork, recordings of songs, etc. for the class in Greece to view and vice versa. With the correct database filters in place, the classroom could change to one in Romania, Portugal or further afield. Other youth and community groups such as the Ynysybwl Regeneration Partnership have taken responsibility for their own trail within the project incorporating physical activity, local landmarks and challenges relating to nature and the local environment. As more groups and schools become involved, the diversity of challenges increases and so too does the potential for sustainability. The project consortium will maintain and update the whole system for a period of at least five years, after which it is hoped that the community groups will continue to update and maintain the content whilst the consortium maintains the infrastructure.

You can view the pilot project at www.dysguponty.wordpress.com and follow the progress of Erasmus+ Our Town via social media or the project website www.our-town.eu.

References

European Commission Directorate-General for Education and Culture (2014). Study on the effective use of early childhood education and care (ECEC) in preventing early school leaving (ESL). Luxembourg: Publications Office of the European Union. Retrieved from www.cccw.ie/wp-content/uploads/2014/04/Effective-use-of-early-childhood-education-and-care-in-preventing-early-school-leaving-Final-Report.pdf.

Kossey, J., Berger, A., & Brown, V. (2015). Connecting to educational resources online with QR codes. *FDLA Journal*, 2(1). Retrieved from https://nsuworks.nova.edu/fdla-journal/vol2/iss1/1.

McInerney, P, Smyth, J. & Down, B. (2011) 'Coming to a place near you?' The politics and possibilities of a critical pedagogy of place-based education, *Asia-Pacific Journal of Teacher Education*, 39(1), 3–16. doi:10.1080/1359866X.2010.540894.

Network of Experts working on the Social dimension of Education and Training (NESET). (2016). Parental and stakeholder's engagement, whole-school approach. Retrieved from https://nesetweb.eu/en/about-us/policy-themes/parental-and-stakeholders-engagement-whole-school-approach.

Pillai, A., Prakash, D., Al-Marhoobi, N., & Shrivastava, M. (2017) Application of QR codes in tourism industry: A review of literature. *International Journal of Computer Technology & Applications*, 8(6), 678–687. Retrieved from www.ijcta.com/documents/volumes/vol8issue6/ijcta2017080608.pdf.

Stats Wales (2019). Annual population survey – ability to speak Welsh by local authority and year. Retrieved from https://statswales.gov.wales/Catalogue/Welsh-Language/Annual-Population-Survey-Welsh-Language/annualpopulationsurveyestimatesofpersonsaged3andoverwhosaytheycanspeakwelsh-by-localauthority-measure.

Traxler, J., & Kukulska-Hulme, A. (Eds.) (2015), *Mobile learning: The next generation*, New York: Routledge (also in Arabic, 2019).

4

DIGITAL INEQUITIES IN RURAL ALASKA

Jonathan T. Bartels and Matthew Bennice

Introduction

Prior to engaging in the topic of this chapter, we must first recognize our roles as educators on Native lands; we teach a language and culture that is not of the place.

At the 2019 Digital Equity Summit, US Federal Communications Commissioner Rosenworcel posed, "No matter who you are or where you live—or where you go to school—you need access to modern communications to have a fair shot at 21stcentury success" (FCC, 2019, para. 2). Rosenworcel went on to note that while smartphones are now widely accessible to lower-income families, the limited capacity and data plans are not adequate to support educational and professional growth. From a Western perspective, it is difficult to disagree with this view; the ability to navigate and work within a variety of digital technologies in post-industrial societies is vital. However, this stance of technological determinism fails to recognize the complexities of technological engagement in many non-Western cultures.

Moving Beyond the Digital Divide

The concept of the 'digital divide' has been a part of our conversations about new technologies since the mid-nineties. Understanding gaps of access in a binary way (haves and have-nots) was appropriate when the internet was still being diffused into society but as access to the internet became more ubiquitous, different forms of nuanced access became clear (DiMaggio & Hargittai, 2001). Attewell (2001) referred to this gap in access—largely constructed along socio-economic lines—as the first digital divide and the "social differences in the ways computers are used at school and at home" as the second (p. 253). DiMaggio and Hargittai (2001) proposed five dimensions of digital inequality to be considered: (a) inequality in technical apparatus, (b) inequality in autonomy of use, (c) inequality in skill, (d) inequality in the availability of social support, and (e) variation in use. These can be broadly categorized as issues of access/use and instruction/support. We would argue that a third issue of inequality can be found in cultural aspects (or lack thereof) in digital spaces.

Access/Use Inequalities

Technological access—in terms of affordability and availability—has historically been the primary focus of much of the work in attempts to address digital inequities (Mossberger et al., 2003). DiMaggio and Hargittai (2001) point to the fact that technological access is not just about the technology an individual can acquire, but also the technological infrastructure they are connected to. Additionally, the physical context of digital access determines the amount of autonomy of use an individual has (DiMaggio & Hargittai, 2001). If an individual is only able to access the internet at school or work, there are likely to be constraints on content that can be accessed and tasks that can be done. Issues of data limits, download speeds, and device capabilities can also pose limits to autonomous use. Howard, Thomas, and Schaffer (2018) point to progress that has been made in ensuring quality internet access at schools across the United States, but suggest that the next step for a school's ability to address digital inequities may be providing mobile hotspots for students who lack internet access at home.

As potential uses of the new technologies and the internet continue to expand, the question is about how individuals or groups make use of these tools. They could be used for educational, professional, or creative pursuits; or they could be used for passive consumption and entertainment (DiMaggio & Hargittai, 2001). Studies have illustrated a gap in internet usage along socio-economic lines in which the economically disadvantaged are less likely to use the internet for capital-enhancement (DiMaggio et al., 2004; Tsetsi & Rains, 2017).

Instruction/Support Inequalities

The internet and related technologies require a new set of skills (or literacies); these skills are vastly different, more complex, and more varied than those of previous communicative mediums. Development of these skills and literacies requires explicit instruction and support. DiMaggio and Hargittai (2001) suggest three different forms of support: (a) formal technical assistance, (b) social technical assistance, and (c) emotional reinforcement. The groundwork for support can begin with sound formal instruction in school addressing technological, content, and cultural needs (Kelly, 2008).

Cultural Inequities

Kelly (2008) went on to identify a third divide, comparable to the third issue we mention earlier, as a divide in access to culturally sensitive technologically mediated instruction. While this point is initially addressing instructional practices, it can be conceptually expanded to culturally relevant content. Warschauer (2003) points out that the internet seems like a limitless expanse of information and content, particularly from a white, middle-class, American perspective. The reality is, while the exact figures are debated, the structural backbone of the internet is based on English and the content of the internet is dominated by Western languages, mostly English, and culture (Baasanjav, 2014).

Digital Inequity

Combining these factors, we can see a "significant difference in the access to and equity of technology experience based on categories such as income, race, gender, location, or education" (Swain & Pearson, 2001, p. 10). This systematic division goes beyond simple differences in access to technology, it constitutes a digital inequity in our society. Ultimately, digital equity is a social justice issue focused on "ensuring that everyone has equal access to technology tools, computers and the Internet, as well as the knowledge and skills to use these resources to enhance their personal lives" (Resta & Laferrière, 2015, p. 744).

Case Study

Data from a recent study will be shared as a means to illustrate the issues of digital inequity present in rural Alaska. The data presented—collected as a part of a larger collective case study investigating the new literacies practices of early career English/Language Arts (ELA) teachers—will share elements of a first-year teacher's experience in rural Alaska. New literacies provide a particularly useful theoretical lens for analyzing the usage of new technologies as it combines socio-cultural and technical components.

The field of new literacies is one that is continuing to be developed, expanded, and refined (Coiro, Knobel, Lankshear, & Leu, 2008). The framework of new literacies used within the context of this study approaches literacy as socio-cultural engagement (Gee, 1991, 1996; Street, 1995, 1998) influenced by new technologies (Lankshear & Knobel, 2006, 2011; Mills, 2010). The central focus of this theoretical frame is to "[study] new types of literacy beyond print literacy, especially digital literacies and literacy practices embedded in popular culture" (Gee, 2010, p. 31). These practices are both internal and external to the technologies themselves.

Additionally, critical practices are situated at the core of this type of new literacies work. Luke (2012) states that the act of engaging in critical literacy uses the technologies of communication to analyze, critique, and transform norms, rules, and the practices that shape our everyday lives. In this, Luke identifies that practices associated with new literacies have the potential to "change relations of power, both peoples' everyday social relations and larger geopolitical and economic relations" (p. 9). As such, to analyze new literacies practices is to analyze power differentials alongside new technologies.

Participant

The participant of this study was Steve (pseudonym): a white male in his early twenties who was born and raised in Alaska. Like many Alaskans, Steve had a true passion for the outdoors and nature; among the limited personal belongings that he was able to move to the village was an expanse of hiking and camping gear. Steve had just graduated with a Masters in the Arts of Teaching after completing his undergraduate studies in English—both degrees earned at an Alaskan university. Upon graduation, Steve accepted his first job as the secondary education (grades 6–12) ELA teacher at the school in River Bend (pseudonym).

Location

The remote-rural village of River Bend is in western Alaska. It has an estimated population of just over 500 residents: nearly all identify as Alaska Native—more specifically, Yup'ik. Approximately 70% or the population holds a high-school degree or higher (more than 20% lower than non-native populations), and the median annual household income is just under $37,000—which is approximately 55% less than the average household income in Anchorage (United States Census Bureau, n.d.).

School

River Bend School (RBS) (pseudonym) serves just over 200 students from pre-kindergarten (early childhood education) through 12th grade and has a total of 15 certified teachers. The school identifies itself as an "English Language School," noting that all classes are taught in English. The students at RBS all identify as Alaska Native—the vast majority of which speak Yup'ik as their first language. Like many schools in rural Alaska, RBS has seen a very high rate of teacher turnover; three of the four core secondary teachers were new to the school along with the entire administration during the study.

Context of Rural Alaska

A week out from the first day of school, I'm flying shotgun in a four-seater prop plane to my new home for the first time. This was my second plane of the day, despite my starting point being in-state, and I still had one more boat ride before I reached my destination. Looking out over the endless sprawl of lakes and streams littered across the tundra, it was not hard to see why this village was so difficult to access. No roads, not even any solid ground; just a maze of water and stubby vegetation in all directions.

I was met at the dock by our school principal, a man who had arrived for the first time himself just a month prior. Trying to keep pace as my rolling luggage caught on exposed nails, he led me down the boardwalk to a teacher housing unit I would share with two colleagues. Standing on the porch, my principal gestured to some points of interest, all within a third of a mile walk from my house; the post office, where everyone collected their mail because there were no street addresses, the store, which sold milk for $10 a gallon, and the school. As he left me to get settled, I wondered how I could live in this state all my life, yet feel like I had just traveled to another planet.

(Steve, research participant)

Defining Rural

Alaska is the largest state in the United States while also one of the least populated. In an effort to better identify the context of ruralness in Alaska, Stevens and Pierson (2017) presented the following framing in a presentation to the state legislator: Urban, Urban Fringe, Rural Fringe, Rural Hub, and Remote Rural. DeFeo and Tran (2019) unpacked these categories further.

- Urban: All of Alaska's cities.
- Urban Fringe: Communities on the road or ferry system within one-hour travel time to a city with amenities.
- Rural Fringe: Communities on the road or ferry system at one or more hours travel time to a city with amenities.
- Rural Hub: Communities only accessible by plane and serve as the central transportation center for the surrounding region.
- Remote-Rural: Communities that are off the road system and have small populations.

Remote-rural communities typically have a population between 200 and 800 residents—a vast majority of which are Alaska Native. Variations between the villages and people of Alaska are as vast and diverse as the land; the village discussed in this chapter is one village among many.

Traditional Native Ways of Learning

Prior to colonial intervention, the educational practices of Alaska Native people groups were driven by traditions deeply rooted in culture, experience, and place.

This is described by some as "the way of the human being", or *Yuuyaraq* in the Yup'ik language (Napoleon, 1996).

The way of the human being is critical to survival in the arctic regions and requires a thorough and nuanced understanding of the area in which one lives. Living a subsistence lifestyle requires a person to be aware of minute physical changes in land, climate, animal behavior, and more. Additionally, one must be able to contextualize this information into previous observations about the past, the interdependence of the natural world, and the cycle of seasons (Roderick, 2010). This knowledge is crucial in ensuring the health of a community in one of the most unforgiving environments in the world. Roderick describes this as a highly place-based educational system, one that is often at odds with the Western education system that has grown to serve a global market economy.

Effective communication is critical to being able to pass on this knowledge, and historically has been done so through oral mediums. Storytelling and songs document important information regarding subsistence activities, proper social behavior, and morality. Non-verbal gestures and cues play a significant role in daily communication as well (Roderick, 2010).

The educational strategies developed and tested by numerous Alaska Native cultures that ensured the survival of their communities over hundreds of years are strikingly similar to those that many educators strive to implement within their classrooms today; real world application, interdisciplinary knowledge, hands-on experience, modeling, small group learning, and building strong personal relationships with instructors (Roderick, 2010). In 1998, the Alaska Native Knowledge Network (ANKN) published the *Alaska Standards for Culturally Responsive Schools*; designed to supplement the state's content standards for schools, the cultural standards brought focus to the centrality of the Indigenous language and culture of a place in the development of culturally-healthy students (ANKN, 1998).

Brief History of Western Education in Alaska

Western education in Alaska, particularly of Alaska Native students, has had a tumultuous history. For decades, it has been colonizers and outsiders who have decided and dictated educational policy. Though many groups have assumed responsibility for the education of Alaskans over the years, the narrative consistently shows Western culture being the basis on which these decisions were made. Barnhardt and Kawagley (2010) have articulated key historical moments.

The ramifications of decades of one-sided educational policy continues to affect schools, students, and communities. Graduation rates in Alaska have consistently been lower than the national average with Alaska Native students having the lowest rates of graduation. In recent years, the gap between graduation rates of Native and non-Native students has narrowed, but the gap still exists (Tran & Hill, 2019).

The issue of teacher turnover is particularly significant in rural Alaska where the turnover rate is roughly double that of urban districts. Within the rural

TABLE 4.1 Moments in the history of Alaskan education

1784	Russian fur trader, Gregorii Shelikhov, established the first "Western" school for Alaska Natives in Kodiak after colonizing the island through massacre of the native population.
1796	Russian Orthodox Church, with Russian American Company support, began mission schools in order to spread Christianity; vocational schools were created, providing training in exchange for indentured service.
1867	Russia sold Alaska to the United States. The Russian Orthodox Church continued to run mission schools, but is joined by American Protestants and Roman Catholics.
1884	Government officially sponsors the establishment of an educational system for Alaskan children. The stated educational objectives remained to correct Alaska Natives' "improvident habits" and "to abandon their old customs".
1904	After population influx to Alaska from the Gold Rush, the District of Alaska created an educational system for non-native children run by the territorial government creating a segregated educational system.
1931	Control over Alaska Native education was transferred to the Bureau of Indian Affairs (BIA). Despite a stated refocusing of the education system to include "culture, civic tradition, and inherited institutions", the mixed-bag of American curriculum was deemed unsatisfactory and "ill-suited" in meeting the needs of Alaska Native students.
1947	Boarding schools were a common practice in Alaska due to low populations in communities. Many Alaska Native students were forced hundreds of miles away from their villages and families. Some who attended these schools reported being forbidden to express elements of their language and culture, as well as the use of corporal punishment for doing so. Students were encouraged not to return to their communities.
1959	Alaska achieved statehood; the BIA transferred control of schools to the state. Decisions about schools began to play a larger role at the local and tribal level.
1975	The state of Alaska was taken to court over the right to provide K-12 education in a student's own community (ending forced boarding schools). Most communities chose to have their own schools.
1998	*Alaska Standards for Culturally Responsive Schools* approved. These standards are intended to serve as a resource for schools and communities attending to the cultural well-being of students. Included are standards for students, educators, curriculum, schools, and communities.

Source: ANC and AFN (2010).

Alaskan context, the highest turnover rates are in the schools categorized as high poverty (Hill & Hirshberg, 2013). Remote-rural locations see the highest rate of teacher turnover at an average turnover rate of 31% (Stevens & Pierson, 2017).

Technological Access and Use in Rural Alaska

As I sit at home preparing to submit first quarter grades, I get an email notification that my household has nearly reached its monthly data limit. My two roommates and I pay $300 a month for our current usage, and though higher data limits are available, they are prohibitively expensive. This is despite the fact that all three of us are teachers, a job which is not only one of the few available in the remote areas of Alaska, but also elevates us to the highest levels of income percentile in the village. Considering that there are still quite a few days left in our billing cycle, I decide to make the trek to school to use the internet and avoid overage fees.

Outside the building, 20 or so community members sit huddled by the locked doorway, their faces illuminated by screens. Most of them are students, but a handful of older individuals are there as well, all taking advantage of the school's WiFi in order to preserve precious phone data. This is as close to an internet cafe that our village has. Though the internet is not supposed to be accessible on non-school approved devices, passwords travel quickly in our little town. Enterprising students have become masters at learning and teaching each other to use Virtual Private Networks in order to circumnavigate school filters. A few girls are trading Snapchat videos back and forth with their friends across the river. Two students from my class come up to show me something they found on the "Yup'ik Memes" page on Facebook. Another boy shows his father how to navigate Netflix as they binge a show together. All of them are doing so bundled in thick jackets and trying to find a spot that blocks the biting October winds.

(Steve, research participant)

Access to communication technologies in rural Alaska has dramatically lagged behind the rest of the United States as a result of the sparse population, the extreme climate and terrain, and the high cost of infrastructure development. Hudson (2015) tracks this history from the telegraph to modern mobile and broadband services. The infrastructure for many of the early advances in these technologies was constructed and maintained by the military; the more recent advances have been funded through federal projects and financial subsidies. The high cost of the infrastructure required for robust broadband service remains a technological access issue in more remote or developing locations (Resta & Laferrière, 2015). Today, more populated areas of Alaska—urban areas and some rural-hubs—have access to telecommunication services that are comparable to the rest of the United States, but access in remote-rural areas of Alaska continues to lag dramatically behind.

As Steve noted, home internet access in rural Alaska is expensive; but it is also very slow. The most robust internet service available in River Bend costs over $300 for 100GB with an advertised download speed of up to 10Mbps (though the actual download speed was documented to be more like 5Mbps). As a point of comparison, the most minimal internet service from the same provider in Anchorage (the state's urban center) consists of 150GB with download speeds up to 75Mbps for $75—the most robust includes unlimited data, download speeds up to 1GBps at a cost of $175. With in-home internet in River Bend so expensive and restricted, the only feasible option is relying on smartphones and mobile data. Through the main service provider, mobile plans include unlimited talk and text with data rates that range from 4GB for $50 a month to 30GB for $140 a month.

Observing students in the classroom and community members around the village, smartphones seemed to be just as present and functioned in the same ways as any other American city. When considering how this technology was being used by community members, Steve noted that it was mostly social media or watching streaming content. This mirrors Tsetsi and Rains' (2017) findings that individuals with internet access solely through their mobile device are more likely to use their access for social activity.

Technological Instruction and Support in Rural Alaska

I frustratedly instruct my students that it's time to transition. Though our class is 90 minutes long, the highly structured nature of the curriculum leaves little time for flexibility. I had already burnt a good portion of the class struggling to get around the school internet filter in order to play an instructional video, while impatient students slyly watched YouTubers on their phones in the back of class. If they knew a trick for how to fix my dilemma, they weren't sharing it with me. Between the counterproductive internet censor and the malfunctions in my perpetually hobbled SmartBoard, I eventually throw in the towel and move to the next task.

The final portion of our class period is online. Students retrieve iPads and headphones from the closet, and log on to a reading intervention program for low-achieving students. The program is scripted, and my access is limited. I navigate the room and attempt to monitor as best I can, but I can see frantic fingers swiping away games as I approach. I understand the temptation. This class is the only in the whole school that has technology built explicitly into the curriculum. Despite having a 1:1 ratio of devices and students, they are mostly used as a reward or "free time" at the end of a lesson. It is not hard to see why my students may have trouble viewing their device as a learning tool rather than an entertainment machine.

(Steve, research participant)

The result of these issues, coupled with historical context, can be clearly seen in the students' low performance on state-mandated assessments; less than 2% of the RBS students scored a the "Perficient" level on the state mathematics or ELA tests (AK DEED, n.d.). Let us be clear about this: we do not believe that standardized testing is the best way to identify and understand academic achievement—particularly in a context where the educational system put in place is not aligned with the local culture. However, the drastically low scores speak loudly about the local education.

In efforts to address the systemically low levels of achievement, RBS—along with many other remote-rural schools in Alaska—adopted scripted intervention programs to serve as the school's curriculum. This positioned the only robust educational use of technology in the school as a delivery vessel for a scripted curriculum packages that, at best, is culturally disconnected. While this program does use technology, the students' interaction is primarily centered on consumption and formulated responses. As often seems the case, within the school, the most sophisticated student uses of technology were subversive: bypass the school's content filter and rapid navigation of devices to play games.

Technology and Culture

As Steve mentions in his narrative, smartphones are commonplace and regularly used to consume or engage Western content (meaning Netflix, Snapchat, etc.). Exploring the cultural complexities of the digital divide within a technology-rich school in the Alaskan Arctic, Subramony (2007) noted:

> the Native Iñupiat youth, were seen to be in the unique position of straddling two vastly different worlds—a traditional, pre-agricultural one at home drawing deeply from subsistence hunting-gathering heritage, and a postmodern, post-industrial one at school that was based firmly in the information age of the 21st century.
>
> (p. 59)

While the school in Subramony's study had a wealth of technology, this concept of the youth straddling two different worlds—one traditional, one technological—transcends the walls of the school. The question has to be asked, is ubiquitous digital access and connection beneficial or detrimental?

Within the *Alaska Standards for Culturally Responsive Schools*, technology is only mentioned twice. While the standards were written over two decades ago; the significance of technology and the internet was still clear. The first mention is within the student standards; the indicator of the standard focused on the development of knowledge and skills states that students are able to "identify appropriate forms of technology and anticipate the consequences of their use for improving the quality of life in the community" (ANKN, 1998, p. 8). This does not align with—and is potentially even in conflict with—the recent statement presented in the introduction. This does not situate technology as an unquestionable necessity. Grenier (1998) explains, "Indigenous knowledge (IK) refers to the unique, traditional, local knowledge existing within and developed around the specific conditions of women and men indigenous to a particular geographic area" (p. 1). The emphasis on a "particular geographic area" is significant; knowledge is connected to the land and environment. Connective technologies are powerful because they can connect many across vast distances.

The second mention of technology in the cultural standards is within the standards for curriculum. This indicator states that culturally sound curriculum "makes appropriate use of modern tools and technology to help document and transmit traditional cultural knowledge" (ANKN, 1998, p. 17). This curriculum indicator is not about the consumption of content; instead, it is about the creation of content. In their work with a project documenting the Tagish language in northern Canada, Moore and Hennessy (2006) note the power of digital technologies as they allow Indigenous groups to document and disseminate sophisticated representations of their own languages and cultures. Historically, the representation of Indigenous groups has been done by the colonizers of Native lands. Steve's mention of students sharing content from a Yup'ik memes Facebook page could also be situated as this type of dissemination work.

Conclusion

Commissioner Rosenworcel began her comments at the Digital Equity Summit, "I believe the future belongs to the connected" (FCC, 2019, para. 2). This turns a blind eye to those who lack digital accessibility, those who have historically been educationally deprived, and those who are culturally alienated by technological determinism. We must remember that digital equity is an issue of social justice; and it is not just about being connected. Ensuring that communities and individuals have access to the technology is not enough. We must also ensure that they have the education and support needed to reap the most benefit possible from the technologies. We must also consider the cultural affordances and constraints those technologies enact within non-Western cultural settings. It is only through conscious efforts to overcome issues of digital inequities that we can ensure that the future belongs to all.

References

Alaska Department of Education and Early Development (AK DEED). (n.d.). *School and district report cards to the public.* Retrieved September 16, 2019. From https://education.alaska.gov/ReportCardToThePublic/report-card.

Alaska Native Knowledge Network (ANKN). (1998). Alaska standards for culturally-responsive schools. Retrieved from http://ankn.uaf.edu/Publications/culturalstandards.pdf.

Alaska Natives Commission (ANC) & Alaska Federation of Natives (AFN). (2010). Alaska native education. In R. Barnhardt, & A. Kawagley (Eds.), *Alaska native education: Views from within* (pp. 7–30). Fairbanks, AK: Alaska Native Knowledge Network.

Attewell, P. (2001). The first and second digital divides. *Sociology of Education,* 74(3), 252–259.

Baasanjav, U. B. (2014). Linguistic diversity on the internet: Arabic, Chinese and Cyrillic script top-level domain names. *Telecommunications Policy,* 38(11), 961–969.

Coiro, J., Knobel, M., Lankshear, C., & Leu, D. (2008). Central issues in new literacies and new literacies research. In J. Coiro, M. Knobel, C. Lankshear, & D. Leu (Eds.), *Handbook of research on new literacies* (pp. 1–21). New York: Routledge.

Collin, S., & Brotcorne, P. (2019). Capturing digital (in)equity in teaching and learning: A sociocritical approach. *International Journal of Information and Learning Technology, 36*(2), 169–180.

Davis, T., Fuller, M., Jackson, S., Pittman, J., & Sweet, J. (2007). *A national consideration of digital equity.* Washington, DC: International Society for Technology in Education.

DeFeo, D. J., & Tran, T. C. (2019). Recruiting, hiring, and training Alaska's rural teachers: How superintendents practice place-conscious leadership. *Journal of Research in Rural Education, 35*(2), 1–17.

DeFeo, D. J., Tran, T. C., Hirshberg, D., Cope, D., & Cravez, P. (2017). *The cost of teacher turnover in Alaska (Report No. 1634).* Anchorage, AK: Center for Alaska Education Policy Research.

DiMaggio, P., & Hargittai, E. (2001). From the 'digital divide' to 'digital inequality': Studying Internet use as penetration increases (Working Paper #15). Retrieved from https://culturalpolicy.princeton.edu/sites/culturalpolicy/files/wp15_dimaggio_hargittai.pdf.

DiMaggio, P., Hargittai, E., Celeste, C., & Shafer, S. (2004). From unequal access to differentiated use: A literature review and agenda for research on digital inequality. In K. Neckerman (Ed.), *Social inequality* (pp. 355–400). New York: Russell Sage Foundation.

Federal Communications Commission (FCC) (2019, July 8). Remarks of Commissioner Jessica Rosenworcel, Digital Equity Summit 2019, Richmond, Virginia. Retrieved from https://www.fcc.gov/document/commissioner-rosenworcel-remarks-digital-equity-summit-2019.

Gee, J. P. (1991). *Social linguistics: Ideology in discourses.* London: Falmer Press.

Gee, J. P. (1996). *Social linguistics and literacies* (2nd ed.). Bristol, PA: Taylor & Francis.

Gee, J. P. (2010). *New digital media and learning as an emerging area and "worked examples" as one way forward.* Cambridge, MA: The MIT Press.

Gorski, P. C. (2009). Insisting on digital equity: Reframing the dominant discourse on multicultural education and technology. *Urban Education, 44*(3), 348–364.

Grenier, L. (1998). *Working with indigenous knowledge: A guide for researchers.* Ottawa: International Development Research Centre.

Hill, A., & Hirshberg, D. (2013). *Alaska teacher turnover, supply and demand: 2013 Highlights (Report No. 1563).* Anchorage, AK: UAA Center for Alaska Education Policy Research.

Howard, N. R., Thomas, S., & Schaffer, R. (2018). *Closing the gap: Digital equity strategies for teacher prep programs.* Portland, OR: International Society for Technology in Education.

Hudson, H. E. (2015). *Connecting Alaskans: Telecommunications in Alaska from telegraph to broadband.* Fairbanks, AK: University of Alaska Press.

Kelly, M. A. (2008). Bridging digital and cultural divides: TPCK for equity of access to technology. In AACTE Committee on Innovation and Technology (Eds.), *Handbook of technological pedagogical content knowledge (TPCK) for educators* (pp. 31–58). New York: Routledge.

Lankshear, C., & Knobel, M. (2006). *New literacies: Everyday practices and classroom learning* (2nd ed.). Maidenhead, Berkshire: Open University Press.

Lankshear, C., & Knobel, M. (2011). *New literacies: Everyday practices and social learning* (3rd ed.). Maidenhead, Berkshire: Open University Press.

Luke, A. (2012) Critical literacy: Foundational notes. *Theory Into Practice, 51*(1), 4–11.

Luke, A. (2018). Digital ethics now. *Language and Literacy, 20*(3), 185–198.

Mills, K. A. (2010). A review of the "digital turn" in the new literacy studies. *Review of Educational Research, 80*(2), 246–271.

Moore, P., & Hennessy, K. (2006). New technologies and contested ideologies: The Tagish First Voices Project. *American Indian Quarterly*, 30(1/2), 119–137.

Mossberger, K., Tolbert, C. J., & Stansbury, M. (2003). *Virtual inequality: Beyond the digital divide.* Washington, DC: Georgetown University Press.

Napoleon, H. (1996). *Yuuyaraq: The way of the human being.* Fairbanks, AK: Alaska Native Knowledge Network.

Resta, P., & Laferrière, T. (2015). Digital equity and intercultural education. *Education and Information Technologies*, 20(4), 743–756.

Roderick, L. (2010). *Alaska native cultures and issues: Responses to frequently asked questions.* Fairbanks, AK: University of Alaska Press.

Stevens, D., & Pierson, A. (2017). *Alaska state policy research alliance: Informing issues with data and evidence.* Retrieved from www.akleg.gov/basis/get_documents.asp?session=30&docid=12204.

Street, B. (1995). *Social literacies.* London: Longman.

Street, B. (1998). New literacies in theory and practice: What are the implications for language in education? *Linguistics and Education*, 10(1), 1–24.

Subramony, D. P. (2007). Understanding the complex dimensions of the digital divide: Lessons learned in the Alaskan Artic. *Journal of Negro Education*, 76(1), 57–67.

Swain, C., & Pearson, T. (2001). Bridging the digital divide: A building block for teachers. *Learning & Leading with Technology*, 28(8), 10–59.

Tetpon, B., Hirshberg, D., Leary, A., & Hill, A. (2015). Alaska native-focused teacher preparation programs: What have we learned? *Alaska Native Studies Journal*, 2, 88–100.

Tran, T. C. & Hill, A. (2019). Alaska High School graduation rate trends (ISER Report 20192). Retrieved from https://pubs.iseralaska.org/media/e86650a3-b938-4205-b5af-d2f68ff43068/2019_08-AK_HS_GradRateTrends.pdf.

Tsetsi, E., & Rains, S. A. (2017). Smartphone internet access and use: Extending the digital divide and usage gap. *Mobile Media & Communication,* 5(3), 239–255.

United States Census Bureau. (n.d.). *American factfinder.* Retrieved September 16, 2019, from https://factfinder.census.gov.

Warschauer, M. (2003). *Technology and social inclusion: Rethinking the digital divide.* Cambridge, MA: MIT Press.

5

MOBILE DEVICE LITERACY

Status and Needs of Women in Senegal

Christelle Scharff

Introduction and Background

Millions of people worldwide are now accessing the web for the first time, and uniquely, on mobile devices, smartphones rather than feature phones. Most phone subscribers are in developing and emerging markets. These users are assumed to be proficient in using their phones, including apps, without prior knowledge and assistance. They are asked to know how to access the internet via data or wifi, pay bills, install apps, transfer money, share pictures, recognize genuine content, etc. Mobile devices have also become business tools to gain financial independence, and to be used to contact potential customers, pay suppliers, sell online, etc. (Burrell, & Oreglia, 2015; Akram, Akkireddy, Le Beux, & Kumar, 2018). The reality is that these users are facing significant barriers in using their mobile devices for personal and business purposes. They often perceive using a mobile phone independently and productively as complex, overwhelming, unintuitive, confusing and unsafe.

The generic concept of digital literacy needs to focus on and adapt to mobile device literacy. Digital literacy is defined as the usage and comprehension of information in the digital age (Gilster, 1998; Gillwald & Global Commission on Internet Governance, 2017). Numerous digital skills frameworks have been produced to summarize the fundamental skills necessary to "live, learn and work" in a society where information and communication technology is part of daily life (NETHOPE Solutions Center, 2018; Hague & Payton, 2010). The frameworks emphasize skills such as foundational technical skills to access, manipulate and create content, a mastery of communication to be an active participant, and critical thinking in the face of the plethora of information available to behave responsibly and stay safe on the internet.

We now need to refocus and adapt the framework of digital skills to the era of mobile devices by thinking about scaling strategies, and inclusive and accessible options for training on-the-go. Whereas, before, only a few privileged trained users were accessing digital content from computers, anyone can now access digital content from mobile devices from anywhere at lower costs. Digital literacy is now required to scale and reach everyone (Roggemann & Nurko, 2019). Wyche, Steinfield, Cai, Simiyu and Thieno (2016) attempted to define mobile digital literacy as the "ability to use mobile phones for purposes other than making and receiving voice calls". Traxler (2012) argues that mobile literacy cannot merely be a subset of digital literacy,

> less for technical reasons than because the expectations and experiences built around mobile, massive in number and diverse in quality, are different from those built around computers, and specifically the ways in which mobiles are part of us, embodied and prosthetic.

Mobile literacy includes knowing how to identify, install and use mobile apps. The reality is that, WhatsApp and Facebook notwithstanding, mobile app adoption is low in developing and emerging markets, especially of locally developed ones. Names of apps developed in the Silicon Valley have become part of the everyday vocabulary of people living in Africa, while local apps, even with local names, have difficulty reaching the public.

Burrell and Toyama (2009) consider that research in information and communication technology for development (ICTD) focuses on the potential of existing and the creation of new technological solutions to achieve economic, social and political development in low-resource or low-income markets. Numerous ICTD researchers have studied the obstacles to mobile devices and apps usage (Medhi-Thies, 2015; Sey, Bar, Coward, Koepke, Rothschild, & Sciadas, 2015; Phokeer, Densmore, Johnson, & Feamster, 2016; Dodson, Sterling, & Bennett, 2013), the criticality of training and effectiveness of videos to improve mobile literacy (Wyche et al., 2016; Cuendet, Medhi-Thies, Bali, & Cutrell, 2013) and the use of intermediaries and gamification to support users in their mobile literacy education (Katule, Densmore, & Rivette, 2016). Obstacles to devices and apps usage and comprehension include low literacy, unfamiliarity with the Western metaphor of the app store and iconography (Wagner, 2014), a disconnect between apps purposes and user's needs, user experience (UX) issues (Ndiaye & Zouinar, 2014), difficulty in identifying new apps, low-quality access to the internet and inadequate infrastructures. Dodson et al. (2013) explored the "utility gaps, the spaces between high rates of mobile phone ownership and low use of productive features on mobile phones", in groups of low-literate Berber-Muslim women in a predominantly oral-language community in rural southwest Morocco. They listed and organized barriers including technical, social, cultural and linguistic factors. They also emphasized the gender gap. Wyche et al. (2016)

developed videos for and with female farmers in Kenya to enable them to improve their confidence in using m-agriculture applications and services. The findings show that videos combined with help from facilitators were crucial, but had to include technical content.

This chapter focuses on exploring ways to improve mobile literacy through the development of a toolkit composed of videos available on YouTube. Our toolkit is named AppliCafé to resonate with the CyberCafé term. It is currently only available in French. In comparison, the GSMA Mobile internet Skills Training Toolkit (2018) offers training modules to be taught by trainers. It does not have videos. It is available in six languages including Hindi and Swahili. The kit explains what the mobile internet is, as well as highlighting various points about safety and cost; it also curates a certain number of apps and sites considered useful for users: Facebook, Google, Wikipedia, YouTube and WhatsApp.

Our approach focuses on the development of a generic toolkit that teaches a wide range of topics related to mobile phone usage, from understanding what the internet is to installing an app on the phone. It is intended to be used by users directly, not in training sessions. Our toolkit was tested in a pilot that was conducted with participants (mostly women) in Senegal. We targeted the following research questions:

- How are women in Senegal using their mobile phones?
- How effective is our toolkit in teaching mobile literacy?
- What are women in Senegal's needs in terms of mobile literacy and apps?

The proposed research is important for the ICTD community and industry as there are billions of potential users in emerging and developing countries and women are still marginalized (Dodson et al. 2013; Bellman & Malhotra, 2016). Our research touches on the scalability of teaching mobile device literary skills through videos directly available to users interested in becoming more knowledgeable about mobile technology. This research will ultimately develop and distribute French and local language material (e.g., Wolof) to teach mobile literacy, and its impact on users' skills will be evaluated. To our knowledge, no such material is currently available.

This chapter is organized as follows. The next section presents the mobile literacy toolkit. The third section outlines our research methodology. The fourth section presents our findings. In the final section, we summarize our conclusions and describe our next step.

The Mobile Device Literacy Toolkit

The toolkit, AppliCafé, is composed of videos available on the AppliCafé YouTube channel (2017). The content focuses on Android, as this is the most commonly internationally used operating system, in particular in developing and emerging markets.

The videos are 60 seconds long to take attention span into account. They use free and cited content from the web. They are currently only available in French. It was important for us to use a female voice for inclusion purposes. A woman from Haiti did the voiceover and worked directly with the video editor. The toolkit currently includes eight videos: 1) "What are the web and the internet?"; 2) "What is Google?"; 3) "What is Android?"; 4) "What is Google Play Store?"; 5) "What is an app?"; 6) "What is an email?"; 7) "How to create an email?"; and 8) "How to install an app?". The videos explain the process of installing an Android mobile app on a smartphone step by step.

Research Methodology

The research described in this chapter took part in several stages and included field trips with undergraduate and graduate students to Thiès and St Louis, cities that are, respectively, 70km and 300km from Dakar, the capital city of Senegal.

The first stage occurred when a team of researchers from Pace University traveled to Senegal in January 2017 to conduct exploratory research, and collect data on how users were using their mobile phones, and how developers and entrepreneurs could promote and scale their app businesses (Scharff, Rene, Schoepp, Shah, & Greenberg, 2017). A small pilot took place in which six users were interviewed and shown our four initial videos. The pilot revealed interesting mobile device usage patterns including the use of websites rather than mobile apps to save data and airtime, the use of mobile data rather than wifi, the use of "Chinese" ("fake") phones that lack core features and the wide use of communication apps such as WhatsApp and Facebook rather than local apps. Participants said that training was crucial to improve their mobile literacy skills. They asked for new videos to be included in the toolkit: "What is Google?", "What are the web and the internet?", "What is an email address?", "How to create an email address?" and "What are social networks and Facebook?".

The second stage is the focus of this chapter. The research team, composed of one lead researcher and four students, conducted three focus groups with participants from women's associations in St Louis, Senegal in January 2018. We visited these associations with the help of a local organization called ARADES. The women organize in associations to support themselves and fight poverty, isolation from divorce and diverse hardships. They said that they are often the sole providers for their children as fathers abdicated their responsibilities, and they are striving for a better life. The actions of the associations target continuing education for women, children's education and business opportunities. In the associations, women collaborate on diverse tasks including making soap, dying cloth, tailoring, managing restaurants and selling processed food. The associations collect small monthly fees that can be used for loans, donations and investment. The focus groups gathered 57 participants (including 9 males). The women invited their sons to the sessions because they usually get their assistance in using their mobile phones and the women believed they should share the knowledge of the session with more people. The male participants were mostly students or graduates from university or professional schools looking for work. Table 5.1 describes the participants by focus groups. Some of the participants in Focus groups 1 and 3 were female university or high school students (less than 6).

We taped the sessions and transcribed them. Participants were asked a series of questions in order to understand what apps they use, how they access the internet and what they would like to learn about their phones. They then watched each video on a projected screen. We paused the videos and went through them sentence by sentence for translation purposes. The videos were played several times on demand. Participants could ask questions whilst performing the activities. The sessions lasted between two and three hours, depending on the time it took to go over the following five videos: 1) "What is Android?"; 2) "What is an app?"; 3) "What is an email?"; 4) "What is Google Play Store?"; 5) "How to install an app?". We used qualitative and quantitative methods to evaluate the effectiveness of our toolkit. Participants had to answer a questionnaire, and demonstrate and apply the concepts they learned so that we could assess their retention of the content presented and evaluate the videos. Sample questions (translated into English) are provided in Figures 5.1 and 5.2.

Findings

Before we discuss the effectiveness of the videos, we will describe how participants use their phones. We will also present the motivation of the participants. We present the limitations of the low-end handsets and how they affect mobile literacy. Our research illustrates the routine uses that participants had difficulties with and their concerns about security and privacy.

Mobile Phone Usage Patterns

Participants reported using their phones mainly for making and receiving calls and sending and receiving text messages. Most of the participants access the internet through data rather than wifi. Only five participants (8.77%) knew how to install an app. Participants mainly use mobile apps that are pre-installed by vendors or installed by intermediaries. Their usage of mobile apps focuses on popular apps such as Facebook, WhatsApp, YouTube and Photo. Facebook and WhatsApp come free when buying certain data pass. One of the participants said: "I would

TABLE 5.1 Focus group participants

Focus Group 1	Focus Group 2	Focus Group 3
10 females/3 males 13 participants	21 female participants	17 females/6 males (for support) 23 participants

- Video 1: What is Android?
- **Questions:**
  - **Question 1:** Choose the logo of Android amongst the following pictures:

    <Android> <Facebook> <Gardfiled>

  - **Question 2:** Choose the dessert that corresponds to the current Android version:

    <Nougat> <Macaron> <Chocolate>

- Video 2: What is an application?
- **Activities:**
  - **Activity 1:** Show us the icon of the Facebook app on **our** tablet
  - **Activity 2:** Cite 3 names of mobile applications.
  - **Activity 3:** Show us the icon of your favorite app on **your** phone.

FIGURE 5.1 Sample questions and activities on Android and mobile applications

- Video 3: What is an email?
- **Questions:**
  - **Question 1:** Is senegal@orange.sn a valid email address? Why?
  - **Question 2:** Is senegal&orange.sn a valid email address? Why?

- Video 4: What is Google Play Store?
- **Questions:**
  - **Question 1:** There are only paid apps in Google Play Store. True/False
  - **Question 2:** There are less than 1000 mobile applications in google Play Store. True/False
- **Activities:**
  - **Activity 1:** Show us the icon of Google Play Store on **your** phone.
  - **Activity 2:** Launch the Google Play Store application.
  - **Activity 3:** Make a search with the word "Senegal" in the Google Play Store.

- Video 5: How to install an Android mobile application?
- **Questions:**
  - **Question 1:** What place do you install apps from?
  - **Question 2:** How are mobile apps described in the Google Play Store?
- **Activities:**
  - **Activity 1:** Show us how you would install SeneNews on **your** phone.
  - **Activity 2:** Launch SeneNews.
  - **Activity 3:** Rate SeneNews.

FIGURE 5.2 Sample questions and activities on Google Play Store and mobile application installation

like use more applications but don't know how to proceed". Other participants had heard about Snapchat and Instagram but did not have them on their phones. Participants knew about (but rarely used) a small number of local apps such as Marodi TV that broadcasts soap operas and music; Seneweb and Senenews for news; and Wari to transfer money. They would access Marodi TV directly from YouTube rather than the app. It is interesting to note that participants were consumers of local Senegalese content mainly. Participants said that they were also interested in health, beauty, cooking and children's education apps.

Participants' Motivations

The participants were very motivated in learning how to use their phones. Women thought it was important for them to gain more independence. They thought they relied too much on intermediaries. They have a real desire to educate themselves and become productive users of technology. They said: "The reality of our time is that if you do not use mobile apps, you are like an illiterate person" and

> As women of our age, we are used to using phones just to make and receive calls. Life is progressing and so we need to cope with technology. That is why this session is highly interesting for us. Generally, the things we want to do with our smartphones, we ask for the help of our children. … Of course, we do have smartphones, but sometimes we cannot execute every task we need to execute.

The Limitations of Handsets

Participants faced problems related to the limitations of their handsets. Some participants owned so-called "Chinese" Android phones. This pejorative term refers to cheap (less than $50) and low-quality phones that look like brand name phones, but lack or misplace core features. Installing apps on these phones is probably technically difficult or impossible. The participants who had these types of phones did not have access to Google Play. People will buy these phones without being aware of this. Many participants had low storage space issues on their phones. Interpreting alert messages related to space, deleting apps and pictures, using SD cards and backing up data to the cloud require mobile literacy skills that the participants did not have. Low-end handsets often have slow performance, bad screen resolution and camera quality and limited storage. This raises the issue of the responsibility of phone manufacturers and traders to provide quality and affordable handsets to users in emerging and developing markets. The tradeoff between quality and price has to be given particular attention.

Difficulties with Routine Uses

Participants asked questions on recurring issues they face. These include: dealing with and adding storage space, understanding what a password is, resetting and recovering passwords, understanding alert messages, identifying and dealing with viruses, locating email addresses, deleting an account, connecting to wifi, taking and viewing pictures.

Usability Issues: Alerts and Emails

Participants had difficulty with alert messages that are often presented with technical jargon. For example, one of the participants had an alert message "Cannot connect to server". That participant thought that she had a virus on her phone, but the problem was related to the connection to the internet.

Most of the participants do not need to send and receive emails. Their communications go through WhatsApp and Facebook Messenger. However, Google requires them to have a valid email address to configure their phone and access Google Play, for example. This clearly shows that developing and emerging market users are not at the center of the design of these features, and that it is essential to rethink the need to create an email address to access all the features of an Android phone. An alternative solution is necessary.

Several participants said that they had lost or broken their phones. They could not retrieve their data because they did not know that data were ultimately saved somewhere (in the cloud) and linked to the email and password associated with their phone. They were not aware of the importance of emails to synchronize accounts from one phone to the other.

Security and Privacy Concerns

Some of the participants had their phones configured by intermediaries. These third parties could potentially use the credentials for questionable, even criminal, purposes (Ahmed, Guha, Rifat, Shezan, & Dell, 2016). When checking participants' phones, many of them already had email set up, though they did not know the email address or password. We discovered this after showing the video about Google Play and when participants had to launch the Google Play app. This gave rise to a discussion on security and privacy, and raised many new questions, including: how to choose a password, the difficulty of remembering passwords and the third party's scope of access. To keep things moving during the focus group sessions, we created emails and passwords for many participants and wrote down the credentials on a piece of paper.

Effectiveness of the Videos

The participants went through the videos one by one, and were asked to answer questions on paper and carry out some tasks. The questionnaire and the activities measured the users' learning retention of concepts and practice of using mobile devices. Table 5.2 summarizes our results.

Of the participants 66.6% could recognize the Android logo and 56.14% could provide the name of the Android version after watching the "What is Android?" video.

The "What is an app?" video generated discussions on mobile applications that participants use and presentations of local apps. Only 55.55% of the participants in Focus groups 1 and 3 could recognize the Facebook logo, even when they identified themselves as heavy Facebook app users.

The "What is an email address?" video depicted the syntax of an email address. Twenty-five percent of the participants in Focus groups 2 and 3 could recognize an email address.

The "What is Google Play Store?" video exemplified the issues with emails, and started the conversation on security and privacy. Participants of the focus groups grasped that Google Play offers free and paid apps (70.17%), and that it has a plethora of apps (64.91%). However, only 18.18% of them could recognize the logo of the Google Play app.

The "How to install an app?" video was played two or three times as this was the objective of the focus groups. At the end of the sessions/focus groups a total of 42.10% of the participants managed to install an app. All the focus groups proposed to install Snapchat on their phones.

The quantitative and qualitative data collected makes it clear that the videos have potential but we need to add new ones based on the feedback of the participants and the issues we observed. The focus groups were not very long and having 42.10% of the users successfully installing an app is promising. We, of course, need more in-depth research and to discuss all the parameters that impacted the study.

Enhancing the Toolkit

The videos definitely need to be in Wolof, and probably in other local languages, to reach a wider audience. We could not have managed the focus groups without a translator. The videos should be designed to be ageless as far as possible and to be reusable. For example, we should not mention a specific Android version. One difficulty is that phones are not always alike and there are many Android operating systems.

The "How to create an email address?" video is very important as a foundation as many other concepts build on it. Not knowing how to create an email address can prevent users from doing other things on the phone. This video is not long enough to cover sending and receiving emails. Many different smaller concepts related to emails need to be added (e.g., finding an existing email, recovering a password).

It appears there is a need for more short videos that break down tasks step by step. Based on the use cases that participants had difficulties with, a certain number of foundation and specific topic videos are necessary for participants to

72 Christelle Scharff

TABLE 5.2 Summary of participants' answers to questionnaires

	Focus Group 1 (n=13)	Focus Group 2 (n=21)	Focus Group 3 (n=23)	Total (n=57)
Recognize Android logo	13	13	12	38 (66.67%)
Recognize Android version	11	11	10	32 (56.14%)
Recognize Facebook logo	3	No data	17	20 (55.55%) (n=36, partial data available)
Know Google Play Store has paid and free apps	12	11	17	40 (70.17%)
Know there are more than 1000 apps in Google Play Store	11	11	15	37 (64.91%)
Recognize Google Play logo	No data	4	4	8 (18.18%) (n=44, partial data available)
Recognize an email address	No data	6	5	11 (25%) (n=44, partial data available)
# Number of Snapchat apps installed	5	8	11	24 (42.10%)

gain sufficient skills to be able to use their mobile phone independently. They include: "What is a password?"; "How to be safe on the internet?"; and "What is a virus?"; "How to reset a password?"; "What is an alert?"; and "How to connect to wifi?".

Conclusion and Future Work

This research contributes to the development of effective material to improve mobile literacy skills for users in emerging and developing markets. It is important for the ICTD community and the industry as there are billions of potential users, subscribers and consumers in these markets. While the focus has been on one country (Senegal), the videos are generic and can be translated into different local languages to benefit a wider audience. Users who were part of our study (mostly women) were motivated to improve their mobile literacy skills to increase their independence in performing routine tasks without help from intermediaries. We identified the issues that they face daily in using their mobile phones. Some of these issues are due to hardware limitations (e.g., space); they rise on the low-end and so-called "Chinese" handsets that they use. This raised the issue of responsibility of phone manufacturers and sellers to provide affordable quality phones in emerging and developing markets. Other issues are related to usability (e.g., alert messages). Our research demonstrates that the concept of email is confusing and that users should not be required to create an email account to fully use Android phones as they will never need to do so. The focus groups identified numerous use cases that block novice users. These use cases range from recovering a password to connecting to wifi, locating an existing gmail account on a phone and knowing how to recover contacts and pictures in case of a lost, broken or stolen phone. The focus groups exemplified the issues related to security and privacy when users owned phones that are configured by third parties.

As shown in existing research, videos have the potential to teach users how to use their mobile phones. In this study, the results of the questionnaire and observations of the participants showed evidence of knowledge retention from the videos. The study needs further investigation. It is not confirmed that the effectiveness of the videos came solely from watching the videos, or from the arrangement of the focus groups whereby videos were stopped after each sentence and participants could ask questions.

The next steps of this study will consist of translating existing videos into Wolof and extending the toolkit by adding new videos. Users expressed a desire for videos on using emails, managing pictures, understanding phone storage, backing up data and privacy on the internet. We plan to co-design these videos with users in Senegal. We are considering releasing all the videos on popular Facebook pages and WhatsApp groups in Senegal to establish a direct link with users and gather more feedback. We are also looking at sharing the material with institutions working on similar research. Our goal is to develop and widely distribute French and local language material to teach mobile literacy.

Acknowledgment

Thanks to Pace University Wilson Center, Scholarly Research, Undergraduate Research and Seidenberg; CREU; Dr. Fall, ARADES; Rene, Schoepp, Posner, Sosa, Gade, Ribeiro and all students involved; Gaetana Rene; Chun Hei Cheung. This work has been approved under Pace University's IRB # 994145–1.

References

Ahmed, S. I., Guha, S., Rifat, R., Shezan, F. H., & Dell, N. (2016). Privacy in repair: An analysis of the privacy challenges surrounding broken digital artifacts in Bangladesh. In *Proceedings of the Eighth International Conference on Information and Communication Technologies and Development ICTD '16* (pp. 1–10). New York, NY: ACM.

Akram, A., Akkireddy, J., Le Beux, Y., & Kumar, S. A. (2018, October 23). Entering the era of smartphones for farmers: Surprises and discoveries. *UN Capital Development Fund Newsletter*. Retrieved from https://www.uncdf.org/article/4004/entering-the-era-of-smartphones-for-farmers-surprises-and-discoveries.

AppliCafé YouTube channel. (2017). Retrieved from https://www.youtube.com/playlist?list=PLEKtbS7M4jiYwLshjDOUGWbIFF2iN-epG.

Bellman, E., & Malhotra, A. (2016, October 13). Why the vast majority of women in India will never own a smartphone. Retrieved from https://www.wsj.com/articles/why-the-vast-majority-of-women-in-india-will-never-own-a-smartphone-1476351001.

Burrell, J., & Oreglia, E. (2015). The myth of market price information: Mobile phones and the application of economic knowledge in ICTD. *Journal of Economy and Society*, 44 (2), 271–292.

Burrell, J., & Toyama, K. (2009). What constitutes good ICTD research? *Journal of Information Technologies and International Development*, 5(3), 82–94.

Cuendet, S., Medhi-Thies, I., Bali, K., & Cutrell, E. (2013). VideoKheti: Making video content accessible to low-literate and novice users. In *Proceedings of the CHI'13 Conference* (pp. 2833–2842). New York, NY: ACM.

Dodson, L. L., Sterling, S. R., & Bennett J. K. (2013). Minding the gaps: Cultural, technical and gender-based barriers to mobile use in oral-language Berber communities in Morocco. In *Proceedings of the Sixth International Conference on Information and Communication Technologies and Development ICTD '13* (pp. 79–88). New York, NY: ACM.

Gillwald, A., & Global Commission on Internet Governance. (2017). Beyond access: Addressing digital inequality in Africa. *The shifting geopolitics of internet access: From broadband and net neutrality to zero-rating* (pp. 37–54). Centre for International Governance Innovation. Retrieved from www.jstor.org/stable/resrep05240.7.

Gilster, P. (1998). *Digital literacy*. New York: Wiley.

GSMA Mobile Internet Skills Training Toolkit. (2018, May 3). Retrieved from www.gsma.com/mobilefordevelopment/programmes/connected-society/mistt.

Hague, C., & Payton, S. (2010). *Digital literacy across the curriculum: A futurelab handbook*. Bristol; Futurelab publisher.

Katule, N., Densmore, M., & Rivette, U. (2016). Leveraging intermediated interactions to support utilization of persuasive personal health informatics. In *Proceedings of the Eighth Conference on ICTD'16 (1–10)*. New York, NY: ACM.

Katule, N., Rivett, U., & Densmore, M. (2016). A family health app: Engaging children to manage wellness of adults. In *Proceedings of the Seventh Annual Symposium on Computing for Development ACM DEV '16*. New York, NY: ACM.

Medhi-Thies, I. (2015). User interface design for low-literate and novice users: Past, present and future. *Foundations and Trends Human–Computer Interaction*, 8(1), 1–72.

Ndiaye, M. A., & Zouinar, M. (2014). The usage of mobile phones by low-literate users in Senegal: An ethnographic study. In *Proceedings of Fourth International Conference on Mobile Communication for Development M4D'14* (pp. 272–280). Karlstad, Sweden: Karlstad University Press.

NETHOPE Solutions Center. (2018, March 19). Digital skills framework library. Retrieved from https://solutionscenter.nethope.org/digital-nonprofit/digital-skills-framework-start-page.

Phokeer, A., Densmore, M., Johnson, D., & Feamster, N. (2016). A first look at mobile internet use in township communities in South Africa. In *Proceedings of the Seventh Annual Symposium on Computing for Development ACM DEV '16* (pp. 1–10). New York, NY: ACM.

Roggemann, K., & Nurko, G. (2019, February 14). The (missing) digital principle: Educate the user. Retrieved from https://dai-global-digital.com/the-missing-digital-principle-educate-the-user.html.

Scharff, C., Rene, V, Schoepp, J. G., Shah, N. K., & Greenberg, A. (2017). Exploring mobile device literacy in Senegal. In *Proceedings of the IEEE Global Humanitarian Technology Conference GHTC'17* (pp. 1–7). Piscataway, NJ: IEEE.

Sey, A., Bar F., Coward, C., Koepke, L., Rothschild, C., Sciadas, G. (2015). There when you need it: The multiple dimensions of public access ICT uses and impacts. *Journal of Information Technologies and International Development*, 11(1), 71–86.

Traxler, J. (2012). Context as text in mobile digital literacy: A European university perspective. In M. Specht, M. Shaples, & J. Multisilta (Eds.), *Proceedings of the Eleventh International Conference on Mobile and Contextual Learning 2012* (pp. 289–293). Retrieved from http://ceur-ws.org.

Wagner, S. (2014). Mobile inclusion in the information age: The relevance of indigenous media movements to M4D. In *Proceedings of Fourth International Conference on Mobile Communication for Development M4D'14* (pp. 71–82). Karlstad, Sweden: Karlstad University Press.

Wyche, S., Steinfield, C., Cai, R., Simiyu, N., & Thieno, M. E. (2016). Reflecting on video: Exploring the efficacy of video for teaching device literacy in rural Kenya. In *Proceedings of the Eighth International Conference on Information and Communication Technologies and Development ICTD'16*. New York, NY: ACM.

6

SUPPORTED MOBILE LEARNING IN THE "THIRD SPACES" BETWEEN NON-FORMAL AND FORMAL EDUCATION FOR DISPLACED PEOPLE

Gabi Witthaus and Gill Ryan

Introduction

According to the United Nations High Commission for Refugees (UNHCR, 2001–2019), there are currently more than 70 million refugees, asylum seekers and internally displaced people in the world. An estimated 3% of young adults amongst refugees are enrolled in post-secondary education, and although this figure is small in comparison to the global average of 37%, it is triple the number reported in the previous three years (UNHCR, 2019). The UNHCR attributes this growth to the new opportunities provided by "connected higher education, where digital programmes are combined with teaching and mentoring" (UNHCR, 2019). Elsewhere it has been noted that online and mobile learning can create "normalcy in adversity" (Moser-Mercer 2016, p. 1), and can potentially provide continuity of education and skill-building for refugees during periods of waiting, or during disruptions caused by the precarious contexts that refugees may be in (Traxler et al., 2019). It can offer flexibility and opportunities for creativity and innovation. There is also a wide range of resources available in mobile-accessible formats that are relevant to refugees (Creelman, Witthaus & Padilla-Rodriguez, 2018).

This chapter considers the work being done by organisations that provide mobile learning opportunities for displaced people. Throughout the chapter, the terms "online" and "mobile learning" are both used, as mobile technology enables access to online education for displaced populations with high smartphone ownership (Frouws, Phillips, Hassan & Twigt, 2016). Mobile learning can provide refugees with "access to people and digital learning resources, regardless of place and time" (Kukulska-Hulme, 2010).

For this chapter, insights were sought into displaced people's motivations for learning, and the associated challenges. As this is an emerging area of research, data was gathered from the "grey" literature (e.g. conference proceedings, videos, blogs and newsletters), as well as traditional academic literature. Examples of three organisations offering supported mobile education to displaced people are provided, and Third Space theory (Bhabha, 1990) is used as a conceptual framework to explore them, with the aim of identifying features that enable opportunities for agency for displaced learners.

Motivations for Learning in Displaced Communities

Being competent in the language of the host country is identified as a strong enabler of social integration (Casey, 2016). In the UK, Kearns and Whitley (2015) suggest that educational qualifications, employment and English language proficiency are associated with better social integration. Proficiency is considered essential for navigating the host country's systems and support services, and for engaging with education and employment. For parents with children at school, being able to communicate in the language their children are learning in is a priority (Doyle & O'Toole, 2013). Mobile social learning, in particular, can support language learning and social inclusion (Kukulska-Hulme, Norris & Donohue, 2015; Kukulska-Hulme, 2018). However, the uses of mobile technologies need to be carefully considered by teachers: a finding from the SALSA project was that learners using their phone to listen to language learning prompts in public places felt they were conspicuously behaving differently from local people (Gaved & Peasgood, 2017).

Gaining employment is an important motivator for refugees (Doyle & O'Toole, 2013). Some refugees are motivated to help others by entering the health or teaching professions, or by training as a mentor to other refugees and asylum seekers. However, displaced people often find that their prior qualifications are not recognised by employers. In some countries, there are schemes to address this, for example, the New Refugee Doctors Project, which provides suitably qualified refugees with specialised language support and professional mentoring to practise medicine in Scotland (NHS Education for Scotland, 2017).

Preparing to enter university is another motivation for displaced people to use mobile learning. Pathways into higher education for refugees are limited because of the lack of recognition of prior learning (particularly where documentation is missing), academic credit transfer across different national frameworks and accessing finance for higher education (Charitonos, 2018b). Nevertheless, digital technologies allow for cloud-based storage of credentials, transcripts and portfolios, and are increasingly enabling refugees with partial or complete qualifications to have their credentials recognised (e.g. Council of Europe, 2019). Uninettuno in Italy follows guidelines from Enic-Naric to help recognise prior learning of refugees (Caforio in Witthaus, 2019). Kiron Open Higher Education in Germany partners with massive open online course (MOOC) platforms Coursera (2019) and edX (2016) to curate MOOC-based curricula enabling learners to obtain credit towards formal higher education in their host countries.

Alongside these more instrumental motivations to learn, some refugees and asylum seekers are simply motivated by the sheer enjoyment of learning, while others may seek to enhance their well-being and sense of self-worth. The Scottish Refugee Council (2011, p. 2) describes the relationship between educational access and mental health as "symbiotic", as access to education improves mental health, and improved mental health opens up access to education. Participating in education can instil feelings of self-worth and mental well-being for those who have been refused asylum, and can keep them engaged with services and support (McKenna, 2018). Education can renew a sense of dignity to refugees, and allow them to contribute positively to their community (Crea & Sparnon, 2017). A recurring theme from narratives of Kiron students (Kiron, n.d.) is making their family proud, through their academic achievements or being able to provide for them. For female students education is often viewed as empowering.

Challenges of Online and Mobile Learning

Many asylum seekers and refugees are living in precarious contexts and processing traumatic experiences. Those in the asylum system and refused asylum seekers may not engage effectively with learning due to the impact of destitution, trauma and precarity (McKenna, 2018). Wider issues, such as family turbulence, financial problems, health problems and family demands, can affect refugees' learning and participation (Cosla Strategic Migration Partnership, 2017). National policies can also play a role, for example the Home Office in the UK can attach "no study" conditions when a person is released from immigration detention if they have exhausted their appeal rights or have committed immigration offences (Refugee Council, 2018). For internally displaced people, living environments may be dangerous and inhibit their digital access and ability to learn. Air strikes, blackouts or curfews may make it difficult to maintain learning, and there is "the need to build an online cultural identity as physical cultures are threatened" (Traxler, 2018, p. 3). In such circumstances, Traxler et al. (2019) argue for "the need for a conception of digital literacy that exploits digital technologies to enhance resilience and preserve wellbeing".

Accommodating the diversity of refugees' learning needs, experiences and languages is a challenge for organisations (Cosla Strategic Migration Partnership, 2017). Some learners have a high level of education but need to learn the language of their host country, while others may have literacy issues in their first language. "Some have never been to school prior to arriving to the UK and have no concepts of literacy, others are more comfortable with writing but still struggle with the Latin alphabet" (Belghazi, 2019). There is an identified shortage of English language classes in the UK, which makes it harder for refugees to access other kinds of support, including gaining employment and participating in community activities (APPG, 2017). Using smartphones to support language learning may be one way to address this (The Open University, 2014). For example, Norman (2019) uses mobile technology with learners as a way to overcome the lack of resources for English language teaching available to her organisation. Belghazi (2019) uses WhatsApp to communicate with learners, noting that learners with low literacy find the autocorrect feature, emojis and memes particularly useful.

Mobile learning can be inhibited by a lack of digital literacy, access to wifi or broadband, the cost of data, cultural expectations, language barriers and fear of being online (Potnis, 2015). Many displaced people have mobile phones, with ownership as high as 96% in some refugee camps, although not all have smartphones (Hounsell & Owuor, 2018). In crisis settings, there may be limited access to electricity and connectivity and a dependence on ageing devices. The potential for open educational resources (OERs) for "opening up access to educational opportunity and reconfiguring traditional boundaries between institutions and wider society" has been noted (Cannell, Macintyre & Hewitt, 2015, p. 64). Simpson (2019) describes the adaptation of OERs to enable access from feature phones (internet-enabled phones with limited functionality) for use in refugee contexts. Castaño Muñoz, Colucci and Smidt (2018) suggest mechanisms for circumventing connectivity issues, such as offline and m-learning, and applications that can work with low bandwidth. Moser-Mercer (2014) suggests using lower resolution versions of videos and/or text-only downloads for offline use, and asynchronous engagement with MOOCs. University of Geneva academics use WhatsApp as their main tool for supporting InZone's learners in refugee camps (O'Keeffe in Witthaus, 2019).

Gender inequalities can also be a barrier. The uneven distribution of digital technology can reinforce the exclusion of women and girls from online education (Sambuli, Brandusescu & Brudvig, 2018). Bokai (2017) identified low female participation (<10%) in MOOCs in refugee camps due to childcare, household responsibilities and computer literacy. Practical barriers such as childcare, lack of family support or limited availability of part-time options were also identified by the Scottish Refugee Council (2011). Some organisations providing education for displaced communities, such as Kiron (Buerglen, 2019), are increasingly focusing on ways to support female learners.

Finally, there are cultural and pedagogical barriers for many displaced learners as the pedagogy embedded in learning resources developed in the Global North may be unfamiliar to some refugees, and may need significant adaptation or contextualisation (Moser-Mercer, 2014). The potential of mobile technology to meet refugees' learning needs can also be hampered by a lack of digital capacity among teachers (Charitonos, 2018a). Solutions being explored include involving refugees as co-designers and co-creators of learning programmes, as will be seen in the examples below.

Example 1: Bridges Programmes

Bridges Programmes, based in Glasgow, Scotland, is a voluntary organisation that supports the social, educational and economic integration of refugees, asylum seekers, migrants and other displaced people in Glasgow. They work with partners to support people into work (if eligible) or education. Through partnerships with colleges and universities, they provide formal and non-formal learning opportunities, while their Open Access Centre offers access to digital technology and support for online and blended learning.

Bridges was an early adopter of OERs, partnering with the Open University in Scotland (OUiS) from 2005 (EADTU, 2016). Identifying reflection as a key learning need for refugees, Bridges initially used the *Reflections Toolkit* (The Open University in Scotland, 2017), an existing OER on the OpenLearn Create platform. Following an evaluation of the *Toolkit*, Bridges and OUiS co-created a remixed, bespoke version with learners (Bridges Programmes, 2013). As learners worked through the original OER, their reflections on their journey, and identification of the skills, experiences and strengths they brought to their new country, became the content for the remixed OER – *Reflecting on Transitions* (The Open University in Scotland and Bridges Programmes, 2017).

Locally-based learners can choose to work through the course face-to-face with a case worker or tutor who provides support with language and digital skills. Group support was initially offered but this proved problematic as some learners found it difficult to discuss personal and traumatic experiences, and gender, culture and age differences affected group dynamics, and so support is now provided on a one-to-one or paired basis (Bridges Programmes, 2013). *Reflecting on Transitions* "offers clients the opportunity to take stock in a supported way and in a safe place" (Lennon, 2019).

Example 2: InZone

InZone is an academic centre based at the University of Geneva's Global Studies Institute, focusing on building higher education spaces in fragile contexts, offering formal and non-formal academic programmes to refugees in Jordan and Kenya, primarily in refugee camps, and building capacity in education and higher education in emergencies at the global level. Together with the UNHCR, InZone co-leads the Connected Learning in Crisis Consortium, which was founded in 2016 (CLCC, 2017), and which promotes the provision of higher education in contexts of conflict, crisis and displacement, using a combination of online and mobile technologies and face-to-face learning. Learners can learn from home using their own smartphones with virtual support, or in various physical locations in the camps, including in the InZone Learning Hub building, with face-to-face and online support (InZone, 2019). Learners on certain courses are able to take out tablets on loan to use at home.

InZone's mission is "pioneering innovative approaches to multilingual communication and higher education in communities affected by conflict and crisis" (InZone, 2019). They use OERs for both formal academic courses and non-formal courses, ensuring that all OERs are locally downloadable to overcome connectivity constraints. InZone supports course creators, curriculum designers and assessment experts to collaborate on adapting OERs to meet local needs, and works closely with local higher education institutions to build contextualised academic programmes in fragile contexts. The use of OERs enables InZone to redeploy limited resources towards translating learning materials and increasing efforts for inclusion. In partnership with other universities, InZone aims to develop learning materials that centre the student voice, and to reflect student feedback in any updates. Some graduates take on facilitator roles for new cohorts, supporting students in the classroom as a complement to the online tutorials provided by academics from the University of Geneva (generally delivered via WhatsApp) and occasional face-to-face teaching weeks led by visiting faculty (P. O'Keeffe, Personal communication, 5 November 2019).

Example 3: Kiron

Kiron Open Higher Education was founded as a social start-up in Germany in 2015, with the aim of giving refugees around the world access to a university education. Kiron's core offer consists of "study tracks" in the form of curated MOOCs from universities around the world, which have been matched to programmes offered by higher education institutions in Germany, Lebanon and Jordan. Kiron has its own learning platform, and, where feasible, learners are invited to participate in small-group online tutorials to complement the MOOCs, using online conference technology. Kiron enters into Learning Agreements with universities to guarantee the recognition of credit points from MOOCs, based on a rigorous quality-assurance process (Knoth, Lorenz & Rampelt, 2018). Kiron also offers short skills-focused certificate courses. To date, they have supported over 6,000 learners in over 45 countries (Kiron, n.d.).

An in-depth study with Kiron learners in Germany found that they overwhelmingly appreciated the opportunity to learn flexibly online, despite facing significant challenges (Witthaus, 2018). In addition to the technical, linguistic and cultural barriers mentioned above, some learners also held an unfulfilled desire for traditional, classroom-based teaching, and found learning online to be a lonely experience. Most learners found strategies to overcome these obstacles, such as self-regulating their learning through goal-setting, monitoring progress and reflecting on their learning, while several also sought out a mentor, either through Kiron's mentoring or "study buddy" programmes, or through their own personal efforts. Learners in this study tended to use a combination of smartphones and laptops; some described a strategy of scheduling their learning activities around the availability of devices, for example, reading on their phones whilst commuting to work, and writing when they had access to a desktop computer at work or a laptop at home.

Third Spaces

The examples above will now be explored in terms of "Third Space" theory. The Third Space concept is attributed to Homi Bhabha, a critical and postcolonial theorist. He proposed a "First Space" and a "Second Space", which he suggested were inhabited by the colonised and the coloniser respectively, while the Third Space was an emergent, "hybrid" space in the intersection between the two, in which neither culture was dominant (Bhabha, 1990).

The Third Space has been touched on in the recent literature in relation to open, online education. It has been suggested, for example, that MOOCs are Third Spaces, in that they enable a bridge between the ontological dualities of formal and informal learning (Cronin, 2014a). Potter and McDougall (2017) explored this idea, and provide a nuanced picture:

> Currently our scrutiny does provide rich evidence of some *third space* practices (peer pedagogy, asynchronous 'membraning' between academy knowledge and storytelling from 'publics'), but the majority of interaction is between the student, the technology and the course materials ....
>
> *(p. 128, emphasis in original)*

What appears to be missing from Potter and McDougall's findings is a sense of learner agency in shaping the learning experience. Returning to Third Space theory, it is argued here that the concept of "hybridity" can provide insights into ways in which organisations create an ecosystem that encourages learners to enact agency over their learning.

Bhabha's concept of hybridity differs from western notions of "multiculturalism" and "pluralism" – he interprets these as the dominant culture saying: "[T]hese other cultures are fine but we must be able to locate them within our own grid" (Bhabha, 1990, p. 208). Instead, he focuses on "that productive space of the construction of culture as difference" (Bhabha, 1990, p. 20). The notion of hybridity in the Third Space potentially enables new, empowering positions to emerge or be negotiated by those groups with less power in society. However, in a study on Turkish migrants in Germany, Bauhn and Fulya Tepe (2016) demonstrate that hybridity may result in "good" or "bad" experiences. They argue that the value of hybridity will depend on whether it expands or diminishes people's capacity for agency, and further, that this capacity is related to whether hybridity was chosen or imposed. Critical theorist, bell hooks makes the same point in relation to the notion of marginality: "I make a definite distinction between that marginality which is imposed by oppressive structures and that marginality one chooses as site of resistance – as location of radical openness and possibility" (hooks 1990, p. 153).

The examples will now be discussed in relation to features that all three of them have in common that express hybridity, and that could potentially expand the capacity for agency amongst displaced people. To this end, the focus will be on opportunities for learners to exercise choice over not just what and how they learn, but also over the positionality they are able to exercise in the learning ecosystem (other than merely that of learner), such as that of teacher, designer, knowledge generator, resource creator, facilitator or mentor.

Firstly, partnerships are a major feature of the delivery model in all three cases. Kiron has set up partnerships with over 60 higher education institutions worldwide, many of which recognise Kiron credits. Bridges Programmes partner with NHS Education in Scotland to support New Refugee Doctors, and with colleges and universities to widen access to further and higher education; these partnerships enable non-formal learning to take place within the familiar setting of Bridges until learners are ready to move on to formal study. InZone has partners at all levels – from the transnational (UNHCR and the International Committee of the Red Cross) to a Swiss regional body (the Canton of Geneva), and universities and organisations in Switzerland, the USA, Jordan and Kenya. Such partnerships give refugees the opportunity to engage in multiple ways in their learning – for example as learners and as volunteers, in various kinds of give-and-take relationships with the different partner organisations.

Secondly, all three organisations prioritise openness as a core principle. Bridges and InZone produce, reuse and adapt OERs and provide supported access to OERs as a pathway into further study and employment. Kiron bases its offer on openly published MOOCs as far as possible. Openness potentially allows for learner agency in that, with appropriate support, learners can choose their own learning pathways and can also adapt and remix existing resources to make them more relevant to themselves and others in their communities.

Thirdly, all three organisations use co-creation as a design principle for the ongoing development of their educational offers. The *Reflecting on Transitions* OER illustrates Bridges' co-creation model, which centres the voice of displaced learners and enables them to set their own goals and learning outcomes (Bridges Programmes, 2013). At InZone, course graduates become facilitators for future cohorts, helping to shape the ongoing development of the programmes. InZone's vision of co-creation sees "refugee learners who harness these [mobile] technologies become the producers of educational materials instead of remaining the passive recipients of information designed to prepare them for the host country's higher education system" (Moser-Mercer, 2016, p. 3). Kiron enables learners to help develop their own curricula through user testing and feedback.

Of the three elements of hybridity discussed here, co-creation is perhaps the one that has the most potential to foster the development of agency, as it allows displaced people to actively shape the curriculum and parameters of support for other learners.

Conclusion

The cases described here illustrate that it is not the technology alone which creates "Third Spaces", but that organisations using open tools in online spaces, and engaging in democratic practices "can foster learner autonomy and agency" (Cronin, 2014b). Three such democratic practices have been examined – openness, partnerships and co-creation – all of which have been shown to enable a kind of hybridity which offers opportunities for displaced people to enact agency over their learning in the context of mobile and online education. Returning to the theme of the book, it is important to consider the extent to which mobile devices and applications afford such opportunities. First, in all three of the examples discussed, learners can engage with the organisations mentioned, as well as with the partnership networks of those organisations, through their mobiles: learners in refugee camps in Africa can communicate with academics in Switzerland via WhatsApp; asylum seekers in Scotland can learn from resources produced by The Open University and other partners; and Kiron's MOOC learners can watch lectures by faculty from around the world, from wherever they are located. Secondly, learners in these three contexts can benefit from openness – as readers and viewers of open, online content. Finally, however, mobile devices may not offer the affordances needed to participate fully in higher education, such as writing assignments, nor to access the tools for co-creation. For these activities, laptops or desktop computers are still needed, and are often only available to refugees and asylum seekers as shared resources in fixed (non-mobile) learning centres or support offices, if at all. It is therefore no coincidence that all the examples identified utilise a blended approach, incorporating both mobile and face-to-face learning, where the classroom element includes access to such tools.

This analysis has illustrated some of the affordances and the limitations of mobile devices and applications for fostering Third Spaces of the kind that might enable refugees and asylum seekers to enact agency over their own learning. The examples given demonstrate that it is possible for communities of displaced people and those who work with them to jointly shape educational ecosystems within a social justice ethos. In the words of Martin Luther King: "Injustice anywhere is a threat to justice everywhere. We are caught in an inescapable network of mutuality, tied in a single garment of destiny. Whatever affects one directly, affects all indirectly" (King, Jr., 1963).

Acknowledgements

The authors wish to thank Marguerite Koole, Barbara Moser-Mercer, Paul O'Keeffe, Renata Suter, John Traxler and Markus Wachowski for their feedback on a draft of this chapter.

References

All Party Parliamentary Group on Refugees (APPG). (2017). Refugees welcome? The experience of new refugees in the UK. Retrieved from https://www.refugeecouncil.org.uk/wp-content/uploads/2019/03/APPG_on_Refugees_-_Refugees_Welcome_report.pdf.

Bauhn, P., & Fulya Tepe, F. (2016). Hybridity and agency: Some theoretical and empirical observations. *Migration Letters*, 3(13), 350–358.

Belghazi, M. (2019). WhatsApp as a learning and support tool. . Retrieved from http://refugeelearningstories.org/published/whatsapp-as-a-learning-and-support-tool.

Bhabha, H. (1990). The Third Space. In J. Rutherford (Ed.), *Identity: Community, culture, difference* (pp. 207–221). Dagenham, UK: Lawrence & Wishart Ltd.

Bokai, D. (2017). Insights from using Massive Open Online Courses (MOOCs) in refugee camps. Retrieved from https://challenges.openideo.com/challenge/refugee-education/research/insights-from-using-massive-open-online-courses-moocs-in-refugee-camps.

Bridges Programmes. (2013). The Reflection Toolkit: Early reflections on its usage at Bridges Programmes. Retrieved from www.bridgesprogrammes.org.uk/files/ReflectionToolkitReport.pdf.

Buerglen, C. (2019). Exploring possibilities with online learning. Retrieved from https://kiron.ngo/community/exploring-possibilities-with-online-learning.

Cannell, P., Macintyre, R., & Hewitt, L. (2015). Widening access and OER: Developing new practice. *Widening Participation and Lifelong Learning*, 17(1),, 64–72. doi:10.5456/WPLL.17.1.64.

Casey, L. (2016). *The Casey Review. A review into opportunity and integration*. London: Department for Communities and Local Government.

Castaño Muñoz, J., Colucci, E., & Smidt, H. (2018). Free digital learning for inclusion of migrants and refugees in Europe: A qualitative analysis of three types of learning purposes. *International Review of Research in Open and Distance Learning*, 19(2), 1–21. doi:10.19173/irrodl.v19i2.3382.

Charitonos, K. (2018a). Technology-enabled language learning for refugees and migrants. The Open University. Retrieved from www.open.ac.uk/ikd/blog/inclusive-innovation-and-development/technology-enabled-language-learning-refugees-and-migrants (accessed 10 August 2019).

Charitonos, K. (2018b). OU participation in UNHCR's Connected Learning in Crisis Consortium. Retrieved from www.open.ac.uk/research/news/mygration-ou-participation-unhcrs-connected-learning-crisis-consortium.

Connected Learning in Crisis Consortium (CLCC). (2017). *About us*. Retrieved from www.connectedlearning4refugees.org/about-us.

Cosla Strategic Migration Partnership. (2017). *ESOL good practice guide*. Retrieved from www.migrationscotland.org.uk/esol-resettled-refugees/introduction/1-1-about-guide.

Council of Europe. (2019). European qualifications passport for refugees. Retrieved from https://www.coe.int/en/web/education/recognition-of-refugees-qualifications.

Coursera. (2019). Transforming lives through learning. Retrieved from https://www.coursera.org/refugees.

Crea, T. M., & Sparnon, N. (2017). Democratizing education at the margins: Faculty and practitioner perspectives on delivering online tertiary education for refugees. *International Journal of Educational Technology in Higher Education*, 14(43). Retrieved from https://link.springer.com/content/pdf/10.1186/s41239-017-0081-y.pdf.

Creelman, A., Witthaus, G., & Padilla Rodriguez, B. (2018). *Refugees' Educational Resources (RefER) project final report*. Milton Keynes: The Open University. Retrieved from www.open.ac.uk/research/sites/www.open.ac.uk.research/files/files/Documents/RefER%20Project%20Final%20Report.pdf.

Cronin, C. (2014a). Networked learning and identity development in open online spaces. In S. Bayne, C. Jones, M. de Laat, T. Ryberg, & C. Sinclair (Eds.), *Proceedings of the 9th International Conference on Networked Learning 2014* (pp. 405–411). Edinburgh: University of Edinburgh.

Cronin, C. (2014b). Open education and digital identities. Retrieved from https://catherinecronin.net/reflecting/openeducation-and-identities.

Doyle, L., & O'Toole, G. (2013). *A lot to learn: Refugees, asylum seekers and post-16 learning*. London: Refugee Council. Retrieved from https://www.refugeecouncil.org.uk/wp-content/uploads/2019/03/A_lot_to_learn-Jan_13.pdf.

edX. (2016, February 18). Thousands of refugees to receive college credit online through edX partnership with Kiron. Retrieved from https://www.edx.org/press/thousands-refugees-receive-college.

European Association of Distance Teaching Universities (EADTU). (2016). *Members' policies and activities concerning refugees and migrants (July 2016)*. Maastricht: EADTU. Retrieved from https://eadtu.eu/images/Services/Policies_and_activities_concerning_refugees_and_migrants_EADTU.pdf.

Frouws, B., Phillips, M., Hassan, A., & Twigt, M. (2016). *Getting to Europe the 'WhatsApp' way*. RMMS Briefing Paper 2. Copenhagen: Danish Refugee Council. Retrieved from www.mixedmigration.org/wp-content/uploads/2018/05/015_getting-to-europe.pdf.

Gaved, M. and Peasgood, A. (2017). Fitting in versus learning: A challenge for migrants learning languages using smartphones. *Journal of Interactive Media in Education*, 1, 1. doi:10.5334/jime.436.

hooks, b. (1990). *Yearning: Race, gender and politics*. Boston: South End Press.

Hounsell, B. & Owuor, J. (2018). Opportunities and barriers to using mobile technology and the internet in Kakuma refugee camp and Nakivale refugee settlement. Samuel Hall. Retrieved from: https://www.elrha.org/wp-content/uploads/2018/02/Innovating_mobile_soultions_Report.pdf.

InZone. (2019). What we do. Retrieved from https://www.unige.ch/inzone/what-we-do.

Kearns, A., & Whitley, E. (2015). Getting there? The effects of functional factors, time and place on the social integration of migrants. *Journal of Ethnic and Migration Studies*, 41(4), 2105–2129. doi:10.1080/1369183X.2015.1030374.

King, Jr, M. L. (1963, August). Martin Luther King Jr.'s 'Letter from Birmingham Jail'. *The Atlantic*. Retrieved from https://www.theatlantic.com/magazine/archive/2018/02/letter-from-a-birmingham-jail/552461.

Kiron. (n.d.). Kiron community – meet our students. Retrieved from https://kiron.ngo/community.

Knoth, S., Lorenz, A., & Rampelt, F. (2018). Make MOOCs count for higher education: Approaches to awarding ECTS credits for learning in open online courses. In W. Van Valkenburg, & R. Schuwer (Eds.), *OE Global 2018* (pp. 1–5). Delft: TU Delft.

Kukulska-Hulme, A. (2010). Mobile learning as a catalyst for change. *Open Learning*, 25(3), 181–185.

Kukulska-Hulme, A., Norris, L., & Donohue, J. (2015). *Mobile pedagogy for English language teaching: A guide for teachers*. London: British Council.

Kukulska-Hulme, A. (2018). Mobile learning for mobile populations: Where should we be heading?The Open University. Retrieved from www.open.ac.uk/research/news/mobile-learning-for-mobile-populations.

Lennon, M. (2019). Case study: Co-creating resources with refugees. In *Open learning champions* (p.16). Retrieved from https://www.open.edu/openlearn/sites/www.open.edu.openlearn/files/open_learning_champions_olc_guide_19_accessibility_checked.pdf.

McKenna, R. (2018). *From pillar to post, destitution among people refused asylum in Scotland*. Glasgow: Destitute Asylum Seeker Service. Retrieved from https://www.rst.org.uk/wp-content/uploads/2019/03/From-Pillar-to-Post-Feb-2019.pdf.

Mercer, B. (2016). *Participatory innovation – mobile and connected learning as a driving force in higher education in emergencies*. Geneva, Switzerland: InZone, University of Geneva.

Moser-Mercer, B. (2014). MOOCs in fragile contexts. In U. Cress, & C. D. Kloos (Eds.), *Proceedings of the European MOOC Stakeholder Summit 2014* (pp. 114–121). Lausanne, Switzerland: Ecole Polytechnique Federale de Lausanne (Swiss Federal Institute of Technology in Lausanne). Retrieved from http://hdl.voced.edu.au/10707/340125.

NHS Education for Scotland. (2017). Scottish Government funding supports refugee doctors to re-train to work in NHS Scotland. Retrieved from https://www.nes.scot.nhs.uk/newsroom/media-releases/refugee-doctors-programme.aspx.

Norman, L. (2019). An English lesson with refugee learners – a treasure hunt in the town centre. Retrieved from http://refugeelearningstories.org/published/an-english-lesson-with-refugee-learners-a-treasure-hunt-in-the-town-centre.

Potnis, D. (2015). Inequalities creating economic barriers to owning mobile phones in India: Factors responsible for the gender digital divide. *Information Development*, 32(5), 1332–1342. Retrieved from https://journals-sagepub-com.libezproxy.open.ac.uk/doi/full/10.1177/0266666915605163.

Potter, J., & McDougall, J. (Eds.). (2017). *Digital media, culture and education: Theorising Third Space literacies* (1st ed.). London: Palgrave Macmillan.

Refugee Council. (2018, July). *Immigration bail and right to study*. Retrieved from https://www.refugeecouncil.org.uk/wp-content/uploads/2019/03/Immigration_Bail_briefing__July_2018_.pdf.

Sambuli, N., Brandusescu, A., & Brudvig, I. (2018). *Advancing women's rights. Gaps and opportunities in policy and research*. Washington: World Wide Web Foundation. Retrieved from http://webfoundation.org/docs/2018/08/Advancing-Womens-Rights-Online_Gaps-and-Opportunities-in-Policy-and-Research.pdf.

Scottish Refugee Council. (2011). *Scottish Refugee Council integration study – education briefing*. Retrieved from http://www.scottishrefugeecouncil.org.uk/assets/0000/3512/Stage_2_Briefing_-_Education_SRC_Refugee_Integration_study_Dec2011.pdf.

Simpson, K. (2019). *Access to higher education for refugees in crisis settings: Adapting an OER to mLearning*. Retrieved from https://cloudworks.ac.uk/cloud/view/11965.

The Open University. (2014). *Why mobile phones for learning?* Retrieved from www.open.ac.uk/blogs/salsa/?p=21.

The Open University in Scotland. (2017). *Reflection toolkit*. Retrieved from https://www.open.edu/openlearncreate/course/view.php?id=843.

The Open University in Scotland and Bridges Programmes. (2017). *Reflecting on transitions*. Retrieved from https://www.open.edu/openlearncreate/course/view.php?id=1840.

Traxler, J. (2018). Digital literacy: A Palestinian refugee perspective. *Research in Learning Technology*, 26(26), 1–21. Retrieved from https://doi.org/10.25304/rlt.v26.1983.

Traxler, J., Khaif, Z., Nevill, A., & Affouneh, S., et al. (2019). Living under occupation: Palestinian teachers' experiences and their digital responses. *Research in Learning Technology*, 27, 1–18. Retrieved from https://doi.org/10.25304/rlt.v27.2263.

United Nations High Commissioner for Refugees (UNHCR). (2001–2019). *Figures at a glance*. Retrieved from https://www.unhcr.org/uk/figures-at-a-glance.html.

United Nations High Commissioner for Refugees (UNHCR). (2019). Tertiary education – out of reach. In *Stepping up: Refugee education in crisis*. Retrieved from https://www.unhcr.org/steppingup/tertiary-education-out-of-reach.

Witthaus, G. (2018). Findings from a case study on refugees using MOOCs to (re)enter higher education. *Open Praxis*, 10(4). Retrieved from https://openpraxis.org/index.php/OpenPraxis/issue/view/33/showToc.

Witthaus, G. (2019). *Enabling equity and inclusion for refugees and asylum seekers through open education*. Retrieved from https://www.youtube.com/watch?v=6OV7myvLV90&t=572s.

7

TOWARDS PARTICIPATORY MOOCS

Amit Pariyar, Narayanan Kulathuramaiyer and Poline Bala

Introduction

The recent development in MOOCs (Massive Open Online Courses) and mobile learning has shaped a landscape of potential educational breakthroughs for rural communities. Koller (2012) and Agarwal (2014), the leaders of mainstream MOOCs, see huge potential from MOOCs passing on the specialized knowledge of the world class universities in the global north to the learner communities in the global south. However, Sharples, Delgado Kloos, Dimitriadis, Garlatti, and Specht (2015) foresee MOOCs embracing various forms of mobile technologies offering new methods of learning that are better suited to rural learners, for instance context-sensitive, geo-located and crowd learning. The optimism about inclusive learning with MOOCs is increased by the growth in mobile penetration and internet connectivity. The International Telecommunication Union (ITU) has reported a general upward trend in developing countries in the percentage of the population using the internet, which increased from 7.7% in 2005 to 45.3% at the end of 2019 (ITU, 2019). These promising figures, together with the MOOCs' philosophy of democratizing education through technology echoed in Rhoads, Berdan and Toven-Lindsey (2013), Wulf, Blohm, Leimeister and Brenner (2014), Rambe and Moeti (2016), have sparked interest among development practitioners in considering MOOCs as a viable way of meeting the learning needs of developing countries.

However, as the educational paradigm MOOCs evolves in line with technology, recent developments show signs of departing from their original philosophy. From a commercial point of view, MOOCs are moving slightly away from the notion of openness to a revenue generation business model through certification and specialized programmes. For southern learners, the added financial burden can give rise to a suboptimal learning experience (Kalman, 2014). The founder of class central[1] aggregate courses Shah (2017) also reinforces the need for true innovation in pricing to enable the people who can benefit the most. From a community perspective, the pedagogical design of MOOCs is being replicated to broaden its reach, however, in the majority of cases, the format of MOOCs formats is simply being repackaged (Chadaj, Allison & Baxter, 2014; Onah, Sinclair, Boyatt & Foss, 2014), which is marginalizing rural communities even further.

The earlier MOOCs, which Rodriguez (2012) categorized as xMOOCs, were mostly led by university instructors or experts, covered mainstream courses, and were meant to engage learners with a specific background. The pedagogical design itself has not changed much except that subject materials outside the standard academic curriculum are increasingly covered to target diverse groups of learners. The initiatives by Udacity to upskill the American workforce (Udacity, 2015) and SDG Academy to inform the general public of the global challenges to reaching sustainable development (SDG Academy, 2018) are examples of MOOCs going beyond the mainstream. Similar trends are also noticed elsewhere in meeting the learning needs of rural communities, for instance, education to empower rural learners (Panyajamorn, Kohda, Chongphaisal, & Supnithi, 2016), and to capacitate rural health care workers (Warugaba, Naughton, Gauthier, Muhirwa & Amoroso, 2016). The underlying intention of many such initiatives is to deliver globally relevant skills to rural communities in response to the assessment of their knowledge gaps, mostly executed in a top-down fashion. This objective of pushing global knowledge at grassroots level can lead to a situation where the value of the local knowledge of certain groups within rural communities gets ignored. Further, the local knowledge is not prioritized in the mainstream knowledge exchange platforms and goes underutilized.

Such concerns are also validated by the 'outside-in' course focus, for instance MOOCs from established universities in the global north are integrated into the curriculum of developing countries. Altbach (2014) critiques the western dominance of education in the global south and Adams (2013) argues that southern learners find themselves in a take it or leave it situation. Such a predominant one-way knowledge flow phenomenon further reduces the ability of rural communities to contribute their local knowledge. Besides this, MOOCs' learning outcomes also tend to be based on individual driven activity. This misses the value of togetherness that the community seeks in fulfilling their learning goals. Content based learning remains the core component of MOOCs. Problem-based (Ally & Samaka, 2013; Maitland & Obeysekare, 2015) and project-based learning (Nkuyubwatsi, 2014) is a necessary component for MOOCs to connect with the experiential learning needs of the rural community. With these developments in MOOCs, replicating the current model to deliver an inclusive learning experience for rural communities seems impractical.

The challenges and context of rural communities are unique, and therefore should not be overlooked in designing the MOOCs. The rural communities deal with issues and problems that may seem small in scale and could be considered trivial from an outsider's perspective. This means, repurposing lectures/content as learning material is not appropriate for them, as they are more inclined towards a problem solving approach to learning. The local culture, customs and traditional knowledge are an integral part of their lives. Failing to assimilate their cultural elements and local knowledge in the learning process will result in dropouts. The knowledge generation mostly happens on the ground with local interaction, consquently one-way knowledge flow is not going to generate social interaction. Two-way knowledge flow is necessary to recognize the local potential and reinforce their learning interests. The learning outcomes based on individual driven activity do not capture the notion of unity and communal bonding. This demands learning outcomes that are oriented towards community driven activity and produce collective benefits for the community. Mutual trust and co-partnership is essential to sustain the development of MOOCs. The pedagogy which evokes community participation at all levels –production, delivery and consumption – is necessary to create an 'inside-out' focus in learning. Figure 7.1 highlights the gaps in the replicated MOOCs' model for inclusive learning. Given these gaps, MOOCs need to be reshaped so that they take into account the context and challenges faced by the rural communities and fulfil their promise to serve a social purpose. Furthermore, the intricate relationship between the indigenous knowledge and knowledge inquiry models leading to the harnessing of tacit and implicit knowledge needs to be developed to generate and transfer knowledge from the ground (Zaka, Kulathuramaiyer, Balke & Maurer, 2008). The holistic knowledge modelling as practised in the remote indigenous communities (Zaman, Yeo, & Kulathuramaiyer, 2011; Zaman, Yeo, & Kulathuramaiyer, 2013) serves as a playground for knowledge inquiry. Such inherent mechanisms should also not be overlooked in reshaping the learning process.

This chapter presents the initiative of the COMPETEN-SEA project in deploying our proposed 'Community Led MOOCs' design model to serve the cultural knowledge preservation needs of the single mother communities in Bario, a remote and rural region in Borneo.

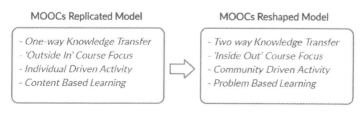

FIGURE 7.1 Gaps in MOOCs' delivery of inclusive learning

MOOCs: From Assumption to Inclusion

The social impact of MOOCs, in general, is simply interpreted from its technological capability to deliver global knowledge to huge audiences. This view positions MOOCs as a technical system, and devalues its ability as a social system to capture the networked relationship between individuals, groups and institutions. MOOCs as a socio-technical system combines the power of people's networks and technological sophistication to maximize the social impact. With this view and the gaps highlighted in Figure 7.1, the assumption that MOOCs can deliver an inclusive learning experience to the rural community overlooks three important elements: *community participation, learning context* and the *community's way of life* (see Figure 7.2).

Community Participation

The necessity for community participation in development projects sounds quite cliché. The participation is ensured at various stages from consultation to empowerment by integrating local resources, local capacities and local knowledge in the overall process (World Bank, 2015) but overall the underlying intention is to operationalize a global knowledge perspective. In such a participatory process, the global knowledge theme subsumes the local knowledge, and even subsides the value of local knowledge that the community has carried for generations. This happens as a result of the hierarchies that intuitively develop when two bodies of knowledge shaped by distinct backgrounds, worldviews, lifestyles and experiences collide with each other. This leads to a non-inclusive participation in which knowledge flow is not levelled up to build collective understanding. (King, Pegrum, & Forsey, 2018) raise concern about MOOCs reproducing existing inequalities by reinforcing a 'top-down' approach in their knowledge flow from global north to global south. The exclusion of the rural community happens at many levels.

FIGURE 7.2 Inclusive learning for participatory MOOCs

Macro Level Exclusion

The instructor-led pedagogy itself leads to a notion of hierarchy and imbalance in the knowledge exchange. The roles have to be reversed so that the learners can play the role of teachers. This will recognize their potential as contributors of local knowledge in the learning process. The instructors are not from the locale where MOOCs are being administered, which further widens exclusion due to lack of personal connect. Such exclusion is bridged when locally trained community champions take on the role of instructor in sharing knowledge with the community.

Micro Level Exclusion

The components of MOOCs such as learning materials are prepared by experts, mostly from universities, with a view to enriching the skills and upgrading local knowledge of learners which may not add value to the community and lead to their exclusion in the learning process. This happens when the assessment of the knowledge gaps of local communities is carried out in a top-down fashion. There is also a danger that the beneficial outcomes of these newly introduced skills can become so overpowering that the community starts to devalue their own local knowledge which they have preserved for generations.

The challenge is maintaining a balance whereby MOOCs do not ignore local knowledge in an attempt to bridge the education disparities. This concern is more apparent with xMOOCs as the learning is guided by the instructors. Conversely, the emphasis by cMOOCs on connecting knowledge resources dispersed in a digital space (Rodriguez, 2012) increases the chances of local knowledge being integrated in the learning process. However, to allow connection between global and local knowledge resources, cMOOCs need to support the local network of learners in rural areas. This would require strengthening the skills of rural communities to explore digital spaces which may put people off participating in the courses (Liyanagunawardena, Williams & Adams, 2014).

Learning Context

The learning context refers to all those factors that supposedly improve the learning experience. Based on the instructional design and context in Sherman (2002) these can be grouped into physical, social and psychological factors. Physical factors refer to the space in which a learner pursues learning, the medium a learner uses and the subject material a learner accesses. Social factors refer to the leaner's opportunity to interact with the instructor as well as other learners throughout the learning experience. The psychological factors refer to the degree to which the learners are motivated to continue learning.

Physical Factors

Many rural learners have limited or even no access to the internet. They have to go to the telecentre or to the nearest city to access the internet. The assumption of MOOCs that learning can be done 'from anywhere' is unrealistic because the rural learners have to confine themselves to a dedicated space to pursue online learning – which resonates more as a group activity. The learning materials can be accessed directly with mobile phones, or sometime through family and friends. This requires MOOCs to serve both the primary (direct) and secondary (indirect) learners. Rural communities also have task-centric learning needs. The use of generic resources can lead to high dropout rates (Richter & McPherson, 2012). The learning outcomes for rural learners are connected to their livelihood and they anticipate tangible outcomes in a short space of time. The basic skills of using the camera feature of a phone to take photos or record videos can produce instant outcomes for a rural community which can then market their local products. This differs from the majority of MOOC learners who are interested in long term gains, for instance switching profession.

Social Factors

For a rural community, the local networks are a valuable resource which becomes functional in problem-solving activities. These networks usually comprise of a small number of people who represent the voices of many others. The challenge for MOOCs is to identify the local network of co-learners and partners with whom the rural learners can interact in their learning pursuit. The interactions in local networks are equally important in inducing trust amongst the rural learners.

Psychological Factors

Kaplan and Haenlein (2016) have shown that MOOCs require a relatively high level of intrinsic motivation and self-discipline. The extrinsic and intrinsic motivations for both rural learners and typical MOOC learners are unique to their own needs. For instance, the rural learners are drawn towards online courses to gain skills that will help them with their livelihood. The rural community also tends to be drawn by the ability of MOOCs to preserve their local culture and knowledge for future generations. The exploration of such aspects of learning is needed to maintain the continued interest of rural learners.

Community Way of Life

MOOCs largely focus on personalized learning pathways and personalized feedback determined by learning analytics (Sunar, Abdullah, White & Davis, 2015). They can be extended, with flexibility for time-bound commitments or self-paced learning, and working with peers or alone. Such factors certainly enrich the learning experience but these are not sufficient to cater to needs of the global learners – those who have lifestyles different from the most privileged learners.

Intangible Factors

In sociology the 'way of life' or lifestyle stems from the concept of social differentiation, social identity and recognition which places cultural values and belief systems at its core (Berzano & Genova, 2015, pp. 1–217). This gives a reason for a community to distinguish itself from other social strata, and the motivation to preserve it for future generations. Our experience working with the Penan community, well-known for its past nomadic lifestyle, has shown that unity and harmony are their greatest strengths, and they have been cultivated it as its way of life (Pariyar, Kulathuramaiyer, Abdullah, & Chuah, 2019). Therefore, the community responds to external triggers in unpredictable ways. The objection of the Penan community to the road construction project (*The Borneo Post*, 2013), despite it being of economic value to the community, affirms the sensitivity of the community towards their 'way of life'. The community feared disintegration and disputes in the village due to an economic divide and the infiltration of alcohol. With such core values intact, the community tends to think alike, care for each other and ensure that no one is left behind in achieving socio-economic progress. For MOOCs to project such communal core values while maintaining a balance between varying degrees of learning outcomes for the targeted learners and non-learners within a community is a challenge.

In psychology, lifestyle is a reflection of an individual's personality, which develops with personal values, preferences, outlooks, attitudes and worldview (Rahayu, Haslina, & Salina, 2018). The lifestyle of an individual in a rural community has evolved against a backdrop of poverty and hardship. Their priorities are need-based. For instance, for farmers harvesting their crops is more important than attending a MOOC course. Their outlook is experiential, intergenerational and locally driven, which is the reason why they care so much for their social, cultural and ecological resources. Such a lifestyle is constantly threated with growing exposure to information. The challenge is to strike a balance between 'what information goes in' and 'how much' to avoid external influence and follow their lifestyle choices.

Tangible Factors

Lifestyle is also shaped by circumstantial factors. Financial constraints might push a community to follow a lifestyle with limited resources and opportunities. MOOCs have to be delivered without overburdening the community financially. The geographical constraints might push a community to choose a certain profession as its way of life. For Penans, who have lived in proximity with the forests since their nomadic times, these forests are integral to their existence and living with nature is their way of life. MOOCs have to create value add-ons out of existing resources to enrich their lifestyle conditions. The mobility constraints might push one community to live in close proximity to another. This means gathering over light refreshments is a frequent affair and a way for communities to build communal bonding. MOOCs have to blend in with such informal gatherings to maximize the learning outcomes.

MOOCS with a Social Purpose

The COMPETEN-SEA Project (http://competen-sea.eu) funded by the European Commission aims to enable Southeast Asian universities to develop educational services targeted at various unprivileged groups, often excluded from traditional educational outreach, across the region. The project in Malaysia is focused on meeting the technological and pedagogical challenges while addressing the needs of one of the most vulnerable and often overlooked communities in the development agendas – the single mother communities in the rural and remote regions of Borneo.

Community Led MOOCs

MOOCs were designed as a technical system to serve the societal needs further marginalizes communities and recreates exclusion due to the enforcement of one-way knowledge flow, content based learning, 'outside-in' course focus and individual driven activity. However, MOOCs need to be reshaped as a knowledge portal that supports two-way knowledge flow, builds upon an 'inside-out' course focus and makes way for community driven activity and a problem solving approach to learning. In response, we propose a 'Community Led MOOCs' design model as shown in Figure 7.3 that integrates community participation, its learning context and way of life, to deliver MOOCs that support the inclusion of the challenges and contexts of rural communities.

Case Study: Going Digital with the Beads

This case study presents an insight from our attempt to repurpose current MOOCs to change them to 'Community Led MOOCs' to serve the knowledge preservation needs of the single mother communities in Bario (see Figure 7.4) – a remote rural community from the Kelabit Highlands of the Malaysian State of Sarawak, on the island of Borneo.

Remoteness of Bario

Bario is a true representation of extreme rural conditions due to its geographic remoteness and poor infrastructure development. The only practical way to reach

Towards Participatory MOOCs 97

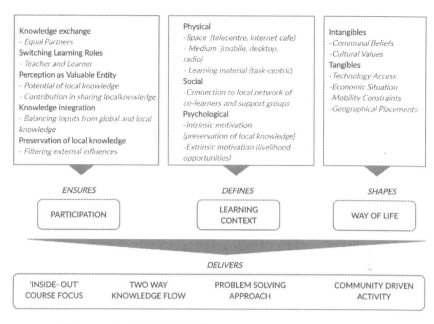

FIGURE 7.3 'Community led MOOCs' for participatory MOOCs

FIGURE 7.4 Members of single mother communities in Bario

Bario is by taking a 19-seater Twin Otter plane from Miri, the closest town on the coast, and the journey takes an hour. Alternatively, there is a logging road that connects Bario and Miri, but the journey takes between 16 and 18 hours over rough terrain which is inaccessible during the monsoon period. Bario is also the site of our pioneering international award-winning rural information and communication technology (ICT) project, e-Bario, which is our collective effort to provide opportunities for local development by providing public telephones and a computer and community telecentre with satellite access to the internet (Harris, Bala, Songan, & Khoo, 2001).

Connectivity via the e-Bario Project

The e-Bario journey began in 1998 as a research project under Universiti Malaysia Sarawak (UNIMAS) which connected the once isolated communities to the world and opened various opportunities for socio-economic growth. e-Bario enabled the Kelabits to communicate with the outside world using the telephone and the internet. The telecentre played an important role in promoting the growth of tourism in Bario (Yeo, Hazis, F. S., Zaman, T., Songan, P., & Hamid,, 2012). The experience of the e-Bario project has been the reference point for our MOOC based intervention.

Telecentre as Knowledge Centre with MOOCs

Over the last two decades, technology has changed dramatically. It is necessary to contextualize the latest technological developments in Bario to create new socio-economic opportunities for the people there. The residents have also gained exposure to the outside world with the influx of tourists. They have come in contact with different cultures and have become aware of the importance of their own Kelabit culture. The communities expect to use various means to safeguard their culture and maintain it for future generations. The digital museum was introduced in Bario to preserve the physical artefacts placed in the community museum as digital formats (*The Borneo Post*, 2017). The community telecentre also needed to be upgraded as a cultural knowledge centre. MOOCs, due to their popularity as a platform for knowledge exchange with the ability to store and disseminate knowledge to the masses, were a perfect reason to revive the telecentre as a knowledge hub for the exchange of global and local knowledge.

This motivated our research team to visit Bario and hold discussions with the local communities to explore how MOOCs could be used to foster knowledge exchange. We identified the significance of beads in the Kelabit culture and the fact that very few measures had been taken to preserve the knowledge and the art of threading them. The bearers of this inter-generational knowledge were in most cases members of the Single Mother Association who devoted most of their time to threading and stringing Kelabit beads (see Figure 7.5).

Kelabit Beads and Their Cultural Significance

Since time immemorial the Kelabits have treasured beads. They are regarded as objects of desire, indicate wealth – family heirloom – and power and carry a

Towards Participatory MOOCs 99

FIGURE 7.5 Members of single mother communities displaying their bead artefacts

coded message of beauty (Bala, 2019). They were also used in barter trade as currency for exchanges. They are carefully threaded into head caps, necklaces and belts as objects of beauty. There are approximately 30 different kinds of beads among the Kelabit. Some are more valuable than others depending on the period. In 1940s mono-chrome glass beads like *ba'o burur* and *ba'o let* (Figure 7.6a and 7.6b) were considered the most valuable beads. In 1980s *ba'o rawir*

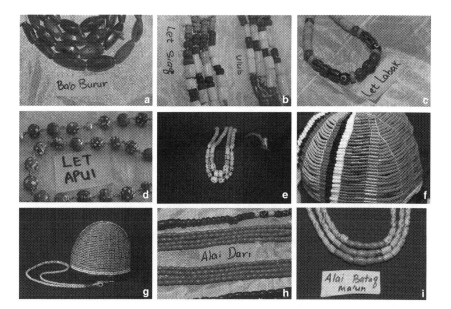

FIGURE 7.6 Bead artefacts representing the Kelabit culture: a) Ba'o burur; b) Ba'o let; c) Ba'o labak; d) Ba'o apui; e) Ba'o let; f) Ba'o rawir; g) Ba'o rawir; h) Ba'o alai

(Figure 7.6f and 7.6g) and *ba'o alai* (Figure 7.6h) were more fashionable and considered priceless. The beaded caps and necklaces are now used as a tourist attraction and sold in the market. But adornment remains the primary use of beads among the Kelabits.

As a result of the shrinking elderly population and the migration of youths to urban areas, the history, knowledge and skills, and the stories associated with the beads were in danger of being lost. This prompted social innovation with MOOCs to meet the cultural knowledge preservation needs and to bridge the knowledge gap between the younger Kelabit population and the rest of the world.

Challenges in Contextualizing MOOCs

Repurposing MOOCs

The current model followed a top-down approach of assessing the knowledge gaps of the community and assuming that the outside knowledge could bridge these gaps. In reality, the local community view themselves as experts in their own ways and are content with the knowledge they have practised for generations. The single mothers in Bario also echoed similar views as they were hesitant to learn new skills, they were more interested in sharing their expertise on beads. This attitude places the community in a teacher role rather than a learner role. In this context, the challenge is to support knowledge generation from the ground by producing MOOCs that engage the community.

Strategizing Community Role

Our earlier assumption before visiting Bario was that the community would need additional skills to match its global need. However, upon interacting with the community, the learning scenarios changed as the knowledge needed to be captured, recorded, organized and uploaded from the ground. This required capacity building training on our part as a mentor to teach basic skills like taking photos with a camera, recording videos, etc. The majority of the actual tasks of recording and uploading videos and contents in the MOOCs was to be completed by the community. The role of the community was to be made explicit. Some were to serve as facilitators helping with the content documentation, some to serve as community scholars and contribute to content generation by sharing their expertise on beads. Some were just to serve as learners to access knowledge shared by their fellow members. Interchangeable roles also needed to be supported to allow the reciprocal benefits of learning and sharing.

Developing Familiarity with MOOCs

A workshop session was conducted to give an overview of MOOCs, how they have been used elsewhere and what they can do for the community (see Figure 7.7).

FIGURE 7.7 Workshop session with single mother communities

The Kelabit language was used in the session to translate and explain the concepts. The task was challenging as the members of the single mother community were mostly illiterate. This required us to use metaphors extensively so that they could build a mental picture of the functional aspects of MOOCs. One of the compelling metaphorical references was comparing MOOCs with a refrigerator. Just as the function of a refrigerator is to preserve the food items in a cool controlled environment for a long time, MOOCs can be thought of as a time machine that freezes knowledge in time. The session was informative and the single mothers were convinced that MOOCs were a suitable platform to preserve their cultural knowledge for future generations.

Cultural Sensitivity

MOOCs needed to be pursued by the community to bring collective benefits not only to single mother communities but also to all the residents. This involved culturally sensitive planning on our side, so that there were activities that would engage with local communities, showed understanding of their local culture and developed trust and mutual understanding. This came to fruition in our workshop session when the project partners, especially the European partners, were invited to participate in cultural performance (see Figure 7.8). This generated a sense of gratitude among the community for our service to help them preserve their cultural knowledge.

The Production of MOOCs

MOOCs as a knowledge platform have great potential to preserve local knowledge but they needed to be reshaped to serve our purpose. The three elements of our "Community Led MOOCs" design model – community participation, their learning context and their way of life – had to be integrated to support knowledge generation from the ground.

FIGURE 7.8 Bonding with local communities

Community Participation

The participation of community as co-partners in producing MOOCs was necessary to deliver the learning outcomes. This led us to initiate a bottom-up approach to knowledge generation and give the control to a group of single mothers to produce MOOC modules on the threading and stringing of Kelabit beads. Our role was more towards the periphery of MOOC production, and focused on capacity building and the training of community members. Two layered MOOC modules were produced, one of which was a general module designed to give an overview of MOOC (see Figure 7.9), and to provide capacity building and training for the community members so that they would be able to generate and populate content for their specialized MOOC module.

FIGURE 7.9 MOOC module on 'Overview of MOOCs' prepared by university experts

We primarily served as mentors and provided teaching for the community members on skills such as creating storyboards, taking pictures, recording videos and uploading content.. For a better understanding of community skills, we compiled the profiles of members of the Single Mother Association and categorized them as facilitators, community scholars and learners. Our training was targeted at facilitators who could serve as technical guides for the community scholars to help them document and share their knowledge. The members could, however, interchange their roles as community scholars to learners and so on. The learners were mostly youths, single mothers and other residents.

We encouraged the participation of the community, positioned the community as equal partners in the knowledge exchange and gave them the ability to switch between teacher and learner roles as they documented and shared their knowledge on stringing and threading beads with other community members. This chimed with the description "by the community, for the community" which encouraged the community to participate in the knowledge exchange.

Learning Context

We had to overcome infrastructure and digital competency issues, in addition to supporting community interaction with local support groups when producing MOOCs. Fortunately, connectivity was not an issue as the telecentre, though partially operational, supported wireless internet. However, the difficulty we faced was organizing content into MOOC modules as the members needed advanced skills to work with a learning management system such as the edX platform. To simplify things, we deployed content management activities in two layers. The activities in the bottom layer were supported with tools that required a minimum learning curve whereas the top layer required advanced skills in using the edX platform. The community members participated in the bottom layer, in which they used a Trello-like platform to upload videos and photos without having to worry about structuring and organizing the content (see Figure 7.10).

FIGURE 7.10 Trello used by the local communities to upload videos

There were also facilitators to support those members who were not able to use Trello and to help those who were illiterate. The uploaded content was then organized into modules and uploaded onto the edX platform with our experts from the university.

The social interaction was also supported with Trello as the members were able to view each other's activities, comment on them and have discussions in informal gatherings. This allowed the community members to get a common understanding of the progress made and the things that needed to be done. The ability to interact with local support groups helped them to assess their knowledge gaps and direct the logical flow of activity needed to bridge the gap. For instance, one youth had to learn about the stories of beads before gaining skills in threading. The community members also interacted with experts from the university to assess their knowledge gaps about what was needed in the global market in order for them to sell their artefacts. The experts gave them training in using social media to market their beads to a global audience. The community members were motivated as they were not only able to preserve their knowledge on beads but were also able to create livelihood opportunities by selling beads.

Way of Life

The community lifestyle was supported as the members were encouraged to add cultural elements such as singing and dance performances to give a context while narrating stories associated with the beads. The community members documented their knowledge while adorning local costumes, showcasing the interiors of their homes and farms, trying out the local delicacies and participating in religious ceremonies. For many, stringing beads was a part of their daily activity, which gave them the added bonus of being able to document their skills in making various artefacts with beads. However, the community members had various other commitments that needed to be fulfilled. To accommodate this, we ensured the community had flexibility in scheduling timings. Also they were free to choose the location in which they documented their knowledge. This meant they could work at home or at informal gatherings usually in the refreshment shop near the Single Mother Association. The repertoire of local knowledge on beads was seen as a local community effort which fostered unity and bonding.

Discussion

Our MOOC based intervention, an ongoing effort to preserve the cultural knowledge of single mother communities in Bario, redirects the MOOCs' approach to inclusive learning in a different direction, by showcasing its ability to foster knowledge creation from the ground, and contributing to bridging the global-local knowledge divide. This is achieved with our 'Community Led

MOOCs' design model which redefines the 'inclusive' and 'participatory' nature of learning in MOOCs, in response to the ones being replicated to serve the learning needs of the marginalized rural communities. The problem with replicating current MOOCs is that it recreates a learning environment biased on one-sided global knowledge transfer with minimal support to integrate local knowledge. This marginalizes the value local knowledge can add to the global community of learners. In our community-led MOOCs design model, we have engaged local communities as both knowledge source and knowledge recipient. The communities were able to switch roles between facilitator, community scholar and learner. The facilitators helped document the local knowledge while the community scholars shared their skills, stories and histories associated with the beads. In addition to their explicit roles, their learning context adhered to their socio-technical challenges, and their way of life was integrated in the model, which maximized the inclusiveness and participation of community members in producing MOOCs.

The outcome of this bottom-up, participatory approach to knowledge sharing translated into the development of a MOOC module on "Threading Beads" led by the group of single mothers in Bario (see Figure 7.11). Our experience has shown that technology transfer is not a solution to the problem, rather power transfer to local communities by enhancing their basic skills such as taking photos, recording videos, can produce solutions that are locally and contextually relevant. We have shown that community members have the ability to use technology on their own terms to bring benefit to them. The MOOC course that the single mothers produced was their collective effort which resonated with the values of unity and bringing benefit to all. Although a thorough assessment of the social impacts of our MOOC intervention is yet to take place, we are clearly seeing positive outcomes. The single mother communities which remained invisible and were sidelined in various local development initiatives are now being pushed to the frontline as valuable members of the community. The single mothers are perceived as pioneers by the youths and other residents in their knowledge preservation efforts. There is also interest among the community members in exhibiting the local knowledge repositories produced by single mothers to invigorate tourism related activities in Bario.

With this novel use case of MOOCs, we offered a new perspective on the participatory role of the community in knowledge exchange, and illustrated that knowledge generation from the ground can be formalized as a communal activity provided that community participation, their learning context and their way of life are integrated in producing MOOCs. This case study also presented a localized view of community led MOOCs, in the context of a cultural knowledge preservation effort by single mother communities in Bario, which can be expanded into other socio-economic contexts to initiate new dialogues and reference points in continuing with MOOC development to serve a social purpose.

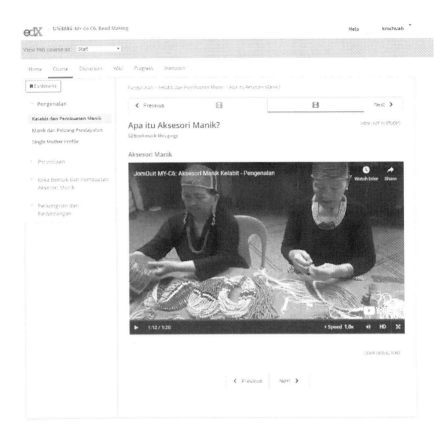

FIGURE 7.11 Videos recorded by the single mother communities

Conclusion

The existing MOOC model is based on a unidirectional global knowledge transfer in a top-down fashion. Replicating such a model for rural communities fails to bring a fresh perspective to address unresolved global problems by integrating local knowledge which the local community has carried for generations. Therefore, a new business model is required to sustain local learning loops, while globally bridging the divide between those who are rich in indigenous knowledge and those who strive to exploit this knowledge.

In this chapter, we have presented bottom-up, inclusive and participatory learning by using the 'Community Led MOOCs' design model. With this model, the local communities were pushed to the forefront in building local knowledge repositories by strategizing their role as community scholars and facilitators. We presented a novel use case of participatory MOOCs with single mother communities in Bario, which is promising in terms of enthusiasm shown by the community in sharing their local knowledge with the global community of learners. The outcome is a MOOC module on "Threading Beads" led by a group of single mothers. Our experience has shown that inclusive learning can be supported with knowledge generation from the ground, provided that the community's participation, learning context and way of life are integrated in producing MOOCs.

Note

1 https://www.classcentral.com/about.

References

Adams, A. A. (2013). The challenges of digital education in the Information Age. *The Possibilities of Ethical ICT*, 6, 6–13.

Agarwal, A. (2014, January 27). *Why massive open online courses (still) matter.* Retrieved September 30, 2019, from https://www.ted.com/talks/anant_agarwal_why_massively_open_online_courses_still_ma tter.

Ally, M., & Samaka, M. (2013). Open education resources and mobile technology to narrow the learning divide. *The International Review of Research in Open and Distributed Learning*, 14(2), 14–27.

Altbach, P. G. (2014). MOOCs as neocolonialism: Who controls knowledge? *International Higher Education*, 75, 5–7.

Bala, P. (2019). *The making of Kelabit beads.* Retrieved October 1, 2019, from https://drive.google.com/open?id=1QhPqtiAWXaHt_IEnTQcerwhHj3CiS8hR.

Berzano, L., & Genova, C. (2015). *Lifestyles and subcultures: History and a new perspective*, Vol. 152. New York: Routledge.

Chadaj, M., Allison, C., & Baxter, G. (2014). MOOCs with attitudes: Insights from a practitioner based investigation. In M. Castro, E. Tovar, M. Cardella, R. Meier, & A. Pears (Eds.), *2014 IEEE Frontiers in Education Conference (FIE) Proceedings* (pp. 1–9). Retrieved from https://doi.org/10.1109/FIE.2014.7044101.

Harris, R. W., Bala, P., Songan, P., & Khoo, E. G. L. (2001). Challenges and opportunities in introducing information and communication technologies to the Kelabit community of North Central Borneo. *New Media and Society*, 3(3), 270–295.

International Telecommunication Union (ITU). (2019). *Measuring digital development facts and figures 2019.* Retrieved August 15, 2020, from https://www.itu.int/en/ITU-D/Statistics/Documents/facts/FactsFigures2019.pdf.

Kalman, Y. M. (2014). A race to the bottom: MOOCs and higher education business models. *Open Learning: The Journal of Open, Distance and e-Learning*, 29(1), 5–14. Retrieved from https://doi.org/10.1080/02680513.2014.922410.

Kaplan, A. M., & Haenlein, M. (2016). Higher education and the digital revolution: About MOOCs, SPOCs, social media, and the Cookie Monster. *Business Horizons*, 59(4), 441–450.

King, M., Pegrum, M., & Forsey, M. (2018). MOOCs and OER in the global south: Problems and potential. In D. Conrad (Ed.), *The International Review of Research in Open and Distributed Learning*, 19(5), 1–20. Retrieved from https://doi.org/10.19173/irrodl.v19i5.3742.

Koller, D. (2012, August 1). *What we're learning from online education*. Retrieved September 30, 2019, from https://www.ted.com/talks/daphne_koller_what_we_re_learning_from_online_education?language=en.

Liyanagunawardena, T. R., Williams, S., & Adams, A. A. (2014). The impact and reach of MOOCs: A developing countries' perspective. *eLearning Papers*, 33, 38–46.

Maitland, C., & Obeysekare, E. (2015). The creation of capital through an ICT-based learning program. In A. Chib, M. Kam, & J. Burrell (Eds.), *Proceedings of the Seventh International Conference on Information and Communication Technologies and Development – ICTD '15* (pp. 1–10). Retrieved from https://doi.org/10.1145/2737856.2738024.

Nkuyubwatsi, B. (2014). Cultural translation in massive open online courses (MOOCs). *eLearning Papers*, 37, 1–10. Retrieved from https://lra.le.ac.uk/bitstream/2381/28554/4/In_depth_37_3.pdf.

Onah, D. F., Sinclair, J., Boyatt, R., & Foss, J. (2014). Massive open online courses: Learner participation. In L. Gómez Chova, A. López Martínez, & I. Candel Torres (Eds.), *Proceeding of the 7th International Conference of Education, Research and Innovation* (pp. 2348–2356). Retrieved from https://doi.org/10.13140/RG.2.1.1222.3520.

Panyajamorn, T., Kohda, Y., Chongphaisal, P., & Supnithi, T. (2016, November). The effectiveness and suitability of MOOCs hybrid learning: A case study of public schools in Thai rural area. In S. Kunifuji, H. Prabowo, & H. Motoda (Eds.), *11th International Conference on Knowledge, Information and Creativity Support Systems (KICSS)* (pp. 1–6). Retrieved from https://doi.org/10.1109/KICSS.2016.7951449.

Pariyar, A., Kulathuramaiyer, N., Abdullah, J., & Chuah, K. M. (2019). Contextualizing learning for rural community using Library-in-a-Box: Experience from Penan community. *International Journal of Innovative Technology and Exploring Engineering (IJITEE)*, 8(8). ISSN 2278–3075.

Rahayu, H., Haslina, H., & Salina, K. (2018). *Easy read on consumer behavior*. Serdang, Malaysia: Universiti Putra Malaysia Press. Retrieved October 1, 2019, from https://ir.unimas.my/id/eprint/22952/1/Easy%20read%20on%20consumer%20behavior%20-%20Copy.pdf.

Rambe, P., & Moeti, M. (2016). Disrupting and democratising higher education provision or entrenching academic elitism: Towards a model of MOOCs adoption at African universities. *Educational Technology Research and Development*, 65(3), 631–651. Retrieved from https://doi.org/10.1007/s11423-016-9500-3.

Rhoads, R. A., Berdan, J., & Toven-Lindsey, B. (2013). The Open Courseware Movement in higher education: Unmasking power and raising questions about the movement's democratic potential. *Educational Theory*, 63(1), 87–110. Retrieved from https://doi.org/10.1111/edth.12011.

Richter, T., & McPherson, M. (2012). Open educational resources: Education for the world? *Distance Education*, 33(2), 201–219. Retrieved from https://doi.org/10.1080/01587919.2012.692068.

Rodriguez, C. O. (2012). MOOCs and the AI-Stanford like courses: Two successful and distinct course formats for massive open online courses. *European Journal of Open, Distance and E-Learning*, 12, 1–13.

SDG Academy. (2018, September 29). *UN sustainable development courses available for free*. Retrieved October 1, 2019, from https://www.humanrightscareers.com/un-sustainable-development-goals-courses.

Shah, D. (2017). *Massive open online courses used to be 100% free. But they didn't stay that way*. Retrieved September 30, 2019, from https://www.freecodecamp.org/

news/massive-open-online-courses-started-out-completely-free-but-where-are-they-now-1dd1020f59.

Sharples, M., Delgado Kloos, C., Dimitriadis, Y., Garlatti, S., & Specht, M. (2015). Mobile and accessible learning for MOOCs. *Journal of Interactive Media in Education*, 1(4), 1–8.

Sherman, G. (2002, January 1). What are learning contexts? Retrieved October 1, 2019, from http://jan.ucc.nau.edu/pt3-p/toolbox/what-are-contexts.htm.

Sunar, A. S., Abdullah, N. A., White, S., & Davis, H. C. (2015). Personalisation of MOOCs: The state of the art. In M. Helfert, M. T. Restivo, S. Zvacek, & J. Uhomoibhi (Eds.), *7th International Conference on Computer Supported Education Proceedings (CSEDU2015), Lisbon, Portugal. 23–25 May 2015* (pp. 88–97). Retrieved from doi:10.5220/0005445200880097}.

The Borneo Post. (2013, August 17). Penans block gas pipeline project in Ulu Baram. Retrieved October 1, 2019, from https://www.theborneopost.com/2013/08/18/penans-block-gas-pipeline-project-in-ulu-baram.

The Borneo Post. (2017, July 15). Kelabit Community Museum in Bario to go digital soon says RKS. Retrieved October 1, 2019, from https://www.theborneopost.com/2017/07/16/kelabit-community-museum-in-bario-to-go-digital-soon-says-rks/.

Udacity. (2015, April 24). Upskill America for the 21st Century. Retrieved September 30, 2019, from https://blog.udacity.com/2015/04/upskill-america-21st-century.html.

Warugaba, C., Naughton, B., Gauthier, B. H., Muhirwa, E., & Amoroso, C. L. (2016). Experience with a massive open online course in rural Rwanda. *The International Review of Research in Open and Distributed Learning*, 17(2), 223–231.

World Bank. (2015, June 8). Some characteristics of World Bank experience with community-driven development (CDD). Retrieved October 1, 2019, from https://advocacy.thp.org/2015/06/some-characteristics-of-world-bank-experience-with-community-driven-development-cdd.

Wulf, J., Blohm, I., Leimeister, J. M., & Brenner, W. (2014). Massive open online courses. *Business & Information Systems Engineering*, 6(2), 111–114. Retrieved from https://doi.org/10.1007/s12599-014-0313-9.

Yeo, A. W., Hazis, F. S., Zaman, T., Songan, P., & Hamid, K. A. (2012). Telecentre replication initiative in Borneo Malaysia: The Coeri experience. *The Electronic Journal of Information Systems in Developing Countries*, 50(1), 1–14.

Zaka, B., Kulathuramaiyer, N., Balke, W. T., & Maurer, H. (2008). Topic-centered aggregation of presentations for learning object repurposing. In C. J. Bonk, M. M. Lee, & T. Reynolds (Eds.), *E-Learn: World Conference on E-Learning in Corporate, Government, Healthcare, and Higher Education* (pp. 3335–3342). Retrieved from https://ir.unimas.my/id/eprint/30163.

Zaman, T., Yeo, A. W., & Kulathuramaiyer, N. (2011). Harnessing community's creative expression and indigenous wisdom to create value. In N. J. Bidwell, & H. Winschiers-Theophilus (Eds.), *Indigenous Knowledge Technology Conference* (pp. 137–148). Retrieved from https://dx.doi.org/10.1504/IJSTM.2013.054202.

Zaman, T., Yeo, A. W., & Kulathuramaiyer, N. (2013). Augmenting indigenous knowledge management with information and communication technology. In Christopher G. Reddick and Saqib Saeed (Eds.), *International Journal of Services Technology and Management*, 19(1–3), 137–148. Retrieved from https://www.inderscience.com/info/inarticletoc.php?jcode=ijstm&year=2013&vol=19&issue=1/2/3.

8

MOBILE INFORMATION LITERACY AND PUBLIC ACCESS IN THE ERA OF POST-TRUTH

Reflections from Community Curricular Experiences in Latin America

Sara Vannini and Isabella Rega

Concerns for a Predominantly Mobile Access

Millions of people, especially in developing countries or within lower income communities, are coming online predominantly via a mobile phone. The poorer people are more likely to be smartphone-dependent, even when mobile devices are not their first technology to access the internet (Pew Research Center, 2019). Development practitioners, advocates of the freedom of the net, scholars and the broader society have been vocal about their concerns related to this smartphone dependency (Shahbaz, 2018).

Mobile technologies have very specific affordances, which influence the way people can access and produce information, and which carry privacy and security implications. Specific smartphone information behaviours include, for example, searching for information through apps versus a browser. Apps may filter information for the user in a less transparent manner and leave the user less free to look for more and different search results – the so called "walled garden" (Clark, Coward, & Rothschild, 2017). Clark and colleagues also claim that accessing the internet via mobile devices is likely to shift information behaviour towards information consumption rather than production, towards a stronger focus on social activities over productivity and towards searching information in more situated but less rigorous ways (Clark et al., 2017).

Mobile-predominant access might also influence the way people conceptualize the internet itself:

> Frequently, mobile users believe a single app or social media platform is the extent of access. As a result, these platforms possess monopolies of the imagination – the ability to shape and control users' perceptions of the Web.

People end up viewing the Web less as a life-changing resource, and more like a television.

(Surman, 2015)

Millions of Facebook users, especially in developing countries, think that Facebook *is* the internet (Mirani, 2015; Vaidhyanathan, 2018).

These facts have potentially disastrous consequences, especially in a world where digital literacy is still one of the main barriers to bridge the digital divide, where disinformation has been used to shift and divide the public discourse and where concerns related to data privacy are impacting the public discourse (Briant, 2018; Coward, 2018). While people are increasingly more vulnerable to surveillance (Briant, 2018) and more likely to be caught in social media "filter bubbles" and "echo chambers" of information and misinformation (Arif, Shanahan, Chou, Dosouto, Starbird, & Spiro, 2016; Starbird, 2017; Vaidhyanathan, 2018), the global internet freedom has reportedly been declining since 2010 (Shahbaz, 2018).

Smartphone-centric access to the internet in a still digitally illiterate world might have dangerous consequences (Nemer, 2019; Vaidhyanathan, 2018). This is especially true for people who are socio-economically marginalized, who have the least resources and ability to discriminate between facts and disinformation and to choose whether or not to provide their personal data and are consequently more likely to be coerced into it (Marwick & Boyd, 2018; Vannini et al., 2019).

Mobile Information Literacy: A Definition

Digital literacy is frequently mentioned as the way forward to counter disinformation and protect people's privacy (Clark et al., 2017; Shahbaz, 2018; Vaidhyanathan, 2018; Vannini et al., 2019). While many digital literacy curricula have been developed over the years, there is a scarcity – with a few exceptions – of curricula that address the issues related to mobile information literacy (MIL), even more so for mobile-only users (Day, 2015). The available mobile courses and curricula in the literature are based on a few case studies, and they are mainly limited to showing the use of the device – neglecting to tackle proper information literacy via the devices (e.g.: Jisc, 2014; GSMA, 2015). On the other hand, the need for MIL-specific experiences has been called for, as using a smartphone requires not only different operational skills, but also specific informational skills (see: Clark et al., 2017; Coward, 2018; GSMA, 2014, 2016).

There are two concepts at the basis of the notion of "mobile information literacy":

- *Information literacy*, defined as a set of abilities requiring individuals to locate, evaluate, select, store and use effectively and ethically the information they need, understand traditional and new information sources, interpret

information in different formats, discriminate information and knowledge, assess and articulate information need (Ala-Mutka, 2011; American Library Association, 1989).
- *Digital literacy*, defined as the ability, knowledge, skills and behaviours to find, evaluate, make informed judgments, utilize, manage, share, and create information and content, using a broad range of information and communication technologies (ICTs), benefit from them for personal life tasks and objectives and understand the value of traditional tools and resources in conjunction with the digital (Ala-Mutka, 2011).

Mobile information literacy is, then, defined as a set of abilities required to "find and evaluate the quality and credibility of information obtained online and understand how to create and share online information effectively, and participate safely and securely" (Day, 2015, p. 5) when using mobile technology, and not PC, environments. MIL must ensure that the so-called "next billion" (of people who will be able to access the internet) will have relevant, meaningful, participatory, free and secure access to the internet.

Two MIL curricula are currently known to the authors:

- Associazione SEED developed a project to familiarize Indian children with ICTs by using tablets instead of computers, leveraging on project-based, problem-solving, collaborative learning and edutainment software (Associazione SEED, 2015; ST Foundation, 2015).
- The TASCHA Group at the University of Washington developed a Mobile Information Literacy Curriculum addressing not only skills, but also concepts and attitudes for two specific contexts of intervention: in Myanmar and Namibia (Day, 2015).

Mobile Information Literacy and Community Technology Centres

Community technology centres (CTCs) are designated and privileged actors in providing digital literacy skills and ICT training to disadvantaged populations, thus bridging the digital divide and contributing to the well-being of such populations. Physical places are still an important component of access to ICTs – and training in their use – for marginalized populations (Best, Thakur, & Kolko, 2010; Kleine, 2013; Parkinson & Lauzon, 2008; Peña-López, 2013). People often go to CTCs even if they have access through mobile technologies or via PC at home, as they value social and peer learning versus individual access (Bar, Coward, Koepke, Rothschild, & Sey, 2013; Gómez, 2011; Rega, 2019; Sey, Coward, Bar, Sciadas, Rothschild, & Koepke, 2013; Vannini, Rega, Sala, & Cantoni, 2013). The popularity of innovation hubs confirms the key value of physical venues in ICT education, innovation and entrepreneurship (European Network of Living Labs, 2014; Friederici, 2014; Jimenez & Zheng, 2018).

The role CTCs play in helping communities develop digital skills is renowned (Bar et al., 2013; Gómez, Ambikar, & Coward, 2009; Sey et al., 2013; Sey & Fellows, 2009). However, as shown by the literature, experiences related to mobile literacy are still at an initial stage, and there are no standard and widely adopted digital literacy curricula based on mobile technologies. Thus the relevance of understanding whether CTCs are innovating their activities by creating and adopting MIL curricula, and whether they share MIL best practices to MIL curricula beyond CTCs. To do so, this study focuses on Latin American CTCs and asks the following questions: What MIL curricular practices are CTCs in Latin America adopting? Are they creating innovative MIL services? Do they share common MIL curricula or best practices? How are they preparing their communities to face the era of disinformation?

Latin American CTCs and Mobile Information Literacy

This chapter focuses on Latin American CTCs, especially in Brazil, Chile and Colombia, and presents an overview of the different ways they engage with MIL activities. We surveyed and interviewed operators of Latin American CTCs, defined as managers and other executive staff members of the venues (see Vannini, Nemer, & Rega, 2017 for further details), mainly working in areas considered to be at partial or high risk of violence and criminality. Their public varied both between and within CTCs, but included the most vulnerable sectors of the population: young people and children, housewives and the elderly. There were only a few cases in which CTCs were collaborating with small enterprises in the area to help them with their capacity building.

Overall, CTCs are starting to offer mobile-related initiatives, many of which are related to education. Their operators showed they see mobile technologies as tools to achieve CTCs' community development goals, particularly in the case of communication and community building. They also indicated that they see a greater role for mobile technologies in education to support CTCs' goals. Indeed, CTCs engage in MIL activities. As a result of our interviews we distinguished five different ways in which MIL is addressed.

Introduction to Mobile Technologies

All interviewees mentioned helping community members perform the most basic functions of mobile technologies in one way or another, according to the context and needs of the community. Activities included: understanding mobile plans, use and consumption of data, configuring the device, installing mobile applications, creating an email address and a social media account and making video-calls using different applications. They often also tackle mobile content creation (e.g.: taking pictures, accessing and using Google Docs), and content sharing (e.g.: via WhatsApp, Social Media, Bluetooth). Finally, they often teach community members how to download and store content on the devices and on the cloud.

Furthermore, operators often explicitly mentioned that they advocate for a meaningful use of the technology:

> This context preaches that technology is the goal and not the means. Owning a mobile is important, but for what? … It will always be relevant to teach people what technology is for and how it can improve their quality of life, for example.
>
> *(Colombia, Participant 15)*

A Context-Relevant Meaningful Use

The context and needs of the community were always the operators' main focus. They mentioned several examples of services they had specifically adapted. These encompass a range of activities, from the use of famous apps like Duolingo to teach English to both young people and adults, to ad-hoc activities; these can be framed as examples of situated learning that proved to be very effective, especially in adult education (Street, 2002). A couple of operators working with housewives mentioned, for example, teaching how them to use mobile devices to learn new sewing techniques:

> So we were delivering [content] about anything that could generate income to people, starting from their daily work. So we showed them some applications that they could access from their tablets and mobile phones.
>
> *(Colombia, Participant 2)*

Another operator from Colombia mentioned teaching at-risk youth how to mix music and create their own tracks, by using mainly cell-phones, tablets and a loudspeaker:

> Well, in my work experience, I worked at a disco … so with this program that I was using, VirtualDJ, I sat down with the young people, and this is a community that is very "salsera" … there is a lot of "salsa choque" and "reggaetón" here. So I tell them "c'mon, guys come here and mix your own, mix songs" … "How does it sound? What is a beat?" … So I saw this possibility and I implemented it … because here it is very common that the youngsters go in the street with speakers listening to music … so I participated in the project of a video … and it is street music, it is "salsa choque", but it is their own! They said "Hear this song? This song plays in a disco". And they are happy to know that they did something, that it is their own.
>
> *(Colombia, Participant 1)*

Mobiles and Computers: Parts of the Same Ecosystem

Sometimes interviewees could not separate their mobile-related learning activities from computer-related ones. Some operators mentioned the need to address mobile-related topics during computer classes. Others address the topic when users can bring their own devices along:

> At times we ask them ... "Can you bring a phone tomorrow?", and [if] they say yes, the course will be focused on mobile, but if they say no, then we will work accessing through a computer.
>
> *(Colombia, Participant 13)*

A few operators admitted using CTC-owned tablets to increase the number of participants in their classes, which would otherwise be limited by the small number of desktop computers available. Others use them to attract a different kind of public, such as the elderly and people with lower literacy levels. Operators' approach to teaching adults and elderly people involves telling them that smartphones and computers are "the same thing" (Colombia, Participant 1), especially relative to performing tasks such as sending emails and access basic information:

> One of my students, both she and her children they have a mobile phone, they don't have a computer at home, they use their phones and they use the computer from the [CTC], so she has a job at the church and she wanted to reply to some emails, send some reports, and it was very interesting because she learned how to write an email. I told her, "it is the same thing as the computer" ... only a question of having more agility with your hands because ... it is touch screen, but the basis is the same, the email appears on your phone, you can attach from your images, select the image, or from your documents.
>
> *(Brazil, Participant 4)*

Finally, a few operators mentioned they believe computers will eventually be replaced by smartphones, which seems to point to a linear perception of technology development:

> Now everything is on [smartphones], so they are never going to disappear, they are just going to improve their quality, their content .... So this is what we say to people, computers per se are going to end, something better will come out. Technology improves, so we are leaving computers on the side and we are starting to use mobile devices.
>
> *(Colombia, Participant 10)*

Mobile Information Literacy Practices

While situated learning MIL practices were widely reported, privacy and security teaching were limited to a few basic behaviours, e.g.: advising children not to share their personal information on social networks:

> We are focusing especially on social networks, because – as you know – the majority of children, even if they shouldn't, they have access to Facebook … we focus especially on Gmail, on shared photos, on security, [we recommend not to] share addresses, where they live … with school kids we focus especially on privacy.
>
> *(Colombia, Participant 11)*

The recommendation is directed to adults as well, who are pressed to check on their children:

> With the parents we worked on that they check on what their children are doing on their phones, we taught them ways to watch them … inside the same social network … for example, who are their friends, that they check on their conversations weekly … but that they do not forbid them to be on the sites. … we are trying to send the message based on what happens in real life.
>
> *(Colombia, Participant 10)*

And to examine their own behaviour:

> It is an issue of raising their awareness since they are young …. The same with the adults … often they do not know the risks because they also make mistakes, and they do not realize that a photo of them naked… this is the internet and then there is nothing to do ….
>
> *(Colombia, Participant 5)*

Operators also want to make sure that users' data is saved in the cloud, perceived as safer than on a device:

> Safe use of mobiles, for example, we teach users to take advantage of their phones but in a secure way … because we can use a phone, but we only save in its internal and external memory, and if we lose it, anyone can access that information. Whereas if we manage the information from … the cloud, others can access but not as easily.
>
> *(Colombia, Participant 13)*

Operators' work on security also includes preventing cyberbullying:

> Last year we worked a lot on cyberbullying and all that has to do with violence on social networks.
>
> *(Colombia, Participant 13)*

It is usually the first class when I explain the rules of the lab, the issues for their security, like on Facebook, of sharing their personal photos, the issue of bullying, of writing [something] on WhatsApp or on Facebook ... and this is a class or half a class that focuses on this and its consequences.] It is the only moment when we have this kind of discussion.

(Chile, Participant 6)

Besides issues of privacy and security, operators stress that a meaningful use of the technology is necessary and important for their communities.

With smartphones, today, as incredible as it may seem, people ask what the internet is and people say "Facebook" (laughing). ... With the ease that smartphones bring, people got used to this use, many times they don't even look for other information ... they are very attached to social media. This is one of the things that we worry about, that the informational world is very vast and people are very limited with social networks.

(Brazil, Participant 9)

However, they mostly do not seem to address issues of information quality evaluation through mobile devices:

We do information literacy, which is how to train users in the search for information by using the necessary sources ... this activity is fundamental with young people, but we do not have a specific activity to help them differentiate [it among the] the different technologies.

(Colombia, Participant 3)

Curriculum design

The design of curricular activities related to MIL and mobile education seems to be mostly entrusted to individual CTCs. CTCs usually read the needs of the community and have different ways of responding to them. Sometimes, operators have to be rather spontaneous:

As [they ask] me "what is WhatsApp, how can I open a PDF, how can I make my WhatsApp private so people don't see my profile picture" ... I sit down with them and explain to them.

(Colombia, Participant 8)

These spontaneous, almost improvised activities leave little space for the operator to tackle the different nuances related to privacy and security, as well as other information literacy issues. Other times entire curricula are created in a more structured way, in response to community's feedback:

> If various users arrive with the same doubt at a certain time, we put them together so that we have to open a training process on that topic, because that is the topic that is of community's concern. And according to the needs that we see up to when we design our working plan, we keep those into account. Still, at any moment a user can come with a specific doubt and we try to offer them a solution.
>
> *(Colombia, Participant 3)*

Among the three countries where our interviewees worked, only in Colombia are ministerial and government directives produced and used to develop curricular materials:

> There are materials that are created by the Ministry of Culture or by the Ministry of Information and Communication Technology in Colombia …. They don't really tell us to use it, what they do is that they create guides and share them online and they let us know that they are there. If a specific unit reckons that it is useful for them, they use it.
>
> *(Colombia, Participant 5)*

However, there don't seem to be established practices for sharing curricula among CTCs once they are created. In only one case did operators mention creating a database:

> But there is nothing that is done … this at the level of Colombia. Yet here in [city name] there is a system that exists only in this city, among us we have content that are generalized, and we are creating guides, and over the years, other [CTCs] can take what [another one] has done and replicate it in their community, not starting from scratch, but starting with something that was tried in another place and adjust it to their necessities.
>
> *(Colombia, Participant 5)*

Discussion and Conclusions

Millions of people are coming online – primarily via smartphone – in an era of post-truth, thus exacerbating issues related to information authenticity and data privacy and security. Communities at the margins are the most likely to lack the skills and resources to choose whether to disclose their personal data, as well as to be able to discriminate between information quality. Mobile information literacy activities have been identified (and called for) as one of the most effective ways of countering these issues. However, MIL-specific curricula are currently lacking.

CTCs play a major role in underserved communities, historically providing them with digital literacy skills training and ICT access. This study focused on Latin American CTCs to ascertain whether and how MIL activities are included in their activities, and to uncover possible best practices for a more widely adopted MIL curriculum.

Outcomes show that although there are numerous mobile literacy services available within CTCs in the region, they are only partial experiences. Also, there is no common framework that comprehensively encompasses MIL topics . MIL experiences in CTCs are mainly limited to explaining the basic functionalities of mobile devices. Users are taught to change their privacy setting, not to share personal information online and where to save their data. However, no distinction is made between personal behaviour in relation to privacy, and issues related to companies' privacy policies – focusing on how personal information published online can be accessed by governments and private companies. Although users are taught how to create and share content via mobile phone, no mention was made about copyright, credits and credibility of content creation and sharing.

Operators did not consider issues regarding the limitations of accessing information via a mobile phone, such as comparing accessing the internet through apps versus a browser or a search engine, or evaluating information quality and authenticity and the propensity of social networks to create information echo-chambers. Their inclination, in some cases, to point out the affinity of mobile devices to computers, without considering in depth the different ways they allow access to information, does not encourage reflection on the particular limitations mobile devices pose in this sense. Finally, the nature of their work, often being required to help users unexpectedly and on very specific issues with their devices, does not leave them space and time to tackle these MIL-relevant topics – particularly in the absence of a MIL-shared curricular framework within which to operate.

Nevertheless, our study shed light on a number of MIL educational initiatives operators are practising in their communities. The way CTCs are responding to their communities' needs and feedback, and the way that technology is portrayed as an instrument that needs to have a relevant meaningful use were emphasized by all operators. Many of initiatives they described might constitute relevant templates from which the mobile-for-learning and mobile-for-development scholarly community could craft contextually appropriate initiatives.

CTCs in Latin America showed a great ability to develop MIL curricula in response to the needs of their communities. However, the work is mostly carried out in individual initiatives, and is still insufficient to respond to the challenges posed by the current mobile-centric post-truth era. We call upon policy makers, scholars and practitioners in the field to support the initiative of CTCs and to share MIL curricula more comprehensively, in order to contribute to the meaningful well-being of underserved communities, as well as the broader society.

References

Ala-Mutka, K. (2011). Mapping digital competence: Towards a conceptual understanding (No. Technical Note: JRC 67075). Retrieved from https://www.dctest.org/uploads/6/8/7/0/68701431/jrc67075_tn.pdf.

American Library Association. (1989). *Presidential Committee on Information Literacy. Final Report*. Retrieved from www.ala.org/acrl/publications/whitepapers/presidential.
Arif, A., Shanahan, K., Chou, F.-J., Dosouto, Y., Starbird, K., & Spiro, E. S. (2016). How information snowballs: Exploring the role of exposure in online rumor propagation. In *Proceedings of the 19th ACM Conference on Computer-Supported Cooperative Work & Social Computing* (pp. 466–477). Retrieved from https://doi.org/10.1145/2818048.2819964.
Associazione SEED. (2015). *DU4K tableting together – India*. Retrieved from http://seedlearn.org/du4k-tableting-together-india.
Bar, F., Coward, C., Koepke, L., Rothschild, C., Sey, A., & Sciadas, G. (2013). The impact of public access to ICTs: Findings from a five-year, eight-country study. In *Proceedings of the Sixth International Conference on Information and Communication Technologies and Development: Full Papers, Volume 1* (pp. 34–42). Retrieved from https://doi.org/10.1145/2516604.2516619.
Best, M. L., Thakur, D., & Kolko, B. (2010). The contribution of user-based subsidies to the impact and sustainability of telecenters—the eCenter Project in Kyrgyzstan. *Information Technologies & International Development*, 6(2), 75–89.
Briant, E. L. (2018). *Building a stronger and more secure democracy in a digital age*. Retrieved from http://data.parliament.uk/writtenevidence/committeeevidence.svc/evidencedocument/digital-culture-media-and-sport-committee/fake-news/written/88559.pdf.
Clark, M., Coward, C., & Rothschild, C. (2017). *Mobile information literacy: Building digital and information literacy skills for mobile-first and mobile-centric populations through public libraries*. Second AfLIA Conference & 4th Africa Library Summit Proceedings, 14–20 May 2017, Yaoundé, Cameroon.
Coward, C. (2018). *A dynamic approach to digital skills*. Keynote presented at the UNESCO Mobile Learning Week, Paris. Retrieved from https://tascha.uw.edu/2018/03/a-dynamic-approach-to-digital-skills-chris-cowards-remarks-at-mobile-learning-week.
Day, S. (2015). *Mobile Information Literacy Curriculum*. Retrieved from http://tascha.uw.edu/mobile-information-literacy-curriculum.
Digital, Culture, Media and Sport Committee (DCMS). (2018). *Disinformation and 'fake news': Interim Report: Government response to the committee's Fifth Report of Session 2017–19*. Retrieved from https://publications.parliament.uk/pa/cm201719/cmselect/cmcumeds/1630/1630.pdf.
European Network of Living Labs. (2014). *Activity Report 2012*. Retrieved from https://www.scribd.com/doc/289562452/ENoLL-Activity-Report-2014.
Friederici, N. (2014). *More art than science? Exploring the roles of technology innovation hubs for urban regions in developing countries*. Presented at the EU-SPRI Forum Early Career Researcher Conference. Retrieved from https://papers.ssrn.com/sol3/papers.cfm?abstract_id=3123868.
Gómez, R. (Ed.). (2011). *Libraries, telecentres, cybercafes and public access to ICT*. Hershey, PA: IGI Global.
Gómez, R., Ambikar, R., & Coward, C. (2009). Libraries, telecentres and cybercafés: An international study of public access information venues. *Performance Measurement and Metrics*, 10(1), 33–48. Retrieved from https://www.deepdyve.com/lp/emerald-publishing/libraries-telecentres-and-cybercaf-s-an-international-study-of-public-fzB6dq0x7t.

Global System for Mobile Communications Association (GSMA). (2014). Digital Inclusion Report 2014. Retrieved from www.gsma.com/mobilefordevelopment/digital-inclusion-report-2014.

Global System for Mobile Communications Association (GSMA). (2016). The mobile economy 2016. Retrieved from https://www.gsma.com/mobileeconomy/global/2016.

Jimenez, A., & Zheng, Y. (2018). Tech hubs, innovation and development: Information technology for development. *Information Technology for Development*, 24(1), 95–118. Retrieved from https://doi.org/10.1080/02681102.2017.1335282.

Jisc. (2014). Developing and delivering a 'mobile skills' training course for staff at the University of Glasgow Library. Retrieved 21 January 2016, from http://www.rsc-scotland.org/?p=4061.

Kleine, D. (2013). *Technologies of Choice?: ICTs, Development, and the Capabilities Approach.* Cambridge, MA: MIT Press.

Marwick, A. E., & Boyd, D. (2018). Privacy at the Margins | Understanding Privacy at the Margins—Introduction. *International Journal of Communication*, 12, 1157–1165.

Mirani, L. (2015). Millions of Facebook users have no idea they're using the internet. Retrieved January 28, 2016, from http://qz.com/333313/milliions-of-facebook-users-have-no-idea-theyre-using-the-internet.

Nemer, D. (2019). WhatsApp is radicalizing the right in Bolsonaro's Brazil. Retrieved August 20, 2019, from https://www.huffpost.com/entry/brazil-jair-bolsonaro-whatsapp_n_5d542b0de4b05fa9df088ccc.

Parkinson, S., & Lauzon, A. C. (2008). The impact of the internet on local social equity: A study of a telecenter in Aguablanca, Colombia. *Information Technologies & International Development*, 4(3), 21–38.

Peña-López, I. (2013). The virtual telecentre and the demand side of unemployment. In P. Prieto, & M. Acevedo (Eds.), *Telecentros 3.0 y la innovacion social en la red* (pp. 72–74). Retrieved from http://ictlogy.net/works/reports/projects.php?idp=2499.

Pew Research Center. (2019). Demographics of mobile device ownership and adoption in the United States | Pew Research Center. Retrieved 21 August 2019, from https://www.pewinternet.org/fact-sheet/mobile.

Rega, I. (2019). Local public access centers. In Renee Hobbs, & Paul Mihailidis (Eds.), *The International Encyclopedia of Media Literacy* (pp. 1–7). Retrieved from https://doi.org/10.1002/9781118978238.ieml0101.

Sey, A., Coward, C., Bar, F., Sciadas, G., Rothschild, C., & Koepke, L. (2013). Connecting people for development: Why public access ICTs matter. Retrieved from http://tascha.uw.edu/publications/connecting-people-for-development.

Sey, A., & Fellows, M. (2009). *Literature review on the impact of public access to information and communication technologies* (p. 10). Seattle, WA: UW Information School. Retrieved from www.globalimpactstudy.org/wp-content/uploads/2010/12/TASCHA_Public-Access-Review_2009.pdf.

Shahbaz, A. (2018). Freedom on the net 2018: The rise of digital authoritarianism. Retrieved from https://freedomhouse.org/report/freedom-net/freedom-net-2018/rise-digital-authoritarianism.

ST Foundation. (2015). Digital unify for kids: First steps into the information society. Retrieved 21 January 2016, from www.stfoundation.org/digital-unify-for-kids-first-steps-into-the-information-society.

Starbird, K. (2017). Examining the alternative media ecosystem through the production of alternative narratives of mass shooting events on Twitter. In *11th International*

AAAI Conference on Web and Social Media (ICWSM 2017) (pp. 230–339). Retrieved from https://aaai.org/ocs/index.php/ICWSM/ICWSM17/paper/view/15603.

Street, B. V. (2002). *Literacy and development: Ethnographic perspectives*. London: Routledge.

Surman, M. (2015, 7 October). Smartphone users in emerging markets deserve better than a watered-down internet. *The Washington Post*. Retrieved from https://www.washingtonpost.com/news/innovations/wp/2015/10/07/smartphone-users-in-emerging-markets-deserve-better-than-a-watered-down-internet/?postshare=7141447426888848&tid=ss_tw.

Vaidhyanathan, S. (2018). *Antisocial media: How Facebook disconnects us and undermines democracy*. New York, NY: Oxford University Press.

Vannini, Sara, Nemer, D., & Rega, I. (2017). Integrating mobile technologies to achieve community development goals: The case of telecenters in Brazil. 8th International Conference on Community and Technologies (C&T) 2017, Troyes, France, 26–30 June 2017.

Vannini, Sara, Gómez, R., Lopez, D., Mora, S., Morrison, J. C., Tanner, J., ... Tafurt, M. del M. (2019). Humanitarian organizations' information practices: Procedures and privacy concerns for serving the undocumented. *The Electronic Journal of Information Systems in Developing Countries*, 86(1), 1–8. https://doi.org/10.1002/isd2.12109.

Vannini, Sara, Rega, I., Sala, S., & Cantoni, L. (2013). Motivations of non-use of telecentres: A qualitative study from Mozambique. *Proceedings: 2013 Pre-ICIS Workshop of the AIS SIG on ICT & Global Development (GlobDev)*. Presented at the 2013 Pre-ICIS Workshop of the AIS SIG on ICT & GlobDev, Milan, Italy, 14 December 2013.

9

AWAKENING SLEEPING LANGUAGES IN SASKATCHEWAN WITH CULTURALLY APPROPRIATE CURRICULA AND TECHNOLOGY

Cheryle Herman, Belinda Daniels, Kevin Lewis and Marguerite Koole

Introduction

As settlers arrived from Europe, their languages began to dominate the social and economic environment of the Canadian prairies. The number of Indigenous language speakers declined rapidly as the people were exposed to new diseases, their land usurped, and their way of life dramatically altered forever. Residential schools (segregated schools in which many Indigenous children were forced to live and study) emerged as early as the seventeenth century (Kirkness, 2013). By the nineteenth century, they had become effective tools in the effort to replace Indigenous language and spirituality with English/French and Christianity. McCarty, Nicholas, and Wigglesworth (2019) argue that colonial schooling was a primary instrument in the purposeful and targeted erasure of Indigenous cultures. Children were forcibly taken from their homes and placed in these schools where they were punished for speaking their maternal languages. The schools were oppressive, and mortality rates were high. As a result of the trauma, some people rejected their language and heritage. Groups who survived or escaped the residential schools continued to speak their mother tongue but still lost much of their linguistic, cultural, and ceremonial knowledge.

It is noteworthy that the last residential school in Canada closed in 1996 (Chrétien, 2013). The long, fraught history of residential schools, government day schools, and system-based policies designed to solve the "Indian problem" has left deep scars amongst the Indigenous people in Saskatchewan and across the nation.

> We encounter a complex web of influences: the punishment and abuse experienced in residential schools, destruction and replacement of traditional

trade and economy, forced participation in public schools with homogenizing policy, and the fear and shame our people accumulated over several generations of assimilation policies.

(Makokis, Shirt, Chisan, Mageau, & Steinhauer, 2010, p. 5)

Fear and shame contributed to the rejection and loss of oral and written language.

For Indigenous nations, language is sacred; it has a spirit and it is alive. It is also essential to identity and nationhood. Language defines who people are and where they come from. The language cannot be separated from land and culture. According to McCoy, Tuck, and McKenzie (2016), "language is not something developed in isolation in human brains" (p. 12). This idea reflects the notion that the land speaks many different languages depending on the Indigenous peoples that inhabit it (Cajete, 1994). Language is a footprint. Footprints indicate where one has walked before and point towards the future; they ground people on the land.

The loss of any language represents a loss to all humanity. "Linguistic systems and practices represent an infinite reservoir of human intellectual, cultural and scientific effort" (McCarty et al., 2019, p. 4). According to Crystal (2000), "About every two weeks another language dies, taking millennia of human knowledge and history with it" (p. 151). This may result in the extinction of 60–90% of the world's almost 7,000 languages in the next century (Romaine, 2007). Yet, there is reason for optimism. Because of the resilience and strength of Indigenous peoples, sustainable and culturally appropriate language maintenance and revival initiatives are emerging. Within the Canadian context, reconciliation and language revitalization are now at the forefront of social and political discourse. Reclamation is the ultimate goal. In this chapter we explore Indigenous language learning tools and strategies relevant to Saskatchewan. We close the chapter with a brief discussion of how current technologies can benefit language revitalization efforts and the main challenges in implementing these technologies.

Language Reclamation in Canada

A Brief History

Indigenous peoples have inhabited the Canadian prairies for at least 13,000 years (Friesen, 2019). By the time Europeans arrived on the east coast of Canada, it is estimated there were millions of people living in Canada with "great multitudes" of people living on the prairies (Dickason, 1997, p. 8). Between roughly 1650 and 1850 the fur trade and the desire for land were among several major impetuses for European expansion westward. This expansion brought disease. Some bands on the prairies, such as the Basquia and Pegomgamaw Cree, lost one-half to two-thirds of their people during the smallpox epidemic of 1781–82

(Waiser & Perret, 2016). In addition to the problem with disease, the bison, a significant source of food and resources, were hunted nearly to extinction by the fur traders. Subsequently, various waves of immigration took place bringing increasingly more Europeans from diverse backgrounds and religious traditions.

Canada has seen a serious decline in speakers of Indigenous languages. "It is estimated that at the time of contact there were an estimated 450 Aboriginal languages and dialects in Canada" (McIvor, 2009, p. 1). Today, of the ten distinct Indigenous language families, approximately 60 languages are still spoken (McIvor, 2009). In terms of population across Canada, there are now 260,550 speakers of these languages (Statistics-Canada, 2017)—less than 1% of the total Canadian population. In the Saskatchewan context, there is additional urgency due to the coming shift in demographics. The Government of Saskatchewan reports that there are 19,020 people who speak Cree and 7,855 who speak Dene as a mother tongue. These two languages are also listed in the top five fastest declining mother tongues in the province with Cree declining by 5,645 speakers and Dene declining by 520 speakers since 2011 (Saskatchewan language: 2016 Census of Canada, 2016). At the same time, it is projected that by 2026, 36% of the Saskatchewan population aged 15 to 29 will be of Indigenous ancestry (Townsend & Wernick, 2008). Strategies and approaches to assist young, Indigenous people reclaim their language and culture are crucial to their future personal wellbeing.

Control over Indigenous Education in Canada

Since Canada was established as a nation via the British North American Act of 1867, the assimilation of Indigenous people was a significant goal of the Canadian government. Through the infamous Indian Act of 1867, the federal government took control of Indian education. (Although education is the purview of the provinces, the federal government remains in charge of Indigenous education to this day.) Churches became heavily involved in managing residential schools in 1892–1893, and attendance at residential schools became mandatory in 1894. It was not until the late 20th century that Indigenous people regained a voice in their own affairs. When Indigenous people gained control of education in 1972, now referred to as First Nations Control of First Nations Education, a policy paper was published outlining how education could include Indian philosophy of education and recommendations. It was at this time that Indigenous language revitalization efforts were initiated in earnest.

The Truth and Reconciliation Commission (2015) proposed 94 calls to action. Eight of the 94 involve language preservation, reclamation, and/or maintenance. These calls to action are congruent with the United Nations Declaration on the Rights of Indigenous Peoples (UNDRIP, 2007), which states that "Article 13.1: Indigenous peoples have individual and collective rights to revitalize, use, develop and transmit to future generations their Indigenous languages" (pp. 12–13). It is interesting that the only countries who voted against the draft were Australia,

Canada, New Zealand, and the United States—speaking volumes about the politics surrounding Indigenous populations in these countries. Indeed, of the nine provinces and three territories in Canada, only three territories and one province currently have some legislation to support the preservation and revitalization of Indigenous languages. (Interestingly, while writing this chapter, on October 24, 2019, the province of British Columbia introduced Bill 41 establishing a legislation framework aligning with the UNDRIP Declaration; the federal government and remaining provinces have yet to follow suit.)

Yet again, there is room for optimism. Indigenous language preservation and revitalization has come a long way in Canada. Indigenous languages are now being spoken in Parliament (Wright-Allen, 2019), which is another positive step in recognizing the importance of Indigenous language use.

Linguistic Characteristics and Writing Systems

Besides colonization, intergenerational trauma, and systemic discrimination, language preservation is hampered by the prevalence of the English language (Makokis et al., 2010), by the complex nature of polysynthetic languages (Kell, 2014), and by the lack of resources for teaching and learning such languages.

Language Characteristics

Many of the Indigenous languages in Canada are *polysynthetic* rather than *isolating* (Kell, 2014). This type of language, also called an *incorporating* language, often has very long words comprised of morphemes (i.e., word parts) (see Figure 9.1). They can have prefixes, suffixes, infixes, and circumfixes. The placement of the morphemes follows regular rules. Compared to more *isolating* languages such as English, the meaning relies less upon sentence structure and/or context. Polysynthetic languages may be either fusional or agglutinative. Fusional languages may have several meanings for one affix and they may combine and change pronunciation. In agglutinative languages such as Cree and Dene, each affix represents one unit of meaning; affixes do not fuse together and affixes do not change pronunciation when combined with other affixes (Kell, 2014).

FIGURE 9.1 Analytic-synthetic language continuum

One cannot translate an English sentence directly into an Indigenous language. For example, in Dene the English sentence 'the girl is playing with her dog' becomes *'ts'ékuaze* (girl) *bets'į* (her) łį (dog) héł (with) *senádher* (play)'. There are no Dene words for 'the' or 'is'. Words from synthetic, agglutinative languages (i.e., in which inflectional morphemes such as affixes express grammatical relationships) will be translated by several words or even by a complete sentence for less synthetic languages such as English (i.e., analytic languages in which meaning is conveyed through word order and helper words).

The relationship between language, thought, and culture is also significant. "Indigenous languages in their symbolic, verbal, and unconscious orders structure Indigenous knowledge" (Battiste, 2013, p. 146). To illustrate, there are animate and inanimate nouns in the Cree language. (The animate/inanimate noun categories are different from the masculine-feminine noun categories seen in some European languages.) While animals and people are animate, there are some objects that are difficult for a non-speaker to predict. For example, rocks and feathers are animate while a river is inanimate. Such differentiation may inform a Cree speaker's worldview. As such, a different mindset and different teaching methods can be helpful.

Writing Systems

Cree and Dene were primarily oral languages passed down through storytelling, prayer, song, and speech. The Cree and other Indigenous groups in North America had additional, highly developed ways of communicating "such as sign language, mnemonic systems, and (more recently) writing systems [including] petroglyphs, petrographs, wampum belts, hide paintings, and syllabics" (Daniels-Fiss, 2008, p. 283). As part of current language learning initiatives, the Standard Roman Orthography (SRO) writing system and syllabics have been used. generally consists of an English equivalent alphabet with some use of symbols and diacritics (i.e., symbols added to characters such as circumflex accents or macrons). Syllabics are based on the use of symbols to show sounds in the Indigenous language. For example, in the Dene language, for the word 'man' is translated as *deneyu* in SRO and ᑌᓀᔪ in syllabics. Among the Cree speaking groups in Saskatchewan, there are three distinct dialects: Plains (y-dialect), Woodlands (th-dialect), and Swampy (n-dialect). In order to meet the needs of each dialect group and to facilitate communication between them, SRO and syllabics require standardization.

Traditional and Emerging Language Teaching and Learning Techniques

There are a range of macro, system-based strategies (as presented in Table 9.1) that support the development and implementation of language-learning

TABLE 9.1 Strategies to support language revitalization

Strategy	Description
Resource creation	Production of resources by language workers and activists for use in language learning and teaching. (McIvor, 1998)
Documentation and preservation	Documentation and preservation of Indigenous languages for future and current us; technology is often used in this process. (McIvor, 1998)
Teacher training	Training of teachers to utilize appropriate teaching methods, to learn the Indigenous writing systems. (McIvor, 1998)
Research	Researching best practices in Indigenous language learning, teaching and current sources of information related to Indigenous languages. (McIvor, 1998)
Policy and political advocacy	A focus on policy change which utilizes strategizing, fundraising, and planning to support Indigenous language initiatives. (McIvor, 1998)
Technology	Utilization of various forms of technology for learning, documentation, preservation, and enhancement of Indigenous languages (such as recordings, websites, and mobile applications).

programs. In other words, at the system level, the lack access to resources or teacher training, for example, may restrict the implementation of teaching and learning strategies (Table 9.2).

Language teachers note that even if they teach the languages in school, the learners may lack an authentic context in which to use the language. Community engagement and *being on their land* is pivotal in Indigenous language maintenance and preservation. Makokis et al. (2010) stress that "it is important to understand that the language is a gift, and [everyone has] a responsibility to teach and to learn it" (p. 43).

Teacher training is also a notable influence on the acquisition of language. Table 9.2 itemises 12 different teaching strategies currently used and advocated by Indigenous language teachers in Saskatchewan classrooms and community contexts. The integration of these strategies into the development of mobile apps and desktop applications may hold significant potential.

Makokis et al. (2010) posit that the best way to learn an Indigenous language is through immersion, land-based activities, ceremony, song, and storytelling. Experiential learning in an Indigenous context is sometimes referred to as land-based learning (i.e., the 'language camp' language-learning strategy). The *nehiyawak* Summer Language Experience in Saskatchewan, founded by Belinda Daniels is an example of land-based learning. It is an annual summer camp based on the land that focuses on building language skills in the original context of the Cree ancestors.

Honouring traditional approaches whilst taking advantage of recent pedagogical techniques requires careful consideration. There should be opportunities for

TABLE 9.2 Language teaching strategies

Teaching strategy	Description	Potential mobile application ("app")
Early childhood language and immersion programming	Includes programs such as language nests where learners are immersed in the Indigenous language (McIvor, 1998). Language nests were first developed in New Zealand (Galley, Gessner, Herbert, Thompson, & Williams, 2016).	Age-appropriate games and activities that reflect curriculum.
Total Physical Response (TPR)	Developed by Dr. James Asher, TPR includes the teaching of vocabulary connected with actions. (First Peoples' Cultural Council, 2016)	Using the accelerometer of a smartphone, an app could be developed that tells a learner to perform an action such as stand, sit, walk forward, etc.
Accelerated Second Language Acquisition (ASLA)	Developed by Dr. Stephen Greymorning, this method has less of a focus on vocabulary and action-related learning activities but more focus on quickly developing learners' ability to understand and produce simple sentences of two or three words. (First Peoples' Cultural Council, 2016)	Apps can be developed that help develop connections between pictures, words, and the development of phrases and sentences (i.e., morphology and syntax).
Picture–Word Inductive Model (PWIM)	PWIM is a strategy for students to develop their reading and writing from a picture. (Calhoun, 1999)	Apps can be developed that help develop connections between pictures, words, and the development of phrases and sentences.
Adult language classes	These are classes that target adult learners at varying levels of language fluency. (McIvor, 1998)	Mobile synchronous and asynchronous communications tools to facilitate authentic dialogue. Automated exercises, audio recordings. Tools for self-checking progress.
Music and song	This strategy references the use of music, song, and dance as a way to teach a language. (Koole & Lewis, 2018)	Apps could play songs along with synchronized lyrics; activities such as quizzes, close exercises, word identification exercises, etc.
Master-apprentice programming	In this immersion method, a fluent speaker is paired with a motivated adult learner to learn the language in a one-on-one setting. (Galley et al., 2016)	Mobile synchronous and asynchronous communications tools to facilitate dialogue.

(*continued*)

TABLE 9.2 (continued)

Teaching strategy	Description	Potential mobile application ("app")
Language houses	Adult language learning immersion programs where adults live with a fluent Indigenous language speaker and only the Indigenous language is spoken. (Galley et al., 2016)	Mobile synchronous and asynchronous communications tools to facilitate dialogue.
Courses for silent speakers	Courses that aim to help speakers who understand the language but do not speak it. (Galley et al., 2016)	Mobile synchronous and asynchronous communications tools to promote dialogue; dictionaries, exercises.
Elder groups	Language learning where fluent Elder speakers teach the language to non-speakers and/or their peers. (Galley et al., 2016)	Mobile synchronous and asynchronous communications tools to facilitate dialogue.
Land-based learning	Encouraging critical thought through interaction with the land and an understanding of nature.	Plant identification apps could help learners identify medicinal plants and other resources for a multitude of day-to-day activities.
Language camps	Opportunities for immersion and/or land-based learning in an authentic context (utilizing a blend of approaches). (Galley et al., 2016)	Mobile synchronous and asynchronous communications tools to facilitate dialogue.

parents, grandparents, Elders, and children to access high-quality resources within authentic, natural language learning contexts such as at home, in the community, and on the land. Implementing a language learning approach requires the building of relationships with a community and, thereby, understanding their needs, goals, and traditions. Finally, communities need an increased number of high-quality language teaching and learning resources—both paper and digital (see examples in Table 9.2).

Technology in Language Teaching and Learning

Over the past two centuries, technological developments have played an important role in language preservation. Recordings of Elders still exist on wax cylinders, cassette tapes, floppy discs, and magnetic recordings. Early Indigenous language preservation and teaching methods included handwriting in syllabics and SRO, and distribution through photocopying. As computers became available, coding special characters on older computer mainframe systems, and later, inserting symbols in the early word processors were arduous processes. The production of computerized text in the syllabic system proved to be difficult until the development of the Unicode system in 1987/1988.

Technology can be positively implemented for linguistic and cultural revitalization through the development of relevant and engaging materials as well as communication tools with which to practise the language. Current generations, even in remote parts of Saskatchewan, can connect (albeit sometimes intermittently) with mobile technology, create content, and circulate information at a rapid rate. "Mobile services via LTE (long term evolution) were available to 99.0% of Canadians at the end of 2017. In rural communities, OLMCs (official languages), and Indigenous reserve areas, LTE was available to 95.9%, 99.0%, and 72.8% of the population, respectively" (Canadian Radio-television and Telecommunications Commission, 2019, p. 32). Indigenous reserves in Saskatchewan have 96.3% accessibility to LTE networks (Canadian Radio-television and Telecommunications Commission, 2019, p. 32). However, in northerly regions outside communities and reserves, connectivity can be unreliable at best.

Ready access to the Internet, whether through broadband or cellular networks, opens possibilities for increased interaction, content creation, and content sharing. Wilmarth (2010) has observed that through engagement with social media such as blogs, wikis, podcasts, video, email, text, and the plethora of image sharing apps available, people are now both consumers and producers of content. In this way, youth may become actively engaged in language preservation initiatives through their use of digital technology:

> Community-based language revitalization efforts have the potential to bring together youth, who are more comfortable with digital technology as users and producers, and Elders, who are language and cultural knowledge holders, to

work collaboratively on language initiatives and projects—thus allowing for an intergenerational exchange of ideas, skills and learning opportunities.

(Galla, 2009, p. 108)

Furthermore, technology can make language accessible in day-to-day social interactions and business—in addition to school-based programming. There are other positive aspects of using computer and mobile technology to enhance language learning and teaching, such as working at one's own pace, receiving immediate feedback, and mobility. Writing emails in the target language can contribute to learning to read and write. Synchronous conferencing tools can allow remotely based students to join conversations. Internet access provides opportunities for scanning, locating, synthesizing, retrieving, accessing, and exercising judgement while curating resources and information. Independent and/or communal use of the Internet can create a sense of ownership for learners and communities because they can develop and access resources relevant to their specific communities. Lastly, "students will become multiliterate in their Native language and English, in addition to being literate in information and computer technology" (Galla, 2009, p. 178).

Challenges

Unfortunately, there is a dearth of digital tools for language revitalization. The Digital Tools for Language Revitalization in Canada (DTLRCL https://www.wicehtowin.ca) database contains information and links to websites, video/audio repositories, and apps useful for Indigenous language revitalization in Canada (Koole, Felber, MacKay, & Lewis, 2018; Koole & Lewis, 2018). Initially, 156 online resources were found of which 83 were dictionaries and 73 were audiolingual tools. The researchers were unable to locate interactive apps for learning and practising syntax in any Indigenous-Canadian language. Consequently, communities might consider collaborating with technologists, designers, and researchers to develop much needed digital resources. At the same time, it is important that language acquisition also reflects current words and concepts associated with "modern" life so that the language is fully useful in day-to-day life.

In designing mobile language tools, "it is important to consider how to design pedagogical activities and tools in ways that are respectful of the people's needs, worldviews, protocols, and physical environments" (Koole & Lewis, 2018, p. 2). Although the statistics (above) suggest that First Nations Reserve communities located in Saskatchewan have good LTE access rates, off-reserve and some northerly regions may still lack consistent connectivity to support digital learning technologies; therefore, stand-alone apps are a better choice. Well-designed apps will allow users to update or refresh content while in an area of reliable connectivity and still be able to use the app in poor-bandwidth areas. Cost and travel are also significant barriers for some learners (Parker, 2012). Digital technologies, particularly mobile technology, in remote locations can assist learners to continue educational programs without having to leave their communities. Through technology, language learning content can be accessed and coordinated with land-based and/or community-based activities such as harvesting, hunting, trapping, and fishing, thereby incorporating culturally relevant activities.

It is also advisable to consider the risks of technology in language revitalization. Loss of control over traditional knowledge (i.e., how it is used, by whom, and when) is a serious issue. Some stories, for example, should only be told in certain seasons; some knowledge should only be shared within a ceremony. In addition to inappropriate use, sometimes traditional knowledge and practices are commoditized by people outside the community. Galley et al. (2016) note that "not all communities or Elders that are being recorded have access to data collected by outsiders after projects are completed and sometimes are asked to pay for [resulting] materials and dictionaries" (p. 14). Moreover, there are still Elders who do not want to be recorded with audio or video technology (Koole & Lewis, 2018). For some Elders, the sharing of sacred information, traditionally taught orally, is not something that can be done through social media or other electronic forms of video/audio technology. Indeed, computer technology can be viewed by Elders and communities as potentially destructive and distractive (Galla, 2009). However, Dauenhauer and Dauenhauer (1998) write that "the risks of sharing information are less dangerous at the present time than the risk that it may otherwise be lost forever" (p. 92). Galla (2009) also argues that:

> technology has helped to document and preserve the voices of our people, gifting our future generations with priceless knowledge and wisdom. Since technology is so much a part of today's culture, the future of Indigenous languages will depend partly on technology to engage students in learning.
> (p. 178)

Concluding Observations

Colonization, assimilation, and segregation policies have had a detrimental effect on Indigenous people throughout the world. In Canada "The situation of languages is very diverse ... for some revitalization is needed, for others, maintenance is needed" (Galley et al., 2016, p. 22). Whatever the situation may be, language loss is occurring at a rapid rate and requires action, particularly in Saskatchewan. The development of sustainable resources using *any* technological platform should be done in consultation and collaboration with local, situated communities. The land is life; it is spirit; languages are born on the land. Therefore, language learning must be connected to the land. In addition, the incorporation of both modern and traditional vocabulary will encourage day-to-day use. With proper planning and guidance from Elders, Knowledge Keepers, and Language Sharers in Indigenous communities, materials can be respectfully produced and made available if and when appropriate. Effective integration of technology can help not only to preserve languages, but also to share languages. With language and cultural knowledge intact, Indigenous peoples will be able to heal and move forward towards prosperity and nationhood. In this way, future generations will be able to trace the footprints of their ancestors.

References

Battiste, M. (2013). *Decolonizing education: Nourishing the learning spirit*. Saskatoon, SK: Purlich Publishing Ltd.
Cajete, G. (1994). *Look to the mountain: An ecology of Indigenous education*. Skyland, NC: Kivaki Press.
Calhoun, E. (1999). *Teaching beginning reading and writing with the picture word inductive model*. Alexandria, VA: Association for Supervision and Curriculum Development.
Canadian Radio-television and Telecommunications Commission. (2019). *Communications monitoring report* (Cat. No. BC9–9E-PDF). Ottawa, Ontario.
Chrétien, D. (2013). *An overview of the Indian residential school system*. Ontario: Union of Ontario Indians, Nipissing First Nation. Retrieved from http://www.anishinabek.ca/wp-content/uploads/2016/07/An-Overview-of-the-IRS-System-Booklet.pdf. Crystal, D. (2000). *Language death*. New York, NY: Cambridge University Press.
Daniels-Fiss, B. (2008). Learning to be a *nêhiyaw* (Cree) through language. *Diaspora, Indigenous, and Minority Education*, 2(3), 233–245. Retrieved from https://doi.org/10.1080/15595690802145505.
Dauenhauer, L. A., & Dauenhauer, R. (1998). Technical, emotional, and ideological issues in reversing language shift: Examples from Southeast Alaska. In L. A. Dauenhauer (Ed.), *Endangered languages: Language loss and community response* (pp. 57–98). Cambridge: Cambridge University Press.
Dickason, O. R. (1997). *Canada's First Nations*. Oxford, ON: Oxford University Press.
First Peoples' Cultural Council. (2016). Teaching tools for language nests. Retrieved July 31, 2019, from www.fpcc.ca/language/Resources/Online_Companion_Toolkit/Teaching_Tools_for_Language_Nests.aspx.
Friesen, G. (2019). History of settlement in the Canadian prairies. In G. Friesen (Ed.), *The Canadian encyclopedia*. Retrieved July 31, 2019, from https://www.thecanadianencyclopedia.ca/en/article/prairie-west.
Galla, C. K. (2009). Indigenous language revitalization and technology: From traditional to contemporary domains. In J. Reyhner & L. Lockard (Eds.), *Indigenous language revitalization: Encouragement, guidance and lessons learned* (pp. 167–182). Flagstaff, AZ: Northern Arizona University Press.
Galley, V., Gessner, S., Herbert, T., Thompson, K. T., & Williams, L. W. (2016). *Indigenous languages recognition, preservation and revitalization: A report on the national dialogue session on Indigenous languages*. Victoria, BC: First People's Cultural Council.
Kell, S. (2014). *Polysynthetic language structure and their role in pedagogy and curriculum for BC Indigenous languages*. Vancouver, BC: BC Ministry of Education.
Kirkness, V. J. (2013). Aboriginal education in Canada: A retrospective and prospective. In F. Widdowson, & A. Howard (Eds.), *Approaches to Aboriginal education in Canada: Searching for solutions* (pp. 7–25). Edmonton, AB: Brush Education Inc.
Koole, M., Felber, A., MacKay, G., & Lewis, K. (2018). An online database of Indigenous language learning/teaching tools. Think Indigenous Education Conference 2018:

Inspiring Change through Indigenous Knowledge, Story, and Education, March 13–16, Saskatoon, SK.

Koole, M. L., & Lewis, K. (2018). Mobile learning as a tool for Indigenous language revitalization and sustainability in Canada: Framing the challenge. *International Journal of Mobile and Blended Learning*, 10(4), 1–12. Retrieved from https://doi.org/10.4018/IJMBL.2018100101.

Makokis, L., Shirt, M. V, Chisan, S. L., Mageau, A. Y., & Steinhauer, D. M. (2010). *mâmawi-nehiyaw iyinikahiwewin*. St. Paul, AB: Blue Quills First Nations College.

McCarty, T. L., Nicholas, S. E., & Wigglesworth, G. (2019). A world of Indigenous languages: Resurgence, reclamation, revitalization and resilience. In T. L. McCarty, S. E. Nicholas, & G. Wigglesworth (Eds.), *A world of Indigenous languages: Politics, pedagogies and prospects for language reclamation* (pp. 29–47). Bristol, UK: Multilingual Matters.

McCoy, K., Tuck, E., & McKenzie, M. (2016). *Land education: Rethinking pedagogies of place from Indigenous, postcolonial, and decolonizing perspectives*. New York, NY: Routledge.

McIvor, O. (1998). Building the nests: Indigenous language revitalization in Canada. Unpublished master's thesis, University of Victoria, British Columbia. Retrieved from https://dspace.library.uvic.ca/bitstream/handle/1828/4106/Parker_Aliana_MA_2012.pdf.

McIvor, O. (2009). Strategies for Indigenous language revitalization and maintenance. In *Encyclopedia of language and literacy development* (pp. 1–12). Canadian Language and Literacy Research Network.

Parker, A. V. (2012). *Learning the language of the land*. [Unpublished master's thesis] University of Victoria. Retrieved from https://dspace.library.uvic.ca/handle/1828/4106.

Romaine, S. (2007). Preserving endangered languages. *Language and Linguistics Compass*, 1(1–2), 115–132. https://doi.org/10.1111/j.1749-818X.2007.00004.x.

Statistics-Canada. (2016). Saskatchewan language: 2016 Census of Canada. Retrieved from https://www.saskatchewan.ca/government/government-data/bureau-of-statistics/population-and-census.

Statistics-Canada. (2017). *The Aboriginal languages of First Nations people, Métis and Inuit*. Ottawa, Ontario. Retrieved from https://www12.statcan.gc.ca/census-recensement/2016/as-sa/98-200-x/2016022/98-200-x2016022-eng.cfm.

Townsend, T., & Wernick, M. (2008). In hope or heartbreak: Aboriginal youth and Canada's future. *Horizons: Policy Research Initiative*, 10(1), 4–6.

Truth and Reconciliation Council of Canada. (2015). Truth and Reconciliation Commission of Canada: Calls to action. Winnipeg, MN. Retrieved July 31, 2019, from http://trc.ca/assets/pdf/Calls_to_Action_English2.pdf.

United Nations Declaration on the Rights of Indigenous Peoples (UNDRIP). (2007). *United Nations declaration on the rights of Indigenous peoples*. New York, NY: United Nations. Retrieved from https://www.un.org/development/desa/indigenouspeoples/declaration-on-the-rights-of-indigenous-peoples.html.

Waiser, B., & Perret, J. (2016). *Saskatchewan: A new history*. Markham, ON: Fifth House Press.

Wilmarth, S. (2010). Five socio-technology trends that change everything in teaching and learning. In H. H. Jacobs (Ed.), *Curriculum 21: Essential education for a changing world* (pp. 80–96). Alexandria, VA: Association for Supervision and Curriculum Development.

Wright-Allen, S. (2019, February 6). Helping make House history: Meet Cree translator Kevin Lewis. *The Hill Times*. Retrieved from https://www.hilltimes.com/2019/02/06/helping-make-house-history-meet-cree-translator-kevin-lewis/187072.

10
EMPATHY-DRIVEN MOBILE APP DEVELOPMENT (MAD) WITHOUT CODING

A Case of Citizen Developers

Dick Ng'ambi

Introduction

South Africa has a population of about 59 million of which 22 million (37%) own smartphones and this number is projected to increase by 5 million in the next five years. The ownership and use of smartphones are spread across socio-economic backgrounds, although how these devices are used varies widely. Ng'ambi and Bozalek (2016) observe that mobile phones are ubiquitous technologies in resource-constrained environments and have the highest penetration rate of any technology in history but remain one of the unexplored devices for educational purposes (p. 207).

However, both the government of South Africa and the business sector have exploited the penetration of smartphones for service delivery, marketing and customer support though this has only been effective for the middle-class who generally can afford the high data costs and/or have Wi-fi in their homes. Recently there has been an increase in government-funded free Wi-fi in public spaces to enable the public to have access to the Internet. Although smartphones are ubiquitous in South Africa with most students owning or having access to one, many schools have banned the use of mobile phones in school. One of the reasons for banning smartphones is the alleged abuse of the device by students, instead schools embrace desktop computers and laptops which most students cannot afford and schools are unable to provide enough of them. The unintended consequences are that such actions of demonising smartphones shape students' attitudes towards them, considering smartphones to be an 'evil', and they hinder students from fully exploiting the opportunities that smartphones offer especially with mobile app development in an educational setting. It is ironic that a mobile generation is growing up with a powerful device, i.e. a smartphone, without guidance from either parents or teachers and everything they know about the device, they either taught themselves or learned from peers. Meanwhile, the Government of South Africa has embarked on skills development initiatives for artisans, and in the schooling sector a new subject on coding (using Scratch http s://scratch.mit.edu) has been introduced in primary schools aimed at equipping young people with the skills *needed* for the Fourth Industrial Revolution (4IR). As Butler-Adam (2018) rightly cautions 4IR requires more than coding skills, it requires problem solvers, people who are capable of implementing, managing and working with the new technology, and working collaboratively. However, because coding does not form part of teacher training curricula, in-service teachers are ill-prepared to teach the new subject and schools offering coding are having to depend on the services of the private sector, and the relationship between coding and other subjects appears disjointed. This not only raises questions about pedagogy but also its sustainability and future impact.

Citizen Developers

One of the environments in which citizen developers thrive is in makerspaces. Ng'ambi and Bozalek (2016) commend the do-it-yourself (DIY) or makerspaces for encouraging citizen developers to make new things through collaboration and innovation. However, the realisation of such an outcome in resource-constrained environments requires pedagogies that exploit and cultivate new beliefs, and thus are transformative of both self and the environment. While the introduction of coding in schools is a welcome initiative, it is a future investment and does not help when dealing with the current challenges. Vincent, Driver and Wong's (2019) predict an increase in low-code development activities by 2024. According to (Vincent et al., 2019), 75% of apps for small- to moderate-scale projects will use citizen development initiatives working with low-code development tools. Then it makes sense, in the context of South Africa, that attention is shifted to citizen development initiatives empowered by low-code applications.

According to the 2019 priority matrix for education (Yanckello and Williams 2019), citizen developers will be of great benefit in less than two years globally (see Figure 10.1).

In his blog, Raia (2018) reminds us that a citizen developer is a highly creative and driven problem solver with little or no prior knowledge of coding or app development but who uses rapid application development (RAD) platforms to create fairly advanced applications. The phenomenon of citizen development (see Figure 10.2) removes the need for intermediaries (technical developers as go-betweens) and encourages citizens experiencing a need to design apps that address their immediate needs quickly without waiting for 'developers' or having a budget to develop such apps.

Citizen developers can augment their knowledge of the community based on lived experience (i.e. disposition) with their creativity and problem-solving skills, to

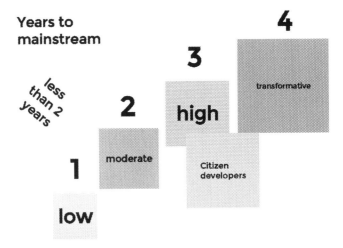

FIGURE 10.1 Citizen development will become a transformative practice
Source: Yanckello and Williams (2019).

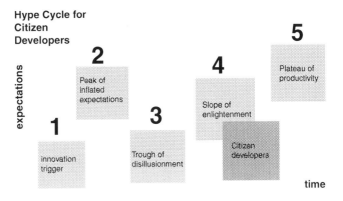

FIGURE 10.2 Hype cycle depicting citizen developers
Source: https://www.gartner.com/document/3953718?ref=solrAll&refval=235351280.

rapidly experiment with building apps at no cost, in fun and playful ways whereby they gain confidence, shifting dispositions and become better developers.

Skills and Dispositions

In her study that identified traits and skills of creative persons, Pitri (2013) found that when children were constantly asked to explain their answers and the decisions they took, explain their plans and argue for what they saw as possible outcomes to their actions, creative thinking was fostered. While it was important to create the right environment, the role of a teacher in modeling the creative problem-solving process was just as critical. "[T]teachers who solve problems creatively are more likely to develop children that are successful creative problem solvers ..." (Pitri, 2013: p. 46).

One of the challenges facing professional development approaches is the focus on skills development with little or no attention paid to the requisite disposition to apply the skills. In order to achieve this duality, a democratic education is needed. To the extent that citizen developers are empowered with practical skills, it is a form of democratic education (Gutmann, 1999) as ordinary people become active participants in mobile apps development to solve context relevant problems in an ever changing world. According to Rogers (1986), the goal of democratic education is to assist students to become individuals: who are able to take self-initiated actions and to be responsible for those actions; who are capable of intelligent choices and self-direction; who are critical, able to evaluate contributions made by others; who have acquired knowledge relevant to the solution of problems; who, even more importantly, are able to adapt flexibly and intelligently to new problem situations; who have internalized an adaptive mode of approach to problems, utilising all pertinent experience freely and creatively; who are able to cooperate effectively with others in various activities; and who work, not for the approval of others, but in terms of their own socialized purposes (pp. 387–388).

It can be inferred that the relationship between dispositions and skills is what Kaspersen (2000) describes as structure and agency in the structuration theory. This is particularly useful in understanding why citizen developers require both skills to design and build solutions quickly but also to develop creative and problem-solving mindsets.

Structuration Theory

Structuration theory states that structure and agency are mutually dependent, like two-sides on a coin. Similarly, skills and dispositions/beliefs are intertwined so that a lasting change to one manifests in the other. McKenney and Reeves (2019) observe that 'to achieve lasting effect, interventions must ultimately address teacher beliefs, norms of social interaction and underlying pedagogical principles' (p. 214). In terms of structure and agency, Kaspersen (2000) put it succinctly, 'the social structure is not simply the sum of individuals' actions. Society is viewed as a structuration process, whereby human actions simultaneously structure and are structured by society' (p. 32). Structuration theory focuses on two of Giddens' theses: "Social practice is constitutive of social life. Social practice constitutes us as actors and embodies and realises structures; and as a result, social practice is the mediating concept between agency and structure, between individual and society" (Kaspersen 2000: 33). The aim of structuration theory is to help explain the relationship between human action and social structures, where the structure is a mindset. According to Giddens (1984), "structure forms personality and society simultaneously – but in neither case exhaustively: because of the significance of the unintended consequences of action" (p. 70). As citizen developers leverage their knowledge and understanding of their contexts to develop mobile apps, their levels of confidence increases, and this has the potential to build transferable skills to build apps to address other needs hence an interplay between human actions and structure.

Unintended Consequence and Unacknowledged Condition

In simplistic terms, structuration theory states that human beings are unconscious of the social structures that inform their actions. Social structures are embedded dispositions that influence actions, and the consequences of these actions, whether intended or unacknowledged, shape the social structures. For example, people who are highly creative and driven problem solvers are unconscious of reality yet they draw upon it in their actions which results in products that embody the designer. These structures, though unconscious, are imprints on the mind, and human actions are a product of these imprints, learning from the unintended consequences as further imprints are made on the mind. Giddens (1984) put it this way, "the unintended consequences of action form the acknowledged conditions of further action in a non-reflexive feedback cycle" (p. 14). It follows that human actions are sandwiched on the one side by the unconscious and on the other hand by unacknowledged conditions and/or the unintended consequences of actions.

Giddens' theory results in us thinking that the use of mobile devices may result in outcomes that are not expected by a user. For example, an unintended consequence of students abusing the mobile phone is that they receive a call or a message while involved in an unrelated activity, the mobile phone being used for cyberbullying when the purpose for which it was purchased was to stay in contact with parents. These unintended consequences become the basis for new actions.

In order to understand the influence of dispositions and why they require a process to change them is that human actors are not only able to monitor their activities and those of others in the regularity of day-to-day conduct; they are also able to 'monitor that monitoring' in discursive consciousness. It is this monitoring of one's own activities and those of others that has made social media relatively popular. It is in the discursive consciousness that actors can justify their actions, explain away outcomes but also express their fears and concerns. Giddens (1984, p. 29) adds that stocks of knowledge which actors draw upon in the production and reproduction of interaction are the same as those whereby they are able to give accounts, offer reasons. etc. It can be inferred from Giddens that the stocks of knowledge from which students draw during empathy is the same knowledge from which they draw to explain their own actions (Giddens, 1984, pp. 4–8).

This argument suggests that there is a relationship between human interaction and human action.

It can be inferred from structuration theory that to fully understand the user needs for which mobile apps are to be designed and developed, a mobile designer needs to have access to the unconscious stocks of knowledge of a user. This is only possible using the discursive consciousness with which actors can justify their actions, explain outcomes but also express their fears and concerns. The methodology for achieving this is through empathy.

Empathy-Led Designs

The term 'empathy' is used to describe eight social actions: knowing another person's internal state, including his or her thoughts and feelings; adopting the posture or matching the neural responses of an observed other; coming to feel as another person feels; intuiting or projecting oneself into another's situation; imagining how the other is thinking and feeling; imagining how one would think and feel in the other's place; feeling distress at witnessing another's suffering; and feeling for another person who is suffering (Batson 2009). When used to inform designs, empathy provides a way of connecting with users and understanding their needs to levels of depth that techno-focused approaches do not. Brown and Wyatt (2010) postulate social challenges require systemic solutions that are grounded in the client's or customer's needs. Thus, the empathy-led design is a human-centered approach to problem solving (Kimbell 2012) and is consistent with design thinking.

The design thinking process has three overlapping spaces to keep in mind: inspiration, ideation and implementation. Think of inspiration as the problem or opportunity that motivates the search for solutions; ideation as the process of generating, developing and testing ideas; and implementation as the path that leads from the project stage into people's lives (Brown & Wyatt, 2010, p. 33). Empathy forms part of the inspiration space where the problem or opportunity that motivates the design of a mobile app solution is uncovered. One of the techniques for doing this is to use an empathy mapping tool (Gibbons 2018). According to Gibbons (2018) an empathy mapping technique is used for visually capturing and presenting what we know about individual users. It serves to make explicit what is ordinarily tacit knowledge. It helps to articulate what is known about a specific user and makes it easy to reach a shared understanding of what a user needs.

The empathy map (see Figure 10.3) mediates the relationship between the environment/context for which the mobile app is to be designed and the world of MADP where the citizen developer is a member of both the environment and the MADP world. Kaptelinin and Nardi (2009) challenge us not to restrict mediation to tool mediation only.

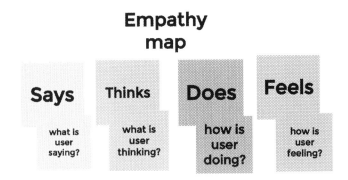

FIGURE 10.3 Empathy map showing four key questions
Source: https://www.nngroup.com/articles/empathy-mapping.

> Tools mediate the relationship between the subject and the object, rules mediate the relationship between the subject and the community, division of labour mediates the relationship between community and the object, and nothing prevents us from considering environments as mediators of human interaction with the world.
> *(Kaptelinin & Nardi, 2009, pp. 255–256)*

One of the aspiration of a democratic education system is to create an openness to experience (extensionality) with an internal locus of evaluation (as opposed to external where value is placed on what people say), but rather asks 'have I created something satisfying to me?' and plays spontaneously with ideas – juggling ideas into impossible juxtapositions (Rogers, 1986). It is in these environments that dispositions are shifted. However, in order to achieve these goals, there is a need for citizen developers to be sensitised to the user's requirements which the empathy map seeks to provide.

Below is a description of how the quadrants in Gibbons' (2018) an empathy map are used:

- The *Says* quadrant contains what the user says out loud in an interview or some other usability study. Ideally, it contains verbatim and direct quotes from research.

During this stage a citizen developer listens to the discursive consciousness of those with a problem / challenge. Note that a citizen developer is a member of a community, so the problem being solved is not alien but engages with others. The aim of this quadrant is to ensure that what is spoken is heard and recorded. It does help to repeat what you have heard so that it can be verified.

- The *Thinks* quadrant captures what the user is thinking throughout the experience. Ask yourself (from the qualitative research gathered): what occupies the user's thoughts? What matters to the user? It is possible to have the same content in both Says and Thinks. However, pay close attention to what users think, but may not be willing to vocalise.

 It is here that creative thinking can be fostered by the citizen developer asking the user to motivate their answers or soliciting explanations to possible contradictions. It is not unusual for a user to default to what they know already hence limiting their thinking about the future possibilities.

- The *Does* quadrant encloses the actions the user takes. From the research, what does the user physically do? How does the user go about doing it?

 The citizen developer uses what they have heard in Says and Thinks to build apps quickly so that the user can be invited to 'Say' and 'Think' again. When using rapid application development (RAD) platforms, a citizen developer may discover limitations in the RAD platform relative to the needs of the user but might also find possibilities of what can be included that was unplanned as far as the user needs were concerned.

- The *Feels* quadrant is the user's emotional state, often represented as an adjective plus a short sentence for context. Ask yourself: what worries the user? What does the user get excited about? How does the user feel about the experience?

 All apps are work-in-progress and in this evaluation quadrant a citizen developer's goal is to meet the emotional needs of a user. The idea here is to listen to words that suggest these feelings in what is said, how it is said, how the user thinks, does and does not – all pointers to feelings.

The general experience of implementing an empathy map and the learning that results from it by the citizen developer and the user is somewhat similar to that of a therapist (citizen developer) and the patient (user) relationship. Rogers (1986) provides nuanced ways of understanding the relationship between a therapist (citizen developer) and patient (user), it is where:

- The citizen developer is able to participate completely in the user's communication.
- The citizen developer's comments are always right in line with what the user is trying to convey.
- The citizen developer sees the user as a co-worker on a common problem.
- The citizen developer treats the user as an equal.

144 Dick Ng'ambi

- The citizen developer is well able to understand the user's feelings.
- The citizen developer always follows the user's line of thought.

Reflections

Participants at the Educational Technology Inquiry Lab (ETILAB) at the University of Cape Town have used empathy-driven app development in sandpit sessions. The sandpits are creative, playful and innovative processes. Figure 10.4 shows the mobile app builder (Fliplet) with the components that citizen developers (participants) employed to build apps without coding. Participants used an empathy map to obtain user requirements.

One of the participants reflected:

> Almost all groups understood the significance of empathising with their client group before suggesting a solution. The use of Fliplet made the design of the solutions seamless, for the group I was in. Although this platform was shown to us briefly, the ease with which we efficiently managed to use it suggests a familiarity with edtech that was not there for many of us at the beginning of the course.
>
> (Extract 1)

The statement ... *Almost all groups understood...* > [Thinks] ... *the use of Fliplet made...* > [Does] ... *the ease with which* ... > [Feels] ... *was not there for many of us at the beginning of the course* ... > [Says]. The point of departure was ... empathising with their client group ... which is critical for an empathy-led app development. There was interaction with the tool (i.e. Fliplet) and the reference to the *familiarity with edtech* speaks to the stocks of knowledge that were drawn upon. To the

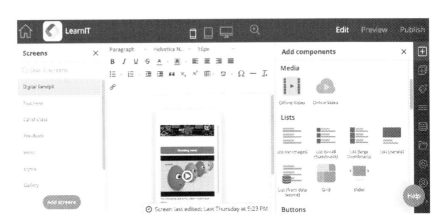

FIGURE 10.4 An example of mobile app building blocks (Fliplet)
Source: https://fliplet.com

extent that human interaction (empathy) led to human action (design of apps using Fliplet) the process was reflective and educative.

One of the unintended consequences and unacknowledged conditions of the empathy-driven process was the design of an app for moms to express milk for their born babies.

> What stood out for me was a presentation by one of the groups about creating an environment which enables new moms that just returned to work to be able to have privacy and time to express milk for their new born babies. A lot came to my mind about this problem, things like would it have been solved in other ways without involving technology? I am thinking of an app for vegans for example, I wouldn't bother myself about such an app because I'm a meat eater, so if the app for the new mothers is made to also create an awareness about the rights that these mothers have then how can the app reach the intended audience that is colleagues of these new moms because one would never just sign up to the app if they are not breastfeeding for example.
>
> *(Extract 2)*

In the statement ... *what stood out for me* ... [*Thinks*] the unacknowledged condition is how the 'unusual' need for an app to support mothers to express milk led to thinking about a new app for vegans. There is a general sense of empathy for mothers ... *one would never just sign up to the app* ... >[*Feels*] and is mindful of action ... *create an awareness about the rights that these mothers* ... >[*Does*]. The cyclic nature of the empathy map was evident in ... *a lot came to my mind about this problem* ... >[*Thinks*]. It is also useful to note that these apps did not need to be completed but were useful as proof of concepts.

One of the participants wrote the following in a blog after the study:

> The idea of empathy was practically demonstrated. For a group to be able to design/propose a suitable problem-solving app/technology tool, members had to fully understand and live with their client's educational challenge. This demonstrated that without understanding a learning/educational challenge at hand, it would be very difficult to come up with an appropriate solution/design.
>
> *(Extract 3)*

An analysis of the blog shows that the approach was effective. The need to be immersed in understanding the user's needs is underscored. The statement concludes that empathy-driven app development enabled the designs of apps that were appropriate, authentic and contextually relevant and addressed real-problems people experienced. Table 10.1 below summarises an empathy-driven mobile app development process.

TABLE 10.1 Empathy-driven mobile app development process

Steps	Empathy process	App development process
1	Provide a client with an opportunity to talk about how they experience the challenge/difficulty for which they are seeking a solution. - Remember this is not about you, so avoid talking about your experience or offering solutions at this stage. - Not everything you need to know is in the 'Says' quadrant, so try and uncover what is not being said.	Create a safe environment, that is non-judgmental. Collaboratively establish the ground rules with participants. Do not pretend to listen. Use the empathy map to record: Says | Thinks | Does | Feels.
2	Re-articulate what the client said as evidence of having listened. N.B. To confirm what one has understood, this step is about telling back what one understood in order to clear any possible misunderstanding. - Checking that you listened is both reassuring and helps to fill in the gaps. - Sign off the requirements with the client. Note that this will be useful in Step 5.	Update the empathy map with new understanding. Ask questions like ... how does that make you feel? Or what did it feel like when ...? Help to make explicit the tacit knowledge.
3	Make adjustments - Using the client requirements build a mockup. - Remember the mockup should be based on the constraints of the components of the MADP.	Do not chase into building the app. Let the client engage with the mockup. Let the client make suggestions or confirm the thinking as it develops. This increases acceptance of the final app.
4	Find a MADP that is appropriate for your needs. - Remember some MADPs have free components and premium ones. - Only subscribe to the paid version when 100% sure that a specific MADP meets your needs. Exhaust the affordances of a free version before subscribing to a paid version.	Try at least two or more MADPs to ensure you are as close to the spec as possible. Treat all your mobile app developments as work-in-progress. You can improve on any design.

Steps	Empathy process	App development process
5	Populate the app with dummy data. – Demonstrate the app to the client. – Give the client a user manual. – Let the client test the app. – Get feedback on the app and manual. – Use the empathy map to gauge whether the initial brief as signed off in Step 2 has been delivered. If not, discuss with the client why some requirements were not met and plan the way further.	Separate feedback into two components: Comments on the app in relation to the need as expressed in Steps 1 and 2. Comments on further developments (include value added features enabled by the mobile app platform). You need to manage this carefully so that you do not agree to do something that the MADP will not enable you to do.
6	Do a final submission to the client and gauge their level of satisfaction.	Feedback at this stage should be used for further development.

Conclusion

This chapter has shown how a constructed safe environment (sandpit) for citizen developers mediate interaction between clients (citizen developers' peers) and the world of MADP to build mobile apps without code shifts dispositions for both citizen developers and clients. The mediation this work has demonstrated corroborates Kaptelinin and Nardi's (2009) call for work that extends the notion of mediation.

> As designers, we construct environments to help people get something done; we think of them as mediators of activity. Making the relationship between artifacts, environments and the world an object of analysis and extending the notion of mediation beyond tools are promising and much-needed directions for further development of activity theory. Future work in this direction is likely to make activity theory a more powerful approach for studying a variety of information technologies such as media spaces, electronic workplaces, and games.
> *(Kaptelinin and Nardi 2009: 256)*

In the context of resource-constrained environments where there is neither a budget to contract professional developers to develop apps, nor skills to build in-house apps, citizen developers are an attractive alternative and perhaps the only sustainable solution in resource-constrained environments. However, there have not been strategies available to inspire citizen developers and equip them with sound design approaches that would shift their dispositions to become both problem solvers and creative designers. This chapter has presented a model that addresses this problem. The chapter reported on the work of the Educational Technology Inquiry Lab (ETILAB) (http://etilab.uct.ac.za) that has shown that the use of empathy-driven designs has potential to inspire citizen developers to become 'mobile app developers' without writing code. The 'E' in the name ETILAB stands for 'Empathy' as this is the point of departure of our work with students. The Lab is a 'digital sandpit' – a 'play' environment where learning is fun, creativity is fostered MADP and others and all work done in the sandpit is treated as work-in-progress since our focus is on changing action through shifting dispositions, as with a chef every artefact is a learning opportunity. "Construction is akin to the act of cooking. And later, after evaluation and reflection when the chef and selected customers test the food, this phase is revisited to make adjustments, based on feedback" (McKenney and Reeves, 2019, p. 146).

As a final word, the more citizen developers found answers to the questions users had, the more both the citizen developers and the users had new questions about the answers they found. This unintended consequence led to further action of seeking better ways of addressing the challenges. This quest for best ways of addressing the challenges often led to exploring the affordances of other mobile app builders – this process of learning quickly what was feasible, 'throwing away', starting again was possible because of the agile nature of design and development – no-code.

Finally below are some of the mobile app builders a reader might want to try:

Name	URL
Adobe PhoneGap (Cordova)	https://build.phonegap.com
App Inventor 2	http://appinventor.mit.edu
Appscend	http://appscend.com
Appsconda	https://appsconda.com
AppSheet	https://www.appsheet.com
Appypie	https://www.appypie.com
Google App Maker	https://developers.google.com/appmaker
iBuildApp	https://ibuildapp.com
Microsoft powerapps	https://make.powerapps.com
Phonegap	https://phonegap.com.

References

Batson, C. D. (2009). These things called empathy: Eight related but distinct phenomena. In J. Decety, & W. Ickes (Eds.), *The social neuroscience of empathy* (pp. 3–15). Cambridge, MA: MIT Press.

Butler-Adam, J. (2018). The Fourth Industrial Revolution and education. *South African Journal of Science*, 114 (5–6). Retrieved from www.scielo.org.za/scielo.php?script=sci_arttext&pid=S0038-23532018000300001.

Brown, T., & Wyatt, J. (2010). *Design thinking for social innovation – Stanford Social Innovation Review.* Retrieved from https://ojs.unbc.ca/index.php/design/article/viewFile/1272/1089.

Gibbons, S. (2018). Empathy mapping: The first step in design thinking. Retrieved from https://www.nngroup.com/articles/empathy-mapping.

Giddens, A. (1982). *Profiles and critiques in social theory.* London: The Macmillan Press.

Giddens, A. (1984). *The constitution of society.* Cambridge: Polity Press. https://www.gartner.com/document/3882864?ref=solrAll&refval=235149099.

Gutmann, A. (1999). *Democratic education* (2nd ed.). Princeton, NJ: Princeton University Press.

Kaspersen, B. L. (2000). *Anthony Giddens – an introduction to a social theorist.* Oxford: Blackwell Publishers.

Kaptelinin, V., & Nardi, A. B. (2009). *Acting with technology – activity theory and interaction design.* London: The MIT Press.

Kimbell, L. (2012). Rethinking design thinking: Part 1. Retrieved from www.lucykimbell.com/stuff/DesignPractices_Kimbell_DC_final_public.pdf.

McKenney, S., & Reeves, T. C. (2019). *Conducting educational design research.* London: Routledge. Retrieved from https://doi.org/10.4324/9781315105642.

Ng'ambi, D., & Bozalek, V. (2016). Learning with technologies in resource-constrained environments. In N. Rushby and D. W. Surry (Eds.), *The Wiley handbook of learning technology* (pp. 200–220). Chichester: John Wiley & Sons, Inc.

Pitri, E. (2013). Skills and dispositions for creative problem solving during the artmaking process. *Art Education*, 66(2), 41–46. Retrieved from https://search.proquest.com/docview/1355013983?accountid=14500.

Raia, M. (2018). The rise of the citizen developer and its impact on the enterprise. Retrieved from https://www.integrify.com/blog/posts/citizen-developer-impact-on-the-enterprise.

Rogers, R. C. 1986. *Client-centered therapy – its current practice, implications and theory*. London: Constable and Company Limited.

Vincent, P., Driver, M., & Wong, J. (2019). Low-code development technologies evaluation guide. Retrieved from https://www.gartner.com/document/code/381782?ref=imq_grbody.

Wong, J., Baker, V., Leow, A., & Resnick, M. (2018). Magic quadrant for mobile app development platforms. Retrieved from https://www.gartner.com/document/3882864?ref=solrAll&refval=259504701.

Yanckello, R. & Williams, C. K. (2019). Hype cycle for education. Retrieved from https://www.gartner.com/document/3953718?ref=solrAll&refval=235351779&toggle=1.

11
TECHNOLOGY-ENHANCED HIGHER EDUCATION FOR REFUGEES

Meaghan Brugha, David Hollow and Catherine Gladwell

Background

Despite high levels of demand for university-level programmes among refugee students, the United Nations High Commissioner for Refugees (UNHCR) (2019) estimates that only approximately 3% of refugee youth globally are currently able to access higher education. Although this is a significant increase from the 1% of refugees who could access higher education in 2015, it is still well short of the UNHCR target of 15% percent provision by 2030. Refugee learners encounter significant barriers in accessing higher education, including achieving the academic standard necessary for enrolment, the absence of available and accessible information about potential educational opportunities, the prohibitive financial cost of higher education, and lacking the necessary documentation to apply, such as evidence of previous educational attainment as well as the required nationality or identity documents (Dippo, Orgocka, & Giles, 2013; Dryden-Peterson & Giles, 2012; Lorisika, Cremonini, & Safar Jalani, 2015; Watenpaugh, Fricke, & King, 2014). Girls face additional challenges in accessing higher education due to responsibility for domestic work, early marriage, lack of access to sanitary products, and lack of confidence. In addition, camp-based refugees face restrictions on their freedom of movement and ability to come and go from the camp, which impact their ability to pursue higher education opportunities (Dippo et al., 2013).

Access to higher education is a human right referred to in various international conventions, including the Universal Declaration of Human Rights (Article 26.2), the International Covenant on Economic, Social and Cultural Rights (Article 13c), and the Convention on the Rights of the Child (Article 28c) (UNHCR, 2015). The individual and community benefits of higher education are multiple and include: serving as an increased incentive to complete primary and secondary studies; providing protection from harm through helping young people to maintain a sense of hope for the future and providing a powerful 'university student' identity; contributing to post-conflict reconstruction; empowering refugee communities by promoting social, economic, and gender equality; and enabling refugees to be more productive contributors to their host communities (Lorisika et al., 2015; McMahon, 2009; OECD, 2012).

A range of blended learning programmes (also known as hybrid or mixed-mode learning) that combine online learning with face-to-face instruction and independent student learning have been developed in response to the need for innovative new approaches in the provision of higher education for refugees. Blended learning can provide refugees with the opportunity to access an international study programme while remaining within their current location and being part of a supportive local learning community (Tarvainen, 2015). This can provide access to higher education at a lower cost than traditional scholarships, and with more support than that provided through solely online learning options. In addition, the blended learning approach in some ways reflects the campus experience, and can contribute to an increased sense of student identity (Al-Fanar Media, 2015).

The Research Study

In 2016, Jigsaw Consult and Refugee Support Network completed a mixed methods research study on blended learning for refugee higher education in low-resource environments in both urban and camp-based settings (Gladwell et al., 2016). The study focused on 11 programmes across 8 different countries, and included face-to-face in-depth interviews with over 300 refugee higher education students and over 50 academics, programme managers, and policy makers. The research provided insight into the challenges and opportunities that such programmes face, and how they can be designed and implemented to be of maximum effectiveness. The research contributed to the work of the Connected Learning in Crisis Consortium which aims to promote, coordinate, collaborate, and support the provision of quality higher education in conflict, crisis, and displacement situations through connected learning.

This chapter is based on the research conducted and builds on it with a particular focus on the technological learning from the study. The chapter presents a review of the structure, pedagogy, and use of technology by blended learning programmes designed for refugees pursuing higher education. It discusses the perspectives of the students and staff at the research sites, including the key challenges they faced regarding technology use in the programmes. The chapter closes with learning for the sector that provides practical principles for programmes to build on, alongside design considerations.

Programme Structure, Pedagogy, and Use of Technology

The underlying rationale for blended learning programmes for refugee higher education is the conviction of programme designers and implementers that blended learning can be more pedagogically effective than online learning for refugee higher education, and is able to reach more students than can benefit through conventional scholarship programmes. While the use of technology in these programmes means they are dependent on the availability of reliable technological infrastructure, namely electricity, computers, and internet connection, blended learning programmes tend to depend less on high bandwidth connectivity (such as for online video streaming) than programmes that are run entirely through online learning platforms.

These programmes normally operate at physical learning centres based in camps or urban environments, in combination with an online learning platform borrowed or adapted from their accrediting international institution. There is significant variation in programme entry requirements, accreditation, the scale and breadth of the courses offered, the structure of teaching and learning, and programme length. Many programmes are free for refugee students at the point of delivery, while others require some financial contribution. There is also significant variation in the balance and structure of online to offline components, but commonly there is a combination of remote and local staff, tutors, and facilitators.

Some of the blended learning programmes have been built on specific pedagogical frameworks that the designers consider to be particularly applicable for effective blended learning for refugee higher education. One notable example is the Ignatian pedagogy employed in the programmes of Jesuit Worldwide Learning. Staff noted that there is an emphasis on reflecting on their learning and what it means to them, which has helped refugee students develop critical thinking skills. This places value on the knowledge gained through students' lived experiences. At the core of many of the programmes included in the research study is a high degree of contextualisation and personal support for students, as well as a focus on applied learning, non-academic development, and community engagement.

These programmes vary in the balance and structure of online to offline components and use technology in different ways, but all offer an online learning environment as part of their delivery structure. This platform provides access to: online modules or courses for students to manage and complete, distance-based support from academics, and peer learning networks. Technology is also often used to create a more flexible learning environment, where students are encouraged to manage large elements of their own study schedules. This is particularly beneficial for refugee students who often study while maintaining other significant commitments. At a programmatic level, technology is used in a range of ways and for various purposes. For example, more than three-quarters of onsite programme staff interviewed in the study stated that they use the internet to do their own research for lesson preparation, to find additional resources for students, and to communicate with the students. Staff also offered a critical awareness regarding the appropriate place of technology within learning: "it depends on what you are doing – technology can enhance your teaching, but it has to have a purpose – you should not use it for the sake of it" (programme staff, Jesuit Worldwide Learning).

It is clear that the technologies that it is appropriate for a programme to utilise will vary widely according to context and therefore this requires detailed consideration in each instance. Mobile phones, for example, are widely used by some refugee populations. In 2019, Jigsaw Consult led the data collection and analysis for a GSM Association study, which identified over two-thirds of refugees as active mobile phone users (i.e., they had used a mobile phone at least once in the previous three months) in the three research locations: urban refugees in Jordan, Kiziba refugee camp in Rwanda, and Bidi Bidi refugee settlement in Uganda (Casswell, 2019). Where this is the case, mobile phones can be used to enhance programme delivery, either through aiding in the online learning directly, or through facilitating additional peer support mechanisms through apps such as WhatsApp. However, affordability, literacy and digital skills, and charging remain key barriers to mobile phone ownership and mobile internet use in all contexts. In addition, among refugees, women have significantly less access and ownership of mobile phones than men (Casswell, 2019). It is therefore critical for blended learning programmes to be cognisant of how their approach may impact the future use of technology by their students and the communities in which they operate, including mapping out potential unintended consequences to ensure that existing inequalities are not being reinforced through the programme structure, delivery, or technology selected.

Student and Staff Perspectives

Programme Strengths

Student and staff perspectives regarding the ease and value of learning with technology vary widely according to multiple practical issues such as security, sustainability of hardware, availability of electricity, and the reliability and robustness of internet connectivity. The majority of students interviewed expressed overall positive sentiments regarding their participation in technology-enhanced programmes. Students gave various reasons for why they enjoyed learning with technology, including the global connections established through their courses, the participatory methods employed through the programmes, the opportunity to learn information and communications technology (ICT) skills while studying, the flexibility of the learning schedule, and the pragmatic awareness that it is the only realistic option available to them as refugee students.

A significant recurring theme that emerged from discussions with students regarding the ways in which they positively engaged with technology through their programmes is the way in which the pedagogical tools of the learning management systems assist them to build global networks and make them feel connected to a wider community:

> it gives us the chance to share the experience of our reality here as refugees – and we can use [name of learning management system] to talk with people in similar situations in other refugee camps who are also studying the course.
> *(Student in Malawi)*

Students were also keen to note the benefits of working on collaborative projects using various technologies like discussion boards, as well as using social media on their mobile phones (such as Facebook, Viber, and WhatsApp). The use of these technologies enhanced their learning and developed agency by enabling them to connect with onsite staff and students on their programmes and in other locations, creating their own learning networks to discuss and share resources.

Students expressed an appreciation of the participatory, learner-centred methods of their programme that helped them to develop critical thinking skills. In addition, several learners explicitly contrasted the pedagogical approaches employed during their blended learning programme with the more traditional rote learning methods they had previously been accustomed to when learning in a face-to-face context. There was widespread appreciation of the critical thinking skills gained as a result, alongside a recognition that it requires significant time for a student to make the requisite transition in learning approach.

The majority of students also highlighted the value of varied activities that cater for different learning styles and preferences, such as the effective integration of audio and video materials. Success was seen in programmes that adapted the educational structure and content to learners' needs through tailoring online content to make it more accessible, and explored how to work with technologies already familiar to students. Furthermore, the provision of additional support for students is particularly important in refugee contexts, and learners benefit from mentoring (both at a peer and non-peer level), as well as psychosocial and career development support that respond to their unique circumstances and experiences.

Key Challenges

Staff and students discussed numerous challenges they encountered with the technological components of their programme. These are structured into five areas: (1) connectivity and hardware; (2) online content; (3) barriers once enrolled; (4) programme monitoring and impact measurement; and (5) the national legislative environment and accreditation process. Each challenge area is discussed in turn below, with consideration for ways in which they could be overcome.

Connectivity and Hardware

Students identified reliable connectivity as their most significant learning challenge, and almost all students and staff expressed the shared sentiment that they require more stable internet connectivity "as this will speed up the learning process" (staff in Kenya). In a small number of programmes, the connectivity challenges are exacerbated by the surrounding political context and government controls. Helpful examples of ways in which programmes mitigate for unreliable internet include allowing learning activities to be completed in an asynchronous manner so that learners can upload their work when they have a reliable connection, and sending programme materials via CD or USB instead of online where necessary.

The physical infrastructure and hardware within the learning centres is also a continual challenge, with many students and staff expressing frustration at the significant time it takes to receive new parts at the learning centre when computers break. One student noted that many of the computers in the learning centre no longer work and "the ones that do work are not that reliable, they often freeze" (student in Kenya). A staff member in Kenya noted the importance of building programme resilience by including a realistic estimate of hardware lifespan in programme budgeting and forecasting. There is also scope for the use of mobiles and materials specifically designed for mobile delivery to reduce the challenges with computers not working, as well as working to access online resources more easily.

Online Content

Many programmes are designed for one specific location and are therefore applicable to a limited population, making contextualisation of online content time-consuming and costly. However, the contextualisation of online content is imperative in order for technology to be an effective tool to aid refugee higher education. To appropriately contextualise course content, staff and students identified three contributing factors: (1) conducting a local needs assessment in order to examine where and how it might be necessary to adapt international course structure and content; (2) ensuring that onsite staff can add additional local resources to the teaching materials and facilitate student discussion groups grounded in local experiences; and (3) prioritising collaboration between international and local experts, particularly in cases where academics from the country of origin or host community are able to work alongside academics from the accrediting university in order to design or adapt the courses.

Barriers once Enrolled

Students identified multiple and overlapping barriers they faced once enrolled in their higher education programmes, such as the challenge of adapting to the online components of the programme. Students explained that their lack of experience with using computers means it is hard to develop subject-specific skills at the same time as developing the necessary ICT skills. Others said they were frightened before starting the course: "I had never heard of this thing called 'online' so it took me a long time to adapt to the idea of studying online. I was so afraid that I might not succeed" (student in Jordan).

Students also explained the difficulty of balancing intensive studies with their other commitments (e.g., family or employment), and largely felt that distance-based staff did not understand or respond appropriately to the challenges they faced. Approximately two-thirds of students thought that distance-based, online staff either "did not understand the challenges they face in life at all", or "understood very little". In contrast, over three-quarters of students reported that the onsite staff within their programme had a good understanding of the difficulties and challenges that they faced. It is clear that it is not easy for staff to develop high levels of empathy and contextual awareness if they only engage with students at a distance, interacting through digital technologies. Students suggested that distance-based staff would benefit from an increased understanding regarding the challenges commonly faced by refugees and the nuances of these across a variety of contexts.

Despite the barriers faced by students following enrolment, respondents exhibited strong motivation for continued study. This was aided by the flexibility of course structure, pastoral support, and encouragement from programme staff and peers. Similarly, financial stipends (e.g., to assist with transport or living costs) also helped reduce pressures on refugee students.

Programme Monitoring and Impact Measurement

Lack of funding, staff capacity, expertise, and prioritisation can make it challenging to measure the longer term impact of programmes on individuals and communities. Yet, the lack of a strong evidence base creates challenges in securing funding and planning for the future. Appropriate technology-based data collection systems could make a significant contribution in this regard, helping to build a more robust evidence base for the sector for the benefit of students, staff, accrediting bodies, and donors. The capabilities of such systems have not yet been fully utilised in any programme with which the research study engaged.

The National Legislative Environment and Accreditation Process

The appropriateness and use-value of technology-enhanced learning is influenced by the national legislative environment within which the programme is operating. The research study found that future employment prospects are a significant consideration for students engaging in higher education, with students noting that the most important factors in selecting a programme are the level of accreditation, and the local and international recognition of the available qualification. The majority of students place high value on internationally accredited courses; however, the accreditation process is challenging and the transferability of credits often lacks clarity.

Recommendations

This section presents practical principles for programmes to build on followed by key programme design considerations. While these recommendations are focused on technology-enhanced refugee higher education, they are also useful principles and design considerations for the sector as a whole.

Four Principles to Build On

Programmes require a clear identity and rationale and should be clear from the outset about what they plan to achieve, how they intend to operate, and how this fits within and is informed by the wider sector. This will aid in understanding whether the programme objectives are feasible given the technology and support available, and what the provision of higher education means to the futures of the refugee learners. The programme should also present a clear rationale for: (1) the pedagogical approach employed, aligning curriculum with intended learning outcomes, and (2) the technology selected to achieve the programme objectives, providing an analysis of its appropriateness within the given context.

Programmes should have a commitment to accessibility and inclusivity throughout all the steps of programming from the marketing of courses, entry requirements and application processes, to course delivery and appropriate support to aid student retention. International staff should have a good understanding of refugee contexts to create inclusive and accessible environments. In addition, holistic approaches with the provision of additional non-academic support such as mentoring, psychosocial support, and career development can help to create a sense of community and safety for students, and can have a significant impact on student wellbeing, empowerment, and their ability to learn.

Programme models should be suitably contextualised as the nature of effective higher education for refugees works differently in each host country, and for different groups of refugees within a host country. Programmes should be designed and implemented in light of the implications of these differences. In order to be effective, technology needs to be introduced in a phased, contextualised approach, with multiple entry points for users. Programmes should consider enabling factors such as connectivity, electricity supply, climate, and security. In addition, the viability of technology-enhanced learning is significantly influenced by national legislative environments, as some countries do not recognise the credibility of online learning. Local staff should be engaged from the outset of programme design to ensure a contextually relevant course model and course materials.

Programmes should have a significant and sustained focus on training and support for all technology users, including basic ICT literacy. Many students do not have this on entry and therefore require substantial initial training and ongoing, in-person support so that they can realise the potential learning benefits of the programme and develop key ICT skills that they can use for their personal lives, work, or further online study. Without such support, technology-dependent programmes risk excluding the most marginalised students who have had less prior exposure to technology. It is also important to prioritise the training needs of staff, as many come to programmes without all the relevant skills and experience for blended learning in place. Programme providers should consider what practical, pastoral, and academic support is required, and monitor closely the course structure and intensity to ensure it is manageable for students. Groups of students at higher risk of withdrawing from the course should be identified and offered targeted support. This is likely to include working students, students with a key support role within their families, and students with lower levels of education prior to engagement in the programme.

Design Considerations for Programmes

Six design considerations are presented below, five of which are directly linked to technology and it is critical that all of them are reflected on for effective decision making about programmes.

What level of accreditation is offered? This can range from full accreditation from an international institution to certification from a national institution. It is necessary to consider the specific host-country regulatory environment to know what proportion of online study is permitted for a higher education qualification.

What depth of academic impact is anticipated? This may be a deep impact for a small number of students through a high cost-per-beneficiary approach or a broad impact for a large number of students through a low 'cost per beneficiary' approach. The appropriate investment in technology – both hardware and software – will vary according to the proposed impact and linked cost per beneficiary.

Where will the programme be located? A programme may locate in an (often) urban area which has a large number of refugee students who are ready to participate in higher education or locate where there are very few refugee students who are ready to participate in higher education. The types of technology that it is possible to use in a secure and sustainable manner will be significantly influenced by the supporting technological infrastructure (such as reliable connectivity and electricity) available within the locality.

To what extent will the programme be integrated? A programme may be delivered that is bespoke for a refugee population or more integrated within the national education system of the host-country.

What will the admission criteria be? Some programmes have standard admission criteria while others are more flexible because of the challenging circumstances of refugee students. Programmes need to consider the minimum levels of ICT literacy that are required for a student to participate in their higher education institution, and may offer specific preparatory courses to help ensure refugee students are equipped to learn within a blended learning environment.

What is the extent of course contextualisation? Some programmes choose to focus on the current context and priorities of their students while others focus on the anticipated future context and priorities. This decision influences the type of online content that will be appropriate within the course in question.

There are many different valid models and approaches to providing higher education for refugees and technology is only one contributing component. Each of the technology-enhanced models has a range of associated benefits and challenges. In order to deliver effectively within a specific context it is necessary for a programme to be able to articulate the rationale for, and understand the consequences of, its selected approach.

References

Al-Fanar Media. (2015, October). Strengthening delivery of higher education to Syrian refugees. Workshop Report. Retrieved from https://www.al-fanarmedia.org/wp-content/uploads/2015/12/Strengthening-Delivery-og-Higher-Education-to-Syrian-Refugees.pdf.

Casswell, J. (2019). The digital lives of refugees: How displaced populations use mobile phones and what gets in the way. Retrieved from https://www.gsma.com/mobilefordevelopment/wp-content/uploads/2019/07/The-Digital-Lives-of-Refugees.pdf.

Dippo, D., Orgocka, A., & Giles, W. (2013). Feasibility study report. Reaching higher: The provision of higher education for long-term refugees in the Dadaab camps, Kenya. The Borderless Higher Education for Refugees Partnership, Toronto, Canada. Retrieved from http://refugeeresearch.net/ms/bher/workshops /feasibility-study-report.

Dryden-Peterson, S., & Giles, W. (2012). Higher education for refugees. *Refuge: Canada's Journal on Refugees*, 27(2), 3–9. Retrieved from https://refuge.journals.yorku.ca/index.php/refuge/article/view/34717.

Ferede, M. (2016, May 24). Virtually educated: The case for and conundrum of online higher education for refugees. Retrieved from https://gemreportunesco.wordpress.com/2016/05/24/virtually-educated-the-case-for-and-conundrum-of-online-higher-education-for-refugees.

Gladwell, C., Hollow, D., Robinson, A., Norman, B., Bowerman, E., Mitchell, J., Floremont, F., & Hutchinson, P. (2016). *Higher education for refugees in low-resource environments: Research study.* Jigsaw Consult, United Kingdom. Retrieved from https://hubble-live-assets.s3.amazonaws.com/jigsawconsult/attachment/file/5/Jigsaw_research_study.pdf.

Lorisika, I., Cremonini, L., & Safar Jalani, M. (2015). Study to design a programme / Clearinghouse providing access to higher education for Syrian refugees and internal displaced persons: Final report. European Commission. Retrieved from https://research.

utwente.nl/en/publications/study-to-design-a-programme-clearinghouse-providing-access-to-hig.

McMahon, W. W. (2009). *Higher learning, greater good: The private and social benefits of higher education.* Baltimore, MD: Johns Hopkins University Press.

Organisation for Economic Co-operation and Development (OECD). (2012). *Education at a glance 2012: OECD indicators.* OECD publishing. Retrieved from https://www.oecd.org/edu/EAG%202012_e-book_EN_200912.pdf.

Tarvainen, J. (2015, September). The contribution of higher education to strengthening communities. In H. Perkins (Chair), Higher education, global wellbeing and the refugee crisis. Seminar conducted at the International Centre for Higher Education Management, University of Bath.

United Nations High Commissioner for Refugees (UNHCR). (2015, July). Higher education considerations for refugees in countries affected by the Syria and Iraq crises. Education Brief, Geneva. Retrieved from https://www.unhcr.org/uk/protection/operations/568bc5279/higher-education-considerations-refugees-countries-affected-syria-iraq.html.

United Nations High Commissioner for Refugees (UNHCR). (2019). *Stepping up: Refugee education in crisis.* Retrieved from https://www.unhcr.org/steppingup/tertiary-education-out-of-reach.

Watenpaugh, D. K., Fricke, A., and King, J. (2014). *We will stop here and go no further: Syrian university students and scholars in Turkey.* Institute of International Education, University of California Davis. Retrieved from https://data2.unhcr.org/en/documents/download/54527.

12
DISADVANTAGED LEARNERS AND THE DIGITAL CONTRACTOR

A Critical Perspective on Mobile Learning in the Global South with Reference to Paolo Freire

Stephen Haggard

The experiences of a contractor working in 2018–2019 on projects aimed at marginal and disadvantaged mobile learners form the basis for this and the next chapter. The company, Digital Learning Associates Ltd, is a commercial developer and licensor of learning content for government, school, and publisher clients. The company also has a commitment and track record in contract content development for Global South mobile education projects. The learners addressed through these projects are characterised by absolute and relative disempowerment across multiple domains, by precarity or marginality, and by exclusion through technological and cultural barriers.

We offer different perspectives in two separately authored chapters. This present chapter is a critical analysis of contractor roles in mobile learning projects for learners in situations of extreme disadvantage. The next chapter, by my colleague Elena Deleyto, reports evidence in detail from three projects. All our observations are situated in recent work that we have directly produced. Disclaimer: we are players in the global EdTech industry, whose dominant narrative is an upbeat "solutionist" shtick in which technology appears to solve problems. Possibly, as such, we might be partisan – although we do make great efforts to stand aside from the EdTech's hype and myths. As conscientious practitioners we pay close attention to how that solutionist narrative plays differently (or unravels completely) when situations of great adversity are the setting for mobile learning's mix of pedagogical, technological, financial, and political factors. Nevertheless we underline that we are offering reportage from involved commercial participants rather than analysis as academic scholars. Since we cannot change this outlook we make no apology for it.

The three mobile learning projects we were contracted to deliver in 2018–2019 in Global South settings are reported in full in the following chapter but for context I list them here with the utmost brevity:

1. The 2018 contract for monitoring and evaluation of a mobile learning course for 1000 state sector teachers in India
2. The 2018–2019 development and delivery of a mobile learning course for teachers in refugee camps in Ethiopia
3. The writing of a full curriculum for around 600,000 refugee students of the Rohingya community of Myanmar, resident in exile in Bangladesh, along with the training of their learning facilitators to teach it, based on a policy-driven framework.

The projects were all commissioned through the British Council, which regularly contracts Digital Learning Associates for educational projects with a technology dimension. Local and international organisations, including the United Nations Children's Fund (UNICEF), the United Nations High Commissioner for Refugees (UNHCR), ministries, local and international non-governmental organisations (NGOs), had mandated or approved the British Council to supervise the delivery. The British Council is a government-funded agency of the United Kingdom (UK) and brings a principles-based approach to advancing education and culture overseas. It is guided by independent expertise, subject to public scrutiny, and makes extensive use of qualified and vetted specialist suppliers. Its use of learning contractors is widely considered (and we would agree) to exemplify best practice worldwide. We are grateful to this unique organisation for its willingness to have the production processes behind these projects reported independently and critically discussed here in research literature.

The Production of Mobile Learning

The production of mobile learning, as opposed to its consumption and outputs in learning activity, is the focus of our reflections in this chapter. Critical pedagogies of mobile learning have tended to investigate their topic at the moment of consumption, when the programme of learning is already in use as an education tool. Defining mobile learning, Matthew Kearney emphasises the primacy of social and conversational processes, and identifies attributes such as "authenticity, collaboration and personalisation" (Kearney, Schuck, Burden, & Aubusson, 2012), yet does not ask whether this applies equally in the communities that create mobile learning experiences, as distinct from those that consume them. Such a partial perspective might reflect the emergent nature of the field, the importance of gathering evidence of its effectiveness, or perhaps the situatedness of many authors inside teaching institutions. Whatever the reason, we contend that critical pedagogy should properly be exercised across the whole product cycle of learning;

that the modes of production for mobile learning should be of fundamental interest to its scholars, and that it will be rewarding to ask questions about who owns and operates its productive capital, who sets the terms by which services are developed, and how those terms are negotiated.

As an example of insights that can flow from this approach: whereas John Traxler describes how M-learning softens the time-space constraints of formal education (Traxler, 2009), we as its producers attest that on the contrary a hardening and rigidification takes place when it comes to the content production process. The narrative of mobile learning when reported at the production end is mainly about technical exactitude, process efficiency and hierarchically structured workflows. This is interestingly paradoxical when compared to the "social and conversational" character of mobile learning as claimed by authors situated inside an education-centred narrative. The contrast invites us to apply some skepticism around the discourse of mobile pedagogy.

Paolo Freire and the Mobile Learners of Guinea-Bissau 1974–1976

To help us critically reflect on our role as mobile contractors working with disadvantaged learners, we compare our experiences to a different moment in the critical pedagogy literature.

Paolo Freire's classic text *Pedagogy in Process: The Letters to Guinea-Bissau* is, in his words, a "report of a phase of political and pedagogical activity" working in the 1970s with adults disempowered by illiteracies of multiple kinds (Freire, 2016, p. 176). In the Guinea-Bissau literacy project, Freire and his team were engaged by the Revolutionary Government to create a learning solution. Of course the phrase "mobile learning" was not available to Freire's African project, nor were its 2020 connotations of portable devices, networks, and interactivity. However, the educational formats he and his co-workers proposed in 1974–1976 anticipate aspects of mobile learning pedagogy in some surprising ways. Freire calls for interactive group learning in "Culture Circles", has a preference for light infrastructure such as outdoor "forest" classes and itinerant teachers, and emphasises contextualised learning linked to productive activity at the moment of need. These tropes would be familiar to mobile learning practitioners today, echoed in formats such as "interactive webinar", "remote tutoring", or "workplace study".

Contextually, Freire's 1974–1976 intervention in post-conflict Guinea-Bissau also seems resonant at first sight. His projects, like ours in 2018–2019, responded to an urgent crisis of teaching and learning, sparked by violence and resulting in displacement. Institutional reform and teacher training were perceived to be essential to building a new society – yet the context meant public provision struggled to provide educational outputs of quality and relevance.

On the other hand, Freire's theory and praxis go utterly against many approaches which typify today's mobile learning programmes for disadvantaged cohorts. He decries programmes of learning ("passive acceptance of packaged knowledge") and mocks the development of core skills ("campaigns [that] idolise literacy"). Freire rejects any role for "foreign technicians with a mission". Any wish on the part of learners to progress their lives is, for Freire, a manifestation of reactionary bourgeois entryism. He calls the notion of literacy to boost employment prospects "strange". In effect, he damns the entire basis and apparatus of what we would today call the "Learning for Development" (L4D) sector. He likewise deplores the core structures of programmatic education, detecting alienation and assured failure in learning features such as graded progression, courses created by authors, and the selection of topics relating to global culture, including instruction delivered in global languages. So our core paradigms as a mobile learning contractor working with disempowered cohorts would face a heavy indictment from the godfather of critical pedagogy – and we need to consider how to answer such charges.

Context matters. In Freire's projects, the learning designer is an empowered militant, often an ex-combatant, with a mandate endorsed by popular support and backed up by victorious firepower. The revolution in Guinea-Bissau – led by Amilcar Cabral's radical agrarian reform movement which won control in the countryside before overthrowing the Portuguese colonial regime – had no place for external technocrats. The comrades inevitably saw in the learning programmes of the pre-liberation era an "elitist" and "alienating" project that served only the aspirational urban middle class. Half a century on, this revolutionary Marxian framework seems archaic yet also has some surprisingly contemporary dimensions. Freire calls for a literacy syllabus that gives equal status to political literacy and linguistic literacy, and in which knowledge evolves through and alongside productive experience. This chimes with today's contexts including calls for a media literacy syllabus in the formal learning agenda to counter "fake news" and disinformation, and the role of financial and personal education in school curricula. We could even compare the expansion of formats such as BTEC (a vocational programme of study in the UK delivered in part by employers for post-16 education as an option at formal learning stages) which mixes theory with workplace experience.

In today's post-conflict displaced populations, when compared with Freire's Guinea-Bissau learners, we can observe a shift in the locus of power when it comes to shaping the design and content of teaching systems. The provision of syllabus and institutions to a refugee nation or a weakened state sector in the early 21st Century is an endeavour the financial and technical apparatus of which sits outside the target community. By consent or necessity (and sometimes by coercion) the locus of control lies in uncertain coalitions of NGO donors, international agencies backed by the firepower of external peacekeeping forces, and technical specialists. Restoration of political and social power to displaced and disempowered populations is the stated well-meaning aim of these actors (although some might dispute that full restoration is the actual goal). The consensus is universal, that empowerment will be achieved through assimilation to an international paradigm that these external global forces represent. "Progress" (and funding) is linked to an ideology of compliance to learning formats, standards, and pedagogies that originate outside the context. Ministries lend their political authority to the implementations – usually with enthusiasm. As practitioners in mobile learning, we need to be aware that our work and our learning models can form part of such arrangements.

Mobile Learning Mode of Production ca. 2020

In each of the 2018–19 projects we contracted to undertake, whether the activity and learners were located in Bangladesh, Ethiopia or India, the task was to supply English Language Teaching (ELT) assets to cohorts which had been diagnosed with an urgent need for accessing English language skills. The British Council maintains the capacity to meet language learning needs in such cases – and collaborates with funding partners and delivery agencies to achieve this. It is a delivery channel for language training for teachers, providing technical implementation through its staff and contractors, and ensuring alignment of UK-funded programmes with a UK Government policy of support for marginal or disadvantaged groups in development and humanitarian work. In a separate work stream, linked to overt policy goals around soft power projection, cultural diplomacy and international education, the British Council also manages a thriving activity stream supplying English language training to self-funding learners.

It is important to draw out three aspects from this context for a critical analysis of the means of mobile learning production for these disempowered cohorts.

- First, the contractual nature of the arrangements. The projects or services under discussion are procured on behalf of a group of unfunded learners with the British Council acting as the commissioner on behalf of other actors, and then using a contracted supplier to perform the delivery. This set-up, exercised in a climate where public sector financial discipline and accountability have totemic status, subjects mobile learning to the rituals and formats of commercial contractor-supplier relationships.
- Second, these projects are inevitably about the learning of an ex-colonial language in the Global South. The terms for progression are set, in English, from London, however wisely. Determination in the learning design and project delivery of the kind and quality of English, for what purposes and for whose benefit, and who decides on those questions, are points negotiated on a power gradient the fulcrum of which is one of the world's top capital cities.
- Third, a generalised and predominantly Western-centric "ideal" practice of mobile learning (to the extent that such a thing exists) is meeting a complex and unique set of constraints in each local setting. The local implementations display local culture patterns of hierarchy and gender on matters from teacher

authority, to device access and data consumption. Roslyn Appleby's book, *ELT, Gender and International Development: Myths of Progress in a Neocolonial World*, has a winning narrative and insight in to how ELT practice "crashes and burns" in Indonesia and elsewhere in a pre-technology era (Appleby, 2010) – and it reads across neatly to mobile learning practice.

Each of these features bring depth and grit to a critical analysis of mobile learning and we expand them in turn below.

Contract-Based Production of Mobile Learning Materials

The role of contractor can be observed in many aspects of contemporary education delivery and is typically associated with ideologies of process efficiency in routine tasks or specialist functions. Researchers are increasingly paying attention to the impact of contracting on learning outcomes or system structures, for example Margaret Mattes (2017) for the Century Foundation in 2017 critically assessing the outsourcing by universities of their online teaching to external contractors known as Online Program Managers (OPMs). The observations that follow aim to extend such critiques.

Where mobile learning is concerned, the advantages claimed for a contracting model will typically include the specialist technical capacity and workflows required for operations. Additionally, mobile learning projects may justify their financing with claims about scalability, flexibility, or reach. Achievement of such goals in publicly funded projects is subject to key performance indicator (KPI)-type evaluation by metrics like efficiency and value for money, which naturally aligns with commercial transacting. Finally, mobile projects are widely perceived by funders as risky or politically exposed (a "no funding of software" rule operates in many development NGOs). Mobile projects thus attract risk mitigation and arm's-length approaches, which contracting enables. The contractor's role is thus intricately and ideologically linked to the mobile learning model, and this introduces a paradox: the rhetoric of mobile learning dials up features like flexibility in the learning process or a softening of the boundaries of time and role. Yet the production process, because of the contracting model, depends on tightness in definition of parameters, and programmatic management of timelines and content. The background and context information given to the contractor is fragmented by nature, being limited to the immediate technical and practical elements required to develop the task at hand and nothing further.

A full critical pedagogy of mobile learning would need to explore how its production dynamics interact with the programme content and learning design. This is not the place to analyse in detail, but it's worth a note in passing that learning contractors typically assemble education products subject to non-negotiable parameters of quality, time, and resourcing. Any unresolved contradictions and conflicts are passed down to the contractor whose resolution of them will reflect business as well as educational objectives. Underlying these rigid paradigms of contract production is the standard commercial model of the digital technology and content industries, which aims to fully realise the possibilities of specialised short-term labour, payment by results, disintermediation of vertical value chains, intellectual property (IP) acquisition (including sometimes learner data) by project partners, modular components, and re-use of assets.

Whether a contractor's perspective on all this can contribute anything useful to a fuller view of mobile pedagogy is also worth considering. There are good reasons to be cautious. Restrictions on contractors usually include non-disclosure agreements establishing legal penalties in the event of breaching confidentiality clauses, and these clauses often interpret "confidential information" rather broadly. Contractors, if they decide to report their experiences at all, will be reporting through the selective lens of "projects we did", viewpoints firmly situated in time and place. Coverage may emerge somewhat randomly from the concatenation of recent experiences – in contrast to scholarly authors whose knowledge and insight might accumulate programmatically within a disciplinary framework. Commercial KPIs such as cost control, margin, and stakeholder satisfaction leading to further projects may compete with the objective metrics of learning outcome favoured by education professionals (assessment and examination data or student surveys). Contractors are by nature unlikely to bite the hand that feeds them. As a result the learning contractor possesses a hybrid outlook blending whatever they know of education theory and practice with skills and values in content production processes, project management, and business operation. We leave it to others to pass the verdict on whether the contractor's mish-mash of know-how, structural limitations, and commercial optics enable or hinder a useful contribution to critical pedagogy. It is perhaps safe to assume that Freire would have had some doubts.

English Language – Engine of Opportunity or Disempowerment?

English deployed as a medium of instruction (MoI) in developing world education systems is a paradoxical phenomenon in which the former colonial language is alternately or simultaneously an alienating barrier to access to learning through denial of mother tongues, and/or an instrumentalist ladder to opportunity and self-determination in a globalised world. Critical writers have diagnosed a "polarised debate" (Milligan & Tikly, 2018) and the "hegemonic" status of English (Barnard & Hasim, 2018). Every project of mobile learning undertaken by us to some extent frames English as MoI, as well as a learning goal *sui generis*. Access to the English language is a "bordered knowledge" in Foucault terminology and a "potent form of symbolic capital" in Erling and Seargeant's *English and Development: Policy, Pedagogy and Globalization* (Erling & Seargeant, 2013, p. 2). English language instruction is a rich domain in which to investigate how the advent of mobile learning technologies links to disempowerment. If mobile learning does enable access to English for disempowered groups, this could bring socially and economically wider participation in the "language economy" (François Grin in Erling & Seargeant, 2013). Models of development, such as India's industry of (business process outsourcing (BPO) conducted in English, show that colonial languages can be repurposed for broad-based economic progress.

In his 1970s Guinea-Bissau work, Freire characterises education in the colonial tongue as a benefit for urban aspirational youth. This (for him) reactionary group perceives literacy only in a narrow linguistic sense as a tool for securing its own class or individual advantage. For his mission of teaching an empowering literacy that is political as well as linguistic, Freire's initial position is to critique the European language option (biculturism as he calls it) as a "denial of being" for African learners. However, as he gets further into his project he hardens this stance and defines language choice as a major factor, acknowledging that he has given insufficient attention to it. He asserts that liberation will occur only when learners can "reconquer their own word". The policy of delivering content to disempowered learners in English appears problematic, in terms of Freire's central insight, that political power projection finds expression in learning design. Indeed, the learning of English could by some accounts be perceived as a perfect storm of disempowerment for the cohorts that we have been working for in Ethiopia, Bangladesh, and India. English means the following are axiomatic: the involvement of external consultants, low articulacy levels in teachers and students, no local control over the means of content production and distribution. The counter-argument is also often made, that English supports a beneficial shift in the locus of cultural power beyond the recipient communities, bringing opportunities for liberation, broadening of experience, and diversity. The companion chapter following this introduces some grist to this controversy.

The routes by which the disempowered populations we have worked with arrive at English as their language basis are in fact diverse and context-specific. In the case of the exiled Rohingya community, the orientation to English is a continuation or extension of their flight from Myanmar culture. A multilingual approach to language teaching is the current operating solution. This arrangement is not driven by education principles. The use in schools of Bangla (the host country language) is avoided for political reasons, but local teachers are encouraged to lean on Chittagonian, the local language of the area with some common links to the Rakhine language. The UNICEF-administered formal language policy incorporates Myanmar language and English as the written languages, and provides for use of the spoken Rakhine language, as the latter lacks a unified written script. Myanmar, however, being the language of the place of origin to which the refugees feel unsafe to return, of which they also have less experience than may be expected due to their lack of access to formal schooling, in practice has less importance than English. Nevertheless, the attitude towards English within the community is one of scepticism, as shown in the Translators Without Borders comprehension study (Translators Without Borders, 2017), which shows the refugee's tendency to under-report his or her English comprehension skills. The donor community (perhaps understandably frustrated by the lack of other options) is building an education syllabus with a strong focus on a colonial language unknown to the Rakhine people or even to the designated teachers. Hence, a role for external Anglophone consultants to create a curriculum for use in schools and ensure the training of teachers to deliver it in English.

In Benishangul-Gumuz province of Ethiopia, English pragmatically resolves the problem of the wide range of coexisting languages. The language question is acute here, with over 20 languages spoken by assorted refugees from at least 6 countries. We conducted Focus Group Discussions with 31 small groups of either students or parents in 5 refugee camp schools, with the sessions being annotated live by trained local facilitators drawn from school staff. Language was the most common topic of the student discussions and yielded interesting evidence about the role of English. The student focus groups, from Grades 8 to 9 (age around 14 but the year banding is not precise in this setting) elicited mainly optimistic views about the advantage to them of English. These words noted from one of our participants stands as an example for many: "Using English language is good because English is international language and the curriculum is also designed in English. To compete with international students the English language is mandatory to learn and to communicate".

In comparison, parent groups were less likely to identify English as the essential feature of successful learning although the majority of groups believed English was a pragmatic choice of MoI. The following summary by the local facilitator of the position of one of the parent focus groups captures a view in which English is a reluctantly accepted as a leastworst option: "Due to diversified refugee community in the camp teachers should only use English. Whereas, others said that interpreting (English to student's mother tongue) is better for students who do not know English well."

Mechanical processing using TextAnalyser of the top five most frequently reported terms in all focus groups showed that the words which best distinguished student groups from parent groups were "English" and "language". These terms were present in students' top five words and absent from parents' statements. So the language choice inserts a generational wedge through its role in learning.

Mobile Learning and the Disempowered Student's Cultural Environment

Proponents of mobile learning models in the Global North often claim that the ubiquity, reach, and, recently, affordability of the necessary hardware and software in devices and networks amount to a new universal paradigm for reach and access to learning (Kewajiban, Mustaji, & Bachri, 2018). A key metric of impact for mobile learning in cash-rich markets is the measure and concept of "scale". The attractions of scaling are in truth for producers more than learners – the term in the technology industry is a basket word combining factors such as the speed of growth, the extent and depth of market reach, and the leverage of technology for commercial yield. Scaling is widely discussed, and appreciated, in the start-up tech world of Silicon Valley – but how might this play out with disadvantaged mobile learners in our projects, where "scale" by any definition is often not present due to the pilot status of projects, or the disaggregation and isolation of target learners, and the predominance of hard-to-reach groups? In some cases we can report that mobile technology does broaden access. Working with state sector teachers in India we found consistent evidence from feedback and learner reports that women teachers on the course identified mobile learning as the most suitable mode for them: it offered less conflict with domestic roles or genderised social conventions compared to a travel-based mode of attending courses.

However, our experience also shows how access to mobile learning can be restricted by barriers including class, gender, and social-economic factors. The policy to shift the training of teachers working in Ethiopian refugee camps from attendance at college courses to mobile delivery of content takes place in a context where the most significant gender difference our surveys recorded across 6000 data points was on phone ownership. Only one in seven female against 29/95 male teachers reported they owned the necessary technology, a statistically significant difference in our sample (standard: Fisher Exact Test). Mobile learning, then, appears unlikely to increase the representation of women in education in Ethiopia. However, in other categorisations, such as the status gap between Ethiopian national qualified teachers and volunteer refugee teachers, there was no significantly different access to devices. This suggests mobile technology can bridge some social divides, but not all. That said, the cultural preference in many African societies for shared viewings and group practices acts to some extent as a factor mitigating against barriers to access.

Technology reach and user access is one dimension in which to assess mobile's potential for engaging marginal groups. Indeed those metrics are a default setting for determining contractors' success in the learning industry. However, we are talking about disadvantaged and disempowered cohorts, which means we are envisaging learning also as a rebuilding of selfhood and community. As a quality criterion, the social and emotional dimension of content makes for a better vantage point than measurements of delivery mechanics. This wholistic perspective is axiomatic for most learning and development professionals. In the case of British Council projects, which are led by independent pedagogical expertise, mobile learning projects can and do allow contractors to follow a best practice approach of creating relevant localised media to run on the chosen platforms. How does this work in practice for mobile learning contractors?

Freire argued his post-revolutionary literacy syllabus should avoid learner alienation, by being rooted in the daily context of his Guinea-Bissau learners. Freire's preferred approach was to train up educators from scratch, forming a group of local cadres who are authentically from and of the milieux they are aiming to reach. This is not achievable in the short cycle of commercial contracting, especially when the contractor is external to the milieu where the learning will happen. So in 2019, the content development contractor charts a route to cultural and social validity through spending sufficient budget on localised content, and through confirming its authenticity by consulting specialists. That process, as experienced by us as contractor, has some inbuilt contradictions. Financial and time resources – often quite significant resources – were available in our mobile learning projects to ensure socio-cultural relevance of content. Appropriate personas are present on the learning platforms, suitable visuals and localities are featured, and that there is visibility of local people. Yet when the time comes for the ritual of consultation with the appointed cultural specialist, the process is more oriented in reality around obtaining the imprimatur of external stakeholders than around the power of the content to secure learner engagement. Strictures made in the name of localisation in the world of 2018–2019 are typically upon topics like acceptable female dress, judicious choice of terminology to alleviate political sensitivities, and the observation of cultural pieties. The learning contractor exists to deliver a solution not just to the question "how can the learners become engaged?" but also to the problem "how can Authority be persuaded to accept these materials?" Compromise is more likely to be on the side of learner engagement.

Conclusion

We have tried in this chapter to critically discuss with reference to Freire the role of external contracting in mobile learning for disempowered communities in the Global South. Contractors are partially empowered players applying the business methods, the languages, and the technologies of privileged learners – but in the service of disempowered communities. This approach places contemporary contracting at some distance from the critical pedagogy school founded by Freire for educating disadvantaged learners. In several ways, contractors may be actually undermining or going directly against many of Freire's principles. However, this chapter's narrative of a contractor experience offers glimpses of positive learning outcomes for marginalised learners under the mobile learning conditions of 2018–2019. The contracting disciplines of cost control and delivery assurance help to support mobile learning's place in the repertoire of valid educational techniques. But sometimes this is an uncomfortable place. Contractors producing capacity or content for mobile learning are aligned in important ways to the structures that underpin disadvantage, even as they deploy mobile learning content and technology to ostensibly address disempowerment. A paradox, in short.

References

Appleby, R. (2010). *ELT, gender and international development: Myths of progress in a neocolonial world*. Bristol: De Gruyter.

Barnard, R., & Hasim, Z. (2018). *English medium instruction programmes: Perspectives from South East Asian universities*. Abingdon: Routledge.
Erling, E. J., & Seargeant, P. (2013). *English and development: Policy, pedagogy and globalization*. Bristol: De Gruyter
Freire, P. (1978). *Pedagogy in process: The letters to Guinea-Bissau*. New York: The Seabury Press.
Kearney, M., Schuck, S., Burden, K., & Aubusson, P. (2012). Viewing mobile learning from a pedagogical perspective. Research in Learning. Retrieved from https://eric.ed.gov/?id=EJ973806.
Kewajiban, T. H., Mustaji, & Bachri, B. S. (2018). Challenges and solutions of web-based learning on mobile devices. In K. Persichitte, A. Suparman, & M. Spector (Eds.), *Educational technology to improve quality and access on a global scale* (pp. 287–296). Retrieved from https://doi.org/10.1007/978-973-319-66227-5_22.
Mattes, Margaret. (2017). *The private side of public higher education*. New York: NY: The Century Foundation.
Milligan, L. O., & Tikly, L. (2018). *English as a medium of instruction in postcolonial contexts: Issues of quality, equity and social justice*. Abingdon: Routledge.
Translators Without Borders. (2017). Language & comprehension barriers in Greece's migration crisis. Retrieved from https://translatorswithoutborders.org/about-us/resources.
Traxler, J. (2009). Learning in a mobile age. *International Journal of Mobile and Blended Learning (IJMBL)*, 1(1), 1–12.

13

MOBILE LEARNING PROJECT REPORTS

A Contractor Delivery Review of Three Services for Disadvantaged and Marginalised Global South Learners

Elena Deleyto La Cruz

This chapter reports and analyses data and other findings from three separate education projects delivered in 2018–2019 by a mobile learning contractor. The author is leader of the content team at Digital Learning Associates Ltd, a commercial developer and licensor of learning content. Issues around the contractor role in serving disadvantaged learners in Global South settings were addressed in the previous chapter by a colleague. The projects concerned all aimed to deliver learning as part of a system-wide initiative with multiple stakeholders, all of whom are guided and overseen by the British Council. We are grateful to this unique organisation for its openness to independent discussion of the project outcomes in research literature, and we stress that conclusions reached here represent the views of the author and not the British Council.

Let's briefly re-state the three projects we delivered and are reporting here:

1. The 2018 contract for monitoring and evaluating a mobile learning course for 1000 state sector teachers in India
2. The 2018–2019 training needs analysis for teachers in refugee camps in Ethiopia, which led to the development and delivery of a mobile learning course for them
3. The writing in 2019 of a full curriculum for around 600,000 refugee students of the Rohingya community of Myanmar's Rakhine State, resident in exile in Bangladesh, along with the training programme for their learning facilitators to teach it, based on a policy-driven framework.

To give an idea of scale, our role as a contractor in mobile learning services was restricted to the following: content creation, technical delivery and/or evaluation. We did not determine the target recipients, the resourcing, the participants or the goals. The total project value in cash terms to produce the contractor outputs described in this chapter was around £100,000 if aggregated across all three projects. The teams working for and alongside Digital Learning Associates on these projects are themselves international, often subcontracted for specific short term inputs. For example in the case of the Rakhine State syllabus, the writers, designers and layout team are all outsourced companies or individuals in Bangladesh. The content editor team is comprised of freelance global English language teaching (ELT) experts based around the world. Similarly the Ethiopian mobile learning projects involve the subcontracting of services ranging from local consulting and field data gathering, to film production and statistical analysis, and the recruiting in the short term of teachers who were to feature in the content. In reporting these projects, then, we are also describing the work of a network of effective and expert collaborators around the world, too numerous to mention and thank individually, but we acknowledge their input with gratitude.

Mobile Learning for State Sector Teachers in India

The British Council in 2018 funded a large-scale pilot of online professional in-service training for classroom teachers in the Indian state school sector, aiming to train 1000 teachers in English language and learner-centred pedagogy using mobile learning methodology. It had the acronym TOPDI (Teacher Online Professional Development Initiative). In many ways this represents an edge-case for mobile learning with a disadvantaged cohort. The learners are state employees with relatively lower incomes, and lower professional status, than teachers in India's booming private sector. They perform their roles without information technology (IT) support or connectivity – although plans for state school digitisation do exist. The only technology and access platforms available to the learners were what they could provide or borrow using their own means. Their access and familiarity with digital platforms is known to be low. Disempowerment is thus a trait.

In the TOPDI programme, an agreed package of work was subcontracted to Digital Learning Associates following a tender response. This took the form of an independent monitoring and evaluation (M&E) exercise at the close of the project, consisting of analysis of project documents including cost reports, learning session transcripts, and student and teacher evaluations and learner data, resulting in a report that also included a literature survey for contextualisation.

Education Ministries in nine Indian states took the lead in determining which teachers would participate, and signed off on the goals of the mobile learning programme. The state officials wished, as education professionals, to extend the teacher skill set towards learner-centred classroom methodology in line with global recommended policy. States' warm adoption of the TOPDI course possibly reflected a lack of options in the face of several challenges in their wider policy environment. These included a crisis in state sector teacher recruitment, and a decline in state sector enrolments in the face of a growing demand for

English medium of instruction schooling from private education providers. The collapse of funding for traditional training models was also a factor: the profiles of cost, access, capacity and quality associated with legacy college-based training meant that teachers were receiving little or no in-service professional development.

The British Council mobile learning solution was tailored to address these policy concerns, with a formal pitch to states that invoked New Delhi's "Digital India" initiative and invited regional political stakeholders in the Ministries to adopt this

> proven scalable, cost effective, replicable and adaptable model of training and continuing professional development for your teachers. We will closely monitor this project on various metrics, acquiring and sharing learning which can inform similar future projects within your state. We will also provide you with reporting on your teachers' progress through the course.
> *(Internal British Council pitching document inviting State Ministries of Education to submit teachers for the TOPDI course)*

Course content was not a first-order element of the proposition, as the main purpose was to validate consumer mobile platforms for mass training delivery. An existing online syllabus for teachers was recycled to provide an indicative curriculum and avoid the costs of content development.

The task in M&E was to use the project data to assess the efficacy of this mobile learning approach to teacher development, addressing two dimensions of its design:

- the pedagogic structure that mixed screen-based asynchronous learning, online support, weekly tutored webinars in Zoom with encouragement for participants to create peer support groups on social media channels
- the technology structure of learners' own devices, consumer web platforms and telco bandwidth packages, including evaluation of learners' skills and confidence in the course delivery environment.

Much of the key data for monitoring had already been collected before our involvement, including baseline and endpoint self-assessments, but as M&E contractor we were expected to input into scripting evaluation questionnaires and focus group discussions.

Critical reflection around this contribution to the mobile learning model starts with our own roles and performance. Our M&E report concluded with a high level of statistical confidence that the pilot data demonstrated a success for mobile learning. We highlighted several achievements that broke new ground in terms of data-derived insights to learner experience, including rate of course completion, the cost of provision for such a disempowered professional group and the spontaneous creation of peer learning groups online and in standard social networks. Nevertheless – and this is not a negative reflection on the pilot's sponsors – the data set on which we based these positive evaluations was potentially problematic. In particular we lacked comparable metrics for alternative methods of delivering teacher training, and we lacked measurements of impact on school student outcomes. There was anecdotal evidence to suggest that these indicators might well be positive, if they had been available. However, a four-week timeline and a time allocation capped at ten days are not conducive to more than a rapid scan of the proffered data. The project-based model of education policy is driven by data and evidence, so such gaps in the data are significant.

To add context, one finding that contributed to the strength of our positive conclusion was that the cost of acquisition (CAC) of learners was low and commercially competitive, while quality was equivalent or better than comparable courses when measured on the performance indicators of learner retention, satisfaction ratings and participation in activities. These are the data points on which we could obtain comparative metrics, albeit not the best metrics with which to demonstrate learning gains.

However, a critical reflection suggests caution here too. Metrics of uptake, participation and relative cost to treat are useful indicators where healthy markets for learning operate; in a context like state sector teacher development in India, where no market operates, strong uptake may not be an indicator of quality or value in the product. To this extent, assessments of mobile learning for disempowered cohorts are subject to the reality that evidence about any learning format is seldom focused on marginalised learners and the comparative evidence base is therefore inherently weak. The limit-case for evaluating the mobile learning was set more by the social and political constraints of the setting, than by the technical performance parameters of the delivery mechanism.

Mobile Learning for Refugee Teachers in Ethiopia

A concert of multi-agency partners working from 2015–2017 with Syrian refugees identified a role in crisis response for language education under the Language for Resilience (L4R) banner. Language confusion was hampering many good efforts and preventing the formation of durable communities among refugees. Successes in Syria led to the expansion of the original programme of research and delivery to other refugee situations including to Ethiopia in 2017–2018 in a partnership of Ethiopia's Agency for Refugee and Returnee Affairs, United Nations High Commissioner for Refugees (UNHCR) and the British Council. We were appointed as contractors in 2018 to a project for raising teacher skills through mobile learning in the province of Benishangul-Gumuz on the Sudan and South Sudan frontier.

The million-plus refugees sheltering in Ethiopian camps from regional wars and ethnic violence had received a pledge in 2017 that the government would provide access to formal learning as part of a package leading to eventual resettlement in Ethiopia. International agency support and donor funds back this up. As an outcome of the 2017 pledges, government schools now operate in the refugee camps, with teachers being either trained Ethiopian nationals (33%) or untrained refugee community volunteers (66%). They teach the Ethiopian curriculum under Ministry supervision. However, teachers struggle to deliver effective learning. This is largely because of the conditions: classes are huge (up to 100 students) and multi-age with adults and children alongside each other. Children and teachers may share no common language, materials beyond chalk and board are unlikely, while trauma and insecurity adversely affect refugees' readiness to learn. But to the extent that no plausible remedies for these problems are at hand, teacher skills offer the most promising domain in which to seek to improve school practice and outcomes.

Early teacher training interventions by the L4R partners were delivered by the British Council using local contractors and took the form of short courses during school holidays, later extended to a trial of in-school workshops. These first efforts suggested that basic training in English and teaching skills was an effective way to positively impact classroom outcomes in refugee area schools. However, political insecurity made training hard to operationalise even in the most stable camps, and the interventions were small scale. At this point, a British Council formal tender process invited a contractor to develop a training needs analysis (TNA) which could be used to build models and evidence for a possible phase of expansion and scaling in the training of teachers. Digital Learning Associates responded and was appointed.

Working with teachers from 4 camps, we ran a week of training to prepare 20 teachers to conduct field research on the topic of teacher needs. These re-trained researcher/teachers were then deployed in their respective camps under our supervision to use structured questionnaires and focus group methodologies. They gathered around 6000 valid data points on the topic of training needs, recording the opinions of around 200 student and parent stakeholders. From this reasonably robust dataset, we developed recommended content for an expanded training programme in language and classroom methods. Our proposals for delivery centred on mobile learning, based on the discovery of much higher than expected levels of mobile device access (75%) and acceptance of screen-based learning in the teacher community. This was a surprise finding: mobile delivery had not been envisaged at the start of the project. In an agreed variation to the initial contract, we produced in the refugee camp school two video-based trial course units for test distribution in camps on Secure Digital (SD) cards. Side-loading by card to phones is the only feasible content delivery method to devices in these situations. The media format was short (4–5 minute) video tutorials, hosted by a local trainer, in which practical classroom and English content were demonstrated in a typical refugee classroom, with an uncertified refugee teacher taking the class (Figure 13.1).

FIGURE 13.1 Filming model teacher instruction in classes at Sherkole refugee camp
Source: Digital Learning Associates.

Content for a unit on the effective use of English language (Video 1) covered a simple English grammar point and the lexis for instructing and controlling pupils. Content for a unit on classroom techniques (Video 2) covered a method of using students to demonstrate learning points. This unit was available in Sudanese Arabic language and English. The learning design of each video involved observing a model performance, taking notes, trying out any featured techniques, arranging to receive feedback on performance and conducting peer discussions. Subtitling was used throughout: the acoustic environment and audio devices of teachers in the settings are challenging. The resulting videos can be played and viewed at www.digitallearningassociates.com/resilience_english. These videos are designed to reach a quality threshold high enough to ensure that data about their consumption and impact will provide valid insights into the problems of mobile learning adoption, rather than reflect responses on the content itself. Evaluation of the use of the mobile learning pilot course has taken place so far in three camps: Sherkole, Bambasi and Tsore (two further camps did later receive the content but entered lockdown for security reasons at the point at which distribution and evaluation were underway).

A simple pre- and post-exposure test of knowledge among all teachers exposed to the videos confirmed that after three weeks a positive impact on their knowledge of the content could be observed. The baseline knowledge assessment on the content was administered to staff at each school before a three-week period in which the films were in circulation on the cards. An endpoint knowledge test was also administered. The following trend of topic knowledge on each of the two content videos after three weeks of access to the mobile learning media was recorded: Video 1: +20%; Video 2: +7%. This is mildly suggestive of a correlation effect between a three-week period of mobile learning availability and increased subject knowledge. However the finding is subject to methodological caveats including possible observation bias. Ideally a longer observation period with multiple follow-ups would have been possible.

Measuring the importance of scaffolding

The scant available literature suggested that mobile learning in such conditions might depend for success and uptake on heavy scaffolding. Because of this, release in the target schools was designed to test uptake and completion under three distinct conditions of support for mobile learning. Statistical design and analysis were supervised by Dr. Matt Jenkins, Lecturer at University of Newcastle and a specialist in quantitative social science methods, and aimed to investigate variance in usage and learning for the learner cohort dependent on scaffolding and support.

The SD video cards were distributed in each of the three trial schools under different conditions as per Table 13.1.

- A "heavy support" condition in which trainee teachers enrolled on a residential training programme off site in February 2019 also received the SD cards with full instructions on use. These teachers viewed the videos in their formal training programme, and were encouraged to take them home and continue to use them, with their principals being tasked to encourage them to continue viewing.
- A "moderate support" category in which a school-based teacher champion was trained to encourage colleagues to undertake the SD-card based training, and follow them up to ensure they did use the cards that were distributed to them
- A "light support" category in which the school principal was given a handful of SD cards and told to make them available to teachers but without pushing and with no particular instructions and no arrangement to follow up

We had hypothesised, based on the literature, that we might be able to observe variance between the camps in the levels of compliance and learning outcome under each of these category conditions. We hypothesised that stronger

TABLE 13.1 Level of support assigned to refugee camp schools in Benishangul-Gumuz, Ethiopia

Condition	Heavy Support	Moderate Support	Light Support
Refugee Camp School	Sherkole	Bambasi	Tsore

scaffolding would predict better uptake and learning. Other categorical variables we aimed to test across the cohort were:

- Does gender account for different levels of access and impact from phone based learning modes?
- Are the learning experiences of Ethiopian qualified national teachers significantly different from those of community volunteer teachers?
- Does the type of phone ownership affect outcomes significantly?

To obtain measures of variance, 90 teachers balanced for gender phone ownership and status (nationally qualified or volunteer untrained) were served a battery of eight experimental questions, and were additionally focus-grouped by our trained teacher/researcher unit. As a result we have a dataset covering frequency and habits in the mobile learning use, opinions on the training content, and we also know the subjects' recall of content for each video.

We briefly present a selection of summary findings most relevant to this topic. Looking at the cohort as whole, viewing of the courses appears to have been extensive both in the number of viewings and the propensity to view multiple times, the involvement of colleagues and compliance with learning tasks.

- The vast majority (between 65% and 75% depending on the video) were watching the content three or more times. Watching with colleagues was reported on at least half of all viewings and such viewings account for around 70% of responses. Compliance with at least one viewing with recommended learning actions such as "take notes", "practice with a colleague" and "try it" account for 80% of responses. Repeated and compliant group viewing appears to be the default mode of content consumption.
- Watching the videos more often and compliance with suggested learning actions are both correlated with better recall of material from them. However, it is a weak correlation perhaps reflecting the short exposure (three weeks) to the content. This relationship is equally correlated on both videos, suggesting the effects could work across multiple units of content.
- Not owning a phone did not decrease consumption, participation in learning or recall of content. On the contrary, non-phone owners performed slightly better on our indicative measures of learning recall. However, the frequency of taking a recommended learning action after watching a video was (perhaps expectedly) higher for users of smartphones and basic phones, and lower for those with no phones.

To test for significant differences between the responses of various groupings, we conducted correlational investigations of the data across categories of gender, status and the different scaffolding conditions in each camp. Surprisingly, the data disproved our hypothesis about the importance of scaffolding. Respondents from the different camps who had accessed the materials under different scaffolding regimes behaved very similarly on all the variables. In particular, there is no difference between camps in the ability of participants to recall content. Consumption habit variables such as frequency of watching, watching with colleagues and opinions of usefulness of these and future videos also showed no variation across the three different content distribution methods. There was also no observable difference between the two different categories of teacher, national-qualified versus untrained refugee volunteer.

Using the Kolmogorov-Smirnov statistical test to consider the difference of scores on the gender variable, we did find some genderised differences. Female teachers emerged (with significance thresholds as stated) as:

- less likely to watch with colleagues (Z=0.121, p=0.029)
- less likely to respond with action (Z=1.075, p=0.013)
- more likely to believe more videos would be useful (Z=1.064, p=0.028)
- neither more nor less likely to recall the content of both the course videos.

The verdict from the pilot data is that in the extreme and disempowering conditions faced by the refugee camp teachers, the delivery to phones of localised and appropriate video training content, even under an unscaffolded mobile learning model, could be a generalisable and effective component for improving outcomes for the full spectrum of learner categories. Its effectiveness, however, is socially mediated rather than a technological given. The community basis for shared device access, collective viewing, compliance with tasks and broadly comparable access across categories (except gender) is what gives the grounds for optimism about mobile learning as a model for impact in teacher education.

By the highest standards of impact assessment such as those of the 3ie Impact Evaluation community, this conclusion does not have a solid enough methodological basis or sample size to form a foundation for policy making. However, the consistency of positive indicators on content recall, compliance with learning method, learner approval and expression of wish for more content does suggest that further efforts would be justified. The British Council is now extending the SD cards on the mobile phone syllabus for teachers in Ethiopia's refugee areas to a fuller course with around two hours of video, aiming at a ten hour programme of professional development by mobile learning for teachers in five different refugee settings initially.

Refugees from Rakhine State (Myanmar) in Bangladesh

After a period of mass Rohingya refugee arrivals in Bangladesh between 25 August 2017 and July 2018, local and international Education Sector partners made a decision to unify the primary education materials that were being donated for use in the existing temporary learning centres. The British Council was given the task of creating the English language materials, and Digital Learning Associates came into this project in the role of expert contractor to create the learning design in accordance with the framework provided by the sector, and to coordinate a team of international editors and local Bangladeshi writers, designers and illustrators. At this point, a decision had already been made as to the place of the English language as a subject of study in the primary curriculum. The approach might go against many prevailing ideas of best practice, but the outcome was required anyway for reasons discussed in the previous chapter.

Irrespective of the route by which English became the desired object of learning, understanding what type of English might best suit these learners, as well as defining the key competencies specific to the context, became key to the learning design. A prior decision excluded mobile phone delivery from the entire project. The refugee camps are maintained as a no-device no-bandwidth no-connection zone by the authorities. Such unalterable facts on the ground about devices, connectivity, English and thus about second language pedagogy pre-shaped all the detailed decision making around the content. The forced adoption of a paper-only syllabus in English contrasted strongly with the outcome in Ethiopia where in a similar context mobile device and multilingual or translingual learning framed the solution. The contrast, taking into account our own prior bias as digital-by-default content developers, provided some interesting insights. While our content production workflow is mobile, adaptive and technologically based, the output was for a fixed and rigid "dead trees" learning model.

One defining context element for this and other emergency education settings is the "low level of both English and pedagogical training of the teachers and facilitators", to cite the learning framework provided for the Rohingya educational sector. But further detail on the language and experience levels of the teachers, a potentially significant constraint, was not given to the British Council by the frontline partners working in the camps, no doubt for understandable reasons, and has been hard to ascertain. In terms of teacher capabilities, we were able to gather the following information:

- In the written documentation provided, teachers are defined as follows: "The Learning Facilitator is basically a person who facilitates learning of children in the camp. Learning Facilitators are drawn from the local community and from displaced Rakhine population. (As Myanmar is one of the language children will learn, need facilitator for language from displaced community). Facilitators currently working in the centers have either completed their schooling or are graduates. Very few are trained teachers. ... The teacher capacities in both English and Myanmar will have to be built substantially so that they are better equipped to transact the LCFA" (Learning Competency Framework and Approach for children of displaced people from Rakhine State).
- A one-day escorted visit to the camp allowed us to meet teachers from two learning centres managed by two of the many different organisations

operating learning centres across the different camps. In both these learning centres we were able to witness English teaching in action delivered by teachers with acceptable levels of English (A2-B1 Common European Framework of Reference for Languages (CEFR) level approximately). However, this proved to be an exception arranged for our benefit, on the grounds that the teacher language level enabled direct communication. A focus group held with around ten more teachers, none of whom appeared to be able to communicate in English at all, pointed to a different reality.

- A meeting with the United Nations Children's Fund (UNICEF) team in Cox's Bazaar, in charge of technical implementation of education in the camps, confirmed that the assumption in creating the materials should be that teachers do not have any English language or pedagogical skills. Translation of the teacher guides into Myanmar (for displaced teachers) and Bangla (for local teachers) is one of the processes in place to support teachers linguistically and as classroom workers.
- There is probably limited literacy in any language among the teacher cohort, according to information given to us by Translators Without Borders (TWB), an organisation working on language research and support in the area, including translation of materials into Chittagonian (local language of the area, with about 30% in common with the Rohingya language according to research) and Rohingya language.
- A meeting with TWB's leading consultant on Language in Education in Cox's Bazar, which unfortunately only took place after the majority of the materials had been created, suggested that groups of teachers were forming unofficial "teacher circles" to work together to interpret the guides (only available in English at that point). Their motivations were language limitations and lack of experience or pedagogical knowledge. This information, unconfirmed and unofficial, nevertheless helps us to paint a more defined picture of the situation of the teachers and how they approach class planning.

The above information has shaped the content of the paper-based teaching materials and also allows us to compare the impact of this no-technology approach to one in which teacher training could be further supported through digital content (as was the case of the pilot project we carried out for teachers in refugee camps in Ethiopia, and the evaluations of phone and tablet based training in India). The cascade training models delivered with paper-based teacher guides by non-teachers were reported within a few months of the first training cycle to be ineffective. In addition to struggling to read English instructions, teachers did not have a way of working out a classroom format in a Community of Practice.

If, instead, a mobile learning solution had been offered as part of a collaborative learning approach (a plausible scenario given current informal teacher circles), we have some confidence that internationally generated materials placed within the local context could support a peer-based collaborative approach. This might, in turn, have helped to build the required pedagogical knowledge and deliver an increased exposure to English. This initial information does indicate lack of access to mobile phones for learning, at least as a complement to teacher training, represents a hindrance to effective teaching in the camps. Despite the mobile phone ban imposed by the Bangladeshi Government that has prevented legal access to working SIM cards to the Rakhine population in Bangladesh, there are positive indicators of concealed mobile phone ownership in the temporary settlements, though access is gender divided. However, in no way does mobile learning present itself as a game-changer solution. Its strength, in this context, would be in providing additional support for peer collaboration, a system that is imperfect by nature, due to the requirement for speedy delivery in a fluctuating political and social context.

These views cannot be proven for the case of the Rohingya's learning programmes, but the parallels drawn with the Ethiopian refugee context do allow us to hypothesise, once again, that the power of social and political contexts are the defining trait of mobile (or non-mobile) materials development for disempowered learners.

Conclusion

The data we gathered from three contracting experiences in the Global South does show that mobile learning, through its ability in some formats to group cohorts and suggest supportive social habits of learning, can be effective with disadvantaged or displaced learners. Marginalised recipients of mobile learning or training have shown, in these projects, successful learning and the overcoming of barriers to learning.

In all three projects under review, however, any gain of learner capacity cannot confidently be attributed to the mobile content delivery mode per se, or even to the content itself, but rather through peer interaction taking place as a consequence of being inscribed in a programme of training. Whether or not this interaction happens efficiently through a mobile device or in a mobile learning model is mainly a product of situation and circumstance.

14
POST-CRITICAL MOBILE PEDAGOGY IN ABORIGINAL AND TORRES STRAIT ISLANDER CONTEXTS

Greg Williams and Ruth Wallace

Introduction

Digital learning environments that are now finally starting to live up to the promises they offered when they began to be introduced four decades ago are now also demonstrating the need for new pedagogical approaches. On the one hand, the democratisation of technology forces a rethink of pedagogy that relies on authoritative and positivist models of knowledge-making and, on the other hand, discriminatory access to technology behoves those with access to find ways of using technology to facilitate access and re-distribute the power that access affords. This is particularly the case within the field of education with people who have been traditionally marginalised by current pedagogical practice.

This chapter posits that different ways of knowledge making will need to be employed to address the affordances of digital learning environments and mobile technologies and that it is crucial to address these issues in relation to people marginalised by traditional pedagogies and particularly Aboriginal and Torres Strait Islander people in an Australian context. This chapter critiques traditional pedagogies as approaching learning from a colonising frame with a focus on content delivery – transmission pedagogies – and that mobile digital learning environments facilitate a more relational pedagogical approach. Our aim is to consider what kinds of institutional practices need to be effected for meaningful change and what pedagogical practices might be employed in an institutional relational policy framework.

Mobile Digital Learning Environments

The hyperbole that accompanied the advent of digital technologies in the 1970s and 1980s has only now, almost half a century later, begun to be realised.

Promises of a new educational age were slow to emerge as the technology available at the 'chalkface' failed to live up to the expectations that were proffered. Even now as schools and universities are embracing digital technologies more fully and integrating them into the fabric of the learning and teaching experience, Selwyn (2016) suggests research into this process tends to be somewhat superficial and uncritical. He claims that technology is often seen as a neutral tool in the educative process and we would agree with him in his assertion that this is not the case. As educative technologies increase in their sophistication, their agency and their influence become even more powerful and the affordances for learning and teaching are more pervasive.

Notwithstanding the continuing issues of equity of access and the potentially colonising impacts of technology on marginalised people's epistemological practices, an increasingly diverse cohort of people are engaging in and employing digital learning environments. Digital technologies have the potential to democratise access to information and increasingly this is the case (Acemoglu, Laibson, & List, 2014).

Growth in connectivity now also means that there are potential diverse contexts for accessing information and knowledge in places which even ten years ago would have been unthinkable. Remote and regional places in Australia and around the world are increasingly connected to the internet with bandwidth that makes mobile learning and digital communications both possible and even commonplace.

Diversity of Learners in Digital Environments

Changes in the social and political landscapes in educational institutions and pedagogies in recent decades predicted increasingly diverse and complex learning environments. People (and in fact whole cultures and colonised societies) who were traditionally excluded from empowering educational environments are increasingly participating in and shaping institutions that previously had precluded their involvement. The convergence of this diversification of educational clientele and the increasingly functional and pervasive digital technologies provide an opportunity for a rethink of pedagogical practice that shapes educational institution in colonised societies. At no other time in history has a more diverse group of people engaged with the dominant, western system of education and at no other time has it been more evident that the epistemological practices of those institutions require an epistemic overhaul (or perhaps reorientation).

Traditional Pedagogical Models

Pedagogies employed in most learning environments in the 20th and 21st centuries have had at their core what Verran (2001) calls a uniformative approach to learning. These uniformative pedagogies are based upon assumptions which rely upon a singular, uniform and pre-existing universe. Whether it is a positivist or an objectivist approach to learning, or one based on assumptions of a constructivist paradigm, each in some way relies upon a set of pre-existing, assumed conditions and norms, and an authoritative source of those norms and expectations.

The Enlightenment period, so formative in European societies, and their colonial engendered pedagogical methodologies can be described as positivist or objectivist in their approach. Ernst Bloch (1986, in Miyazaki, 2004, p. 10) characterised most contemporary philosophical work as being constrained by its temporal orientation. He said, it is often looking back into the past, contemplating and categorising the universe as it has already been constituted through processes of coming to know. The universe and 'the' knowledge of it is pre-existent to the knowers and this constrains the possibilities of doing things differently by linking knowing (and therefore learning) to a consolidated and ossified frame of reference.

This objectivist approach to teaching has been problematised by a generation of researchers, but it doesn't stop teachers employing objectivist pedagogies within their classrooms and reinforcing their position as teachers as a position of authority. Verran's (2001) analysis can be invoked here and the postmodern, constructivist frame can be critiqued in a similar way. A constructivist approach merely re-affirms the role of the social in knowledge-making and highlights the inherent power relations that are inherent in that process in the classroom. A social construction of knowledge as a philosophical frame confirms a pre-existing condition of subjectivity and makes uniformative claims that are similar to, or echo those of positivists and objectivists. One group claims a uniformative position that there is a real world, whilst the others claim the uniformative position of the exact opposite. When you make a claim for a pre-existing and ordered universe (or if you make a claim of the certainty of an opposite uncertainly and relativist universe), then there are assumptions being made that strike at the core of our reality that make it hard for us to broker alternative conceptions of what that reality might be and apply them to our professional and personal lives.

The diversity of learners in the 21st century educational institutions brings with it a complex and diverse set of ontological assumptions, epistemological practices and translations of these assumptions and practices into the process of engaging in western/Anglo-European educational institutions. Traditionally, educational institutions have been relatively slow to respond to increased epistemological diversity and many have been intransigent to the needs of those who have been labelled as the 'other'.

Educational institutions in the west have traditionally operated from within a transmission orientated pedagogical model that is drawn from an objectivist frame. An objectivist frame makes assumptions that the universe is real and that it pre-exists our conception of it. This seems logical to our minds, probably because we have been trained so comprehensively in this tradition, but other cultures and other ways of knowing don't rely on such a concrete conception of the world.

Objectivists, in knowing the real work, can reliably make distinctions between what is and what isn't. If the work is real and immutable, then the distinctions between things can be identified as clear. Boundaries are clear between what is real and what isn't and between what constitutes something and what doesn't – that sense of seeing the world in a way that prioritises the object(ive) nature of things. It prioritises the claim that there is only one objective pre-existing universe, one authoritative way of engaging with the world and therefore a range of ways of knowing that are relegated to subjective and sub-ordinate social and cultural practices that are not what is 'really' going on. Pedagogical practice that relegates other ways of knowing to the scrap heap are neither inclusive nor empowering. Objectivist pedagogical models perpetuate colonising practices and ensure that people who subscribe to anything other than those models will be excluded from positions of influence and power.

New digital learning environments that are beginning to realise the vision of the affordances of technology are providing both opportunities for new kinds of learning environments which create a disconnect between the active and relational learning that these environments afford, and traditional pedagogies employed in classrooms. We need to enact pedagogical processes that will both allow for making the most of the affordances that mobile technologies and a digital learning environment provide and engage the diverse epistemological landscapes that are wanting to engage with the western academy.

A Relational Frame

If we change the temporal orientation of our frame of reference in the way that Bloch (1986, in Miyazaki, 2004) describes, it affords the potential for us to think about the ways in which we relate to people in educational spaces. Traditional pedagogical orientations have the learners configured as Lockean *tabula rasa* and the teacher as a source of knowledge and curricular authority, but problems arise in a digital classroom and even more so in mobile learning environments, when this ends up not matching the actuality of the learning landscape. Learners in a mobile and digital environment have access to as much knowledge as teachers and can access it almost instantaneous (notwithstanding issues of access and bandwidth). So, what role does an authoritative voice have pedagogically speaking and does this authoritative frame make the most of the learning that is possible?

Bloch's (1986, in Miyazaki, 2004) change in temporal orientation helps to focus upon a more relational frame upon which to hang pedagogical practice. If each of us, both the teacher and the learner come to the learning experience with a frame that allows us to acknowledge the experience and partial authority of that experience, it leaves each of us open to valuing both what we know (and can bring to the learning experience) and what others know and bring to the learning experience as well. If we are looking forward and not constrained by the ossified structures of already existing theory, knowledge and philosophy, then there is the possibility of learning focusing on the 'not-yet' as opposed to the 'always has been'. Nothing is set but, informed by our past (our genealogies) and looking forward into the possibilities of what might be when we interact with others in learning, new possibilities arise.

New possibilities arise if we are able to conceive of our knowledge and experiences (from the past) contributing to a shared understanding of what is to be. This is what Christie and Verran (2013) and Kenney, Viseu, Myers, Martin and Suchman (2015) describe as a *relational empiricism*, a relational knowledge making process where the knowledge and experience of everyone contributes to a 'working imaginary'; a temporary and emerging knowing that draws on the expertise and knowledge of all the participants in the process. The learning (the imaginary) constituted by the collective relation of the 'class' relies upon the partial authority of the empirical knowledge-making processes afforded to each person in the group. Teachers bring particular kinds of knowledge and particular kinds of valuable experience. They bring professional knowledge (both content and pedagogy) but so does every learner – both through their own empirical knowledge-making processes shaped by and potentially enhanced by the democratised learning afforded by a mobile digital environment. Pedagogically speaking, the role of a teacher then (and all the members of the learning group, in so far as they are all teachers and learners at the same time) is to be paying careful attention to the way in which the relationality of the learning space allows for, and constrains, the expression of empirically derived knowledge (imbued with the partial authority of each knower) by everyone in the learning group.

Digital and mobile learning environments need a pedagogy that is comfortable with the process of each participant in a learning process to be both teacher and learner – all contributors to the 'working imaginary' that forms as a product of the relational agency of each person in a learning group. A relational frame for the enacting of a pedagogy that fits more easily with a digital and mobile environment means that there is no set outcome that will arise from learning. People contribute to learning informed by the genealogies of their empirical knowledge-making and the traditions of the cultures from which they participate and there is no knowing beforehand what these contributions will be and how they will relate to (build up or reshape) the contributions of others. The knowledge is a 'work in progress' and something that has likely never been before, because of the varied and diverse configuration of the knowers at that point in time.

In pre-digital and pre-mobile times, the knowledge created in a learning experience relied heavily on the intensity and regularity of physical contact between learners. Once people stop meeting (at the end of semester, for example), then the clotting of knowledge-making – the working imaginary – takes on a different life as each member of the group takes what they have configured in the experience away with them to new interactions and different relationally driven experiences. A mobile digital environment affords the possibility of these 'working imaginaries' being, first, created and configured by people who would never normally be able to interact on a sustained basis, and secondly, being maintained and strengthened by ongoing interactions between people who no longer have to be physically present with each other.

Relational Practice

Relational practice is not a new concept nor necessarily that different from current classrooms and learning spaces that are characterised by activity and opportunities for learning that probably can facilitate the formation of 'working imaginaries' and recognise the value of the input of learners. The role of relationship in Indigenous educational contexts was identified by Wallace, Curry and Agar (2008), who showed:

> developing innovative and successful approaches to training in urban, remote and regional contexts with Indigenous people necessitates effective partnership and the recognition of diverse knowledge systems as they relate to the worlds of work, community engagement and learning.
>
> *(p. 1)*

To connect the concepts of mobile technologies engaging with, and consciously performing relational practice, is perhaps more of a difference in orientation to thinking – the temporal shift away from set and concretised philosophical frames and a conscious attention paid to the 'imaginaries' that are being created (what Bloch might call the 'not-yet') and exploring ways to facilitate contributions to them both through action and inaction.

In an educational context, relational practice is an empirical experiencing of the experience of coming to knowing – not knowing what may emerge, because you haven't constrained what is possible by a past-ward looking temporal orientation that will frame possibilities in an ossified philosophical frame – one that frames the world as something always and already present and enduring.

Institutional Practice

The uptake of digital technologies by Indigenous Australians has been significant, and mobile technologies have provided a mechanism to support engagement, particularly in remote and regional areas where computer ownership and access may be less than in urban households. McNair Ingenuity Research's (2014) study found 70% of Australian Aboriginal and Torres Strait Islander people own a smartphone compared with 66% of the Australian population. Analysed by place of residence, 83% of Aboriginal and Torres Strict Islander people living in urban areas own a smartphone, while 73% of Aboriginal and Torres Strait Islander people in regional communities and 43% of Aboriginal and Torres Strait Islander people own a smartphone.

Mobile technologies are used by Aboriginal people surveyed in metro areas primarily for sending SMS or MMS, making voice calls and browsing the internet (McNair Ingenuity Research, 2014). More recently, Rice, Haynes, Royce and Thompson (2016) found social media was an important part of Indigenous people's use of digital technologies while also noting the potential negative impacts that exist for all populations.

> Indigenous young people use social media to help form, affirm and strengthen identity, to feel a sense of power and control over their own lives and to make and continue community and family connections ... Strengthening identity through social media may therefore offer an opportunity to help improve educational and health outcomes among Indigenous young people. There was good evidence for social media use and uptake in both remote and urban environments, suggesting that it could be utilised in settings across Australia as part of education, engagement and health promotion interventions ... Social media can enable young and old Indigenous people to reconnect and understand each other better through collaborative efforts between the generations – utilizing the skill over digital technology of the young people and the knowledge and wisdom of culture, language, Country and traditions of Elders.
>
> *(Rice et al., 2016, p. 2)*

The prevalence of mobile technologies has provided access to platforms for Aboriginal and Torres Strait Islander people to communicate in media that can be adapted to an individual, group or political purpose, is not regulated by many of the externally managed communication forms (such as online educational services, national newspapers or government communication) or defined by an external body's purpose.

The integration and growth of mobile technologies have challenged the provision of educational services to consider ways of learning, representing and sharing information that are not in the control of the educational institution. The priority to provide appropriate access and support for the practices mobile technologies support has been identified by leading agencies involved in the utilisation and provision of digital technologies with Aboriginal and Torres Strait Islander people.

Institutional Policy

First Nations Media Australia (FNMA) (2019), the nation's peak body for First Nations not-for-profit broadcasting, media and communications has identified the practices that would support Aboriginal and Torres Strait Islander engagement and mobilisation of the digital and particularly mobile technologies. As a result of the 2019 Indigenous Focus Day, Shaping Our Digital Futures – *Apurte*

Akaltye-antheme (Arrernte for 'learning together'), FNMA released a communique that identifies the key policy actions that will support active engagement of Indigenous people in digital technologies:

- Remote data collection to measure access, availability, affordability and digital literacy;
- Improve availability – prioritised roll-out of broadband and mobile coverage to communities with limited access;
- Last mile access – public Internet access through community-wide WiFi; community access computers;
- Affordable access – unmetered access to all key online services; affordable pre-paid mobile options;
- Digital Literacy – culturally and language appropriate skills program in remote communities, locally tailored to needs and existing levels of digital access, engagement and skills;
- Digital Mentors program to provide local jobs and a peer-supported learning model.

(First Nations Media Australia, 2019)

Educational Institutional Action

In a study of Aboriginal and Torres Strait Islander students' experiences of online education, Reedy (2019) found the concept of relatedness to others and content were significant in students' engagement and experience of higher education. Among the findings, participants consistently expressed:

- the difficulty of making connections with others in online learning environments … the shared nature of learning was central to a positive educational experience, … collaborative and collegial educational processes were important … online learning environment was an isolating and lonely place, one where they were left to navigate their educational journeys alone (p. 135);
- that establishing relatedness with other Indigenous students was an important part of the process of establishing their identity and sense of belonging within the academy … there were no mechanisms that enabled them to safely do so (leading) … to a sense of frustration and desperation (p. 136);
- (the value of developing) personal relationships with their teachers. The importance of these relationship increased for external students as it was often the only connection they made online, (a) friendly and supportive teacher presence in the online environment contributed to their feelings of connection (p. 140);
- negative social construction of indigeneity and the participants' personal experiences of racism impacted on their experiences of higher education (p. 141).

Relatedness was a consistent theme in the study that identified gaps in the way online learning is constructed and evaluated which could relate to mobile pedagogy and educational policy.

Adapting Reedy's (2019) educational design principles to guide the development of the mobile learning and education policy that aims to support the learning of the Indigenous student suggests the following key principles:

- Learning experiences and engagement is designed to promote and support social connection;
- Learning experiences and environments are designed to provide abundant opportunities for students to initiate and develop interpersonal connections with each other;
- Learning environments and interactions facilitate opportunities for Indigenous students to safely identify themselves and others and have the tools for ongoing interaction within or beside the learning environment;
- Design learning experiences and environments that engage in cross cultural interactions and encourage shared knowledge construction and understandings across a range of disciplinary and cultural lenses;
- Provide spaces for teachers to have a supportive, pedagogically effective and culturally appropriate presence that is identifiable and tangible to students;
- Make spaces to integrate and reflect the diversity of Indigenous knowledge perspectives and people throughout the content;
- Design learning experiences to be accessible and manageable on mobile devices in ways that also minimise cost and maximise diverse devices and systems. This may include places where mobile connections are discontinuous and expensive.

In addition, we suggest consideration of the matters identified previously in this chapter.

1. Learning experiences need to be safe and ethically managed to promote positive relatedness and engagement;
2. Space for co-constructed content that may challenge the orthodoxies of pedagogy or representations;
3. Design that shares authority, leadership and control at different stages in the learning process.

Conclusion

Pat Anderson AO (Office of the Order of Australia), an Alyawarre woman who is a tireless advocate for Australia's First People, reflecting on the *Uluru Statement from the Heart* (released on 26 May 2017) (Anderson & Leibler, 2017, p. i), a proposal for an Indigenous voice in the Australian Parliament and thereby policies, funding and laws that impact Aboriginal people, said:

It formally acknowledges our place here. We would no longer remain ignored, invisible, powerless and voiceless. It would establish a significant national narrative about working together – about a genuine two-way conversation. And it would also be a place where we could bring our stories and our knowledge to the symbolic centre of contemporary government.

(Anderson, 2019, p. 5)

The development of mobile pedagogical practice and policy that are based on understanding the relational and culturally significant elements of educational practice in Aboriginal and Torres Strait contexts have the potential to provide a place to engage in a significant two-way conversation. A conversation that brings together historical, symbolic and academic understandings of practice. A policy approach that values diversity and shares power. Alternatively, mobile pedagogical practice can replicate the educational practices that have divided and prevented voices from being heard. The relational elements of mobile technologies could provide a pathway to find ways to change and accept this challenge.

References

Acemoglu, D., Laibson, D., & List, J. (2014). Equalizing superstars: The internet and the democratization of education. *The American Economic Review*, 104(5), 523–527. Retrieved January 22, 2020, from www.jstor.org/stable/42920991.

Anderson, P. (2019). Keynote address. 5th Annual Ngar-Wu Wanyarra Aboriginal and Torres Strait Islander Health Conference, Shepparton, October 16, 2019. Retrieved from https://www.lowitja.org.au/content/Document/Pat_Anderson_AO_%20Ngar-Wu_Wanyarra_Shepparton_FINAL_16_Oct_20.

Anderson, P., & Leibler, M. (2017). *Final Report of the Referendum Council* (p. i). Canberra: Commonwealth of Australia. Retrieved from https://www.referendumcouncil.org.au/sites/default/files/report_attachments/Referendum_Council_Final_Report.pdf

Christie, M. J. & Verran, H. (2013). Digital lives in postcolonial Aboriginal Australia. *Journal of Material Culture*, 18(3), 299–317.

First Nations Media Australia. (2019). 6th Indigenous Focus Day Communiqué. Retrieved January 19, 2020, from https://firstnationsmedia.org.au/sites/default/files/files.

Kenney, M., Viseu, A., Myers, N., Martin, A., & Suchman, L. (2015). Counting, accounting, and accountability: Helen Verran's relational empiricism. *Social Studies of Science*, 45(5), 749–771.

McNair Ingenuity Research. (2014). *Media usage amongst Aboriginal and Torres Strait Islander people*. Sydney: McNair Ingenuity Research. Retrieved January 14, 2020, from https://mcnair.com.au/wp-content/uploads/Media-Usage-amongst-Aboriginal-and-Torres-Strait-Islander-People-McNai....pdf.

Miyazaki, H. (2004). *The method of hope*. Stanford, CA: Stanford University Press.

Reedy, A. (2019). Rethinking online learning design to enhance the experiences of Indigenous higher education students. *Australian Journal of Educational Technology Special Issue: Digital Equity*, 35(6), 132–149.

Rice, E., Haynes, E., Royce, P. & Thompson, S. (2016). Social media and digital technology use among Indigenous young people in Australia: A literature review.

International Journal for Equity in Health, 15, 81. Retrieved from https://equityhealthj. biomedcentral.com/articles/10.1186/s12939-016-0366-0#citeas.
Selwyn, N. (2016) *Is technology good for education?* Cambridge: Polity Press.
Verran, H. (2001). *Science and a African logic*. Chicago: The University of Chicago Press.
Wallace, R., Curry, C., & Agar, R. (2008). *Working from our strengths: Indigenous enterprise and training in action and research*. Australian Vocational Education and Training Research Association (AVETRA) 11th Annual Conference, Adelaide, April 3–4.

15
MOBILE ASSISTED THIRD SPACE (MATS) IN THE MARGINS

A Tool for Social Justice and Democracy

Rebecca Kelly

Introduction

This chapter outlines the application of Third Space Theory to support educational outcomes and presents a model for Mobile Assisted Third Spaces (MATS). The concept of Third Space has recently been acknowledged as having relevant applications to the practice of learning with mobile devices (Schuck, Kearney & Burden, 2017). Applying the concept of Third Space to educational practice is not new, studies have highlighted the valuable features the construct offers particularly in the areas of teacher education, language learning and teaching non-traditional students (Flessner, 2014; Gutiérrez, 2008; Moje, Ciechanowski, Kramer, Ellis, Carrillo & Collazo, 2004). The potential of Third Space constructs to advance and enhance thinking in the field of educational technology is much more recent especially in the area of mobile learning (Schuck et al., 2017; Schuck & Maher, 2018). This chapter offers insights into the concept of Third Space and its relevance for pedagogy and particularly mobile specific pedagogy. The first section explores the background of Third Space Theory through the work of three seminal authors in the field. The second section explores the concept of Third Space learning and how this theory has been considered and applied as pedagogy in multiple settings, specifically in the area of supporting non-traditional students. In the following section, the chapter offers an insight into current research exploring the potential of Third Space for mobile specific pedagogy that promotes social justice and democratic educational practices. The concept of MATS is introduced and examined through an example of mobile supported social learning amongst small-scale rural farmers in South Africa.

Third Space – Theoretical Background

The study of Third Space Theory challenges the role of physical location in defining space and prioritises instead the personal and social dimensions that define it. Three key bodies of work: *The Location of Culture* (Bhabha, 1994), *Third Space: Journeys to Los Angeles and Other Real and Imagined Places* (Soja, 1996) and *The Great Good Place* (Oldenburg, 1989) all coin the term each in their own nuanced way, simultaneously acknowledging the importance of human interaction with both sentient and non-sentient aspects in defining space. For example, Soja (1996) describes space as a mutually constituted construction between the physical and the social; arguing that physical elements shape the social interactions within them but also, simultaneously, social activities shape the physical space around them. Thus spatial thinking moves away from the notion of space as a container of activity or existence and moves towards thinking of space as a process, born from the interplay of interactions and intersections within it (Soja 1996). Similarly Bhabha's (1994) interpretation of Third Space discards thinking of spatial dimensions as being homogenous or contained; emphasising the cultural dimensions of space, he argues entities of space or time are never unitary and therefore manifestations of culture and discourse must exist between referential systems and beyond cultural borders. In contrast Oldenburg's (1989) description of Third Space is intrinsically linked to the physical, he explores ideas of a 'Third Place' as locations between home and work which through their neutrality facilitate open, collegial and flexible atmospheres inherent to identity formation, democratic practice and civil engagement.

Both Bhabha (1994) and Soja (1996) are critical of binary concepts; within both iterations of a Third Space Theory it is acknowledged that opposites cannot or should not exist. As a space of intersection any binaries must amalgamate to a greater or lesser degree and create something new. Soja (1996) does not dismiss the concept of binaries completely but instead describes their position as subject to "a creative process of restructuring" (p. 5) within Third Space. Instead of a compromise between binaries true Third Spaces recreate and redefine existing phenomena; in existing between different subjectivities Third Space creates 'multiple beliefs and split subjects' from which new ideas and understandings must evolve (Bhabha 1994, p. 79). Bhabha's (1994) discussion of "hybridity" is critical to understanding the nature of Third Space and the disruption of the binary concept; hybrid understandings and enactments are created when binaries are challenged and new possibilities and spaces for meaning-making are created. Like Bhabha's conception of hybridity, Soja's (1996) concept of "thirding" asks us to "set aside demands to make an either/or choice and contemplate instead the possibility of a both/and also logic" (Soja, 1996, p. 5). Thirding, like Bhabha's (1994) hybridity, produces alternative spaces that are not just an additive combination of binary options, but a restructuring of spatial possibilities. Oldenburg argues the concept of thirding as a site for identity creation and socio-political regeneration. This restructuring of possibilities has been an attractive concept in the field of education where Third Space has increasingly been used to support pedagogical practices.

Educational Applications of Third Space

This reconnoitre into concepts of space has become central to social theory and has begun to permeate thinking around education and pedagogy. From a pedagogical perspective Third Space offers the potential to move away from a focus on prescription towards a focus on process in teaching and learning (Chapman, 2016). Consequently, there has been increasing research exploring the affordances of Third Space Theory to support teaching and learning worldwide. Moje et al.'s (2004) study addresses literacy learning across multiple subjects, it purports the need to create a Third Space, which can join both in school and out of school knowledge/discourse within school knowledges and discourses. Gutiérrez's (2008) work similarly discusses the disjunct between academic literacies and teaching practices and those that are relevant and accessible to students from non-dominant communities. Both studies represent Third Space as a place to increase engagement and achievement amongst students who are traditionally lower achievers through the application of practices that reflect their sociocultural identities. The use of Third Space to support democratic educational practices and promote social justice principles amongst student populations is widely recognised.

Third Space is used to explore the places in education infrastructures in which dominant and marginalised communities and discourses co-exist (Luk-Fong, 2010). The use of Third Space Theory within the featured settings show it to be a useful tool with which to support underachieving students in a wide variety of circumstances. For example, Gutiérrez, Baquedano-Lopez and Turner (1997), Gutiérrez, Baquedano-Lopez and Tejada (1999) and Gutiérrez (2008) have worked both conceptually and empirically for over two decades exploring how social learning and the theory of Third Space can better support the literacy development of marginalised students. They used the work of Bhabha (1994) and Soja (1996) to develop an approach which they term 'a collective Third Space' (Gutiérrez, 2008, p. 148). Within earlier work Gutiérrez, Baquedano-Lopez and Tejada (1999) theorise Third Space teaching/learning as a navigational space in which participants can cross over or draw upon different binaries, discourses or discursive boundaries. Arguably, this enables participants to become more in command of their learning and gain access to alternative knowledge (Gutiérrez et al., 1999). Third Spaces become hybrid learning spaces in which students' linguistic and cultural forms, styles, artefacts, goals or ways of relating all interrelate and combine to transform the official linguistic and cultural forms of the school, teacher or classroom into an individualised and internalised experience (Gutiérrez et al., 1999).

Like Gutiérrez et al. (2008), Moje et al. (2004) advocate the use of Third Space concepts to promote inclusion and widen access to their educational settings. Moje et al. (2004) remind us of the importance of acknowledging the many different funds of knowledge (Moll, Amanti, Neff & Gonzalez, 1992) available in Third Space teaching/learning. Gutiérrez (2008) explored Third Space as a tool to navigate aspects of cultural difference. Congruently Moje et al. (2004) promote the transferability and relevancy of knowledge across settings. These examples highlight the ability of Third Space principles to bridge cultures and promote democracy. Its use has supported students to navigate cultural difference, understand different perspectives and be empowered as active participants in their learning. Such outcomes identified in the literature as a direct result of utilising Third Spaces for learning resonate fully with definitions of global competency and citizenship (OECD, 2018) suggesting its potential to assist in education across the globe. This potential is discussed in greater detail in "Mobile Assisted Third Space (MATS)". Within the literature available several themes arise regarding the pedagogical affordances of Third Space, and why they are being applied. These recent applications of Third Space for learning highlighted six reoccurring affordances and features: Collaboration, Hybrid Discourse, Democracy, Transformation, Reflection and Transferability. These are discussed in detail below.

Collaboration

Learning through social construction and corresponding theories such as Zone of Proximal Development (Vygotsky, 1978) and Communities of Practice (Lave & Wenger, 1991) are widely cited as underpinning Third Space learning principles. Aaen and Dalsgaard (2016) report findings of Facebook as a Third Space of school life, indicating a defined community structure amongst participants through which a shared practice supports and enriches their experiences of school life. Third Space is described as a place where academics and teachers can collaborate as professionals rather than compete for power within teacher education programmes (Williams 2013). Amongst studies reviewed there was a strong tendency towards Third Space concepts encompassing collaborative practice in a variety of ways.

Hybrid Discourse

Collaboration necessitates the interaction of two or more discourses, this interaction is used to create a new *third discourse* (own emphasis) which is built from new knowledge/new understandings and generates a hybrid language between collaborators. In order to operationalise the concept of "Third Space", Kirkland (2008, 2010) calls for a "pedagogical Third Space" in teaching that synthesises traditional school literacies with students' lived literacies. Kirkland (2008) positions "pedagogical Third Spaces" as spaces that challenge and expand what type of knowledge is valued in school and in the world at large. Brown (2016) suggests the need for learning environments to accommodate students' native discourses and cultures alongside academic discourses in order to mediate relationships between and across different types of knowledge. Brown (2016) argues that the dynamic set of discourses brought by the students to the learning situation should be seen and used by educators as a valuable resource not as something separate or irrelevant to academic practices.

Democracy

Not surprisingly with the extensive use of collaboration and a reliance on the amalgamation of difference into hybrid discourses, Third Spaces are described as inherently democratic places. The seminal works of Freire (1970), Foucault (1984) and Giroux (2005) and are used to explore the potential of Third Space concepts for greater social justice in education (Idrus, 2015; Moje et al., 2004). Some studies employ Third Space explicitly with the intent of promoting social justice (Moje et al., 2004; Bustin, 2011; Thomas, Haug & Enstad, 2016; Turner, 2016), whereas for others it is a positive but not necessarily a prescribed outcome (Ai & Wang, 2017). Aaen & Dalsgaard (2016, p. 176) discuss the "democratic potential" of social network sites when used to support a "Third Space of school life" (Aaen & Dalsgaard 2016, p. 163), describing their searchability and asynchronous features as widening the opportunities for participation and thus supporting more democratic educational practices. Dyrness and Hurtig (2016, p. 187) report the existence of "Third Space pedagogies" which form within migrant collectives in the USA to navigate and resist the native neoliberal educative economies which often contradict or impede their educational priorities. Applying the concept of Third Space to migrant education enables practices to transcend the "spatially and temporarily bounded and politically laden binaries of belonging or not belonging, native or other" (Bhabha, 1994, p. 26) and consequently increase focus on the realities and potential of migrant populations instead of resorting to deficit-laden assumptions about their potential achievements and contributions. Third Space pedagogies prioritise collective experiences in an attempt to circumvent the structural inequalities that often shape educational achievement and thus future trajectories.

Transformation

Many studies recognise the potential of Third Space to support transformational outcomes through identity formation (Idrus 2015), through changing attitudes/ understandings of sociocultural issues (Fitts, 2009) and by increasing ability in specific content areas (Flessner 2009). Fitts (2009) explicates the transformation potential of Third Space Theory in his application of it to teaching practices in an American dual language school to inform strategies of using students' discourses in conjunction with academic discourses. They acknowledge transformational educational experiences are difficult to engineer amongst the structural and institutional constraints of formal schooling. They offer a model for using Third Spaces in a way that can support the transformation of curricula and thus enable both students and teachers to bridge official and unofficial discourses to provide increased accessibility to academic language and content. The potential for transformation amongst individual students and teachers and institutionally in terms of educational approaches is evident.

Reflection

The most common setting in which Third Space Theory is applied amongst the literature used to support this chapter is that of teacher education. Almost all of these studies explicate their adaptation of a Third Space as a reflective space. Correspondingly reflection is explored as a key activity in Third Space learning for immigrant education (Dyrness & Hurtig 2016). Reflection around professional roles/personal identities, cultural identities and the structure of society is widely purported as necessary within Third Spaces. Flessner (2014, p. 232) describes his use of a "reflective Third Space" to address dualism of the research and practice divide in his practice as a university-based mathematics teacher educator and a third-grade maths teacher. He proposes Third Spaces lead to purposeful change in both the First and Second Spaces – in this instance in the two settings in which he studies. Reflection is the process in which Third Space concepts are utilised, the way in which Third Space allows for meanings to be bound, re-examined and reformed to generate the learning processes desired.

Transferability

The ability of Third Space concepts to bridge the academic and non-academic world is cited as a crucial feature amongst the articles reviewed. Idrus (2015) provides a strong example in this study by utilising Third Space concepts to actively increase the relevancy of learning to wider contexts outside the classroom. Flessner's work is underpinned by the necessity to create educational experiences that generate "real world" applications for learning. Levy (2008) utilises Third Space concepts as a research tool to explore literacy practices of preschool children between home and school environments. These examples emphasise the use of Third Space concepts to support the transferability of learning and knowledge between multiple settings. This theme is more evident in the use of Third Space Theory in the area of educational technology discussed in the next section.

Mobile Assisted Third Space (MATS)

The potential of Third Space to support educational technologies has been recognised (Levy, 2008). This section exemplifies how Third Space Theory to the use of technology to support learning. Several of the six features of Third Space learning identified in the previous section are present in these studies.

Technology Supported Third Space

Online social networking sites (SNSs) have been described as Third Spaces (Aaen & Dalsgaard, 2016). In their study they report finding a new "Third Space" in student managed online groups that bridge both the physical and virtual/academic and social domains; this space elicits unique differences in "communication structure", "Discourse", "Agency" and "Roles" to those in purely academic (first) or purely social (second) spaces (Aaen & Dalsgaard, 2016, pp. 181–182). Consequently, Aaen and Dalsgaard (2016) argue that distinct student communities evolve in a Third Space which allows progressive opportunities for collaboration, social integration and inclusion. The potential of social networks to develop a socio-educational space is developed in Chau and Lee's (2017) study exploring its use to support higher education (HE) Linguistics learning in Hong Kong. Like Aaen & Dalsgaard (2016) they report the bridging between social and academic discourses within SNS groups as a Third Space. Drawing heavily on Wenger's (1998) Community of Practice Theory, the study documents how student identities are constantly shifting and renegotiating these spaces. This process is described as a "discursive practice" that is made more complex by the online space in which identities are being constructed (Chau & Lee, 2017, p. 38).

Continuing the assertion of Third Space as an opportunity to articulate identity Evolvi (2017, p. 224) describes the articulation of "hybrid identities" by Muslim bloggers on the Italian site Yalla. In this study the blog is found to act as a Third Space in which their individual experience can be made public in a "hybrid space" to safely challenge dominant narrations and be empowered to define their own experience (Evolvi, 2017). Evolvi's study highlights how technology supported Third Spaces can either purposefully or by coincidence subvert hegemony. Howell, Sheffield, Shelton and Vujaklija's (2017, p. 25) work describes how a closed online discussion group provides trainee teachers with "collaborative Third Space" in which they can actively discuss, reflect on and interpret their placement experiences with each other and university-based teacher educators. This study exhibits both the collaborative and transferable features of Third Spaces as it acts as a meeting place for trainees while they are on placement but also as a bridge between the theoretical and conceptual learning in their university setting with the practical experience of the classroom (Howell, Sheffield, Shelton & Vujaklija, 2017). Blended learning is reported as occurring within a Third Space; Lapp, Fisher and Frey (2014) draw on Oldenburg's (1989) concept of a third place between schoolwork and home to describe the use of the internet and media to encourage social interaction, broaden ideas and share new perspectives within blended learning curriculums. Third Space as described by Lapp et al. is transformational in that through engaging with hybrid discourses new meanings and changes in knowing and being occur.

These examples clearly convoke the concepts and interpretations within the Third Space literature. Interestingly all these examples also used technologies afforded through mobile devices. The concept of space is central to much thinking around mobile learning and their potential to create distinctive and new educational spaces has been acknowledged (Burden & Kearney, 2017). There is clear correlation between the affordances and features of Third Space Theory and mobile learning practice, and this is explored further in the following section.

Third Space and Mobile Learning

Mobile learning is rapidly establishing itself as a contemporary pedagogy increasing opportunities for innovation in a variety of educational contexts and practices (Burden & Kearney, 2017). Defined as pedagogy facilitated by portable devices which are ubiquitous, pervasive and offering a diverse range of capabilities (Kearney, Burden & Rai, 2015), mobile learning is situated as learning that untethers users from traditional concepts of time and space (Schuck & Maher, 2018). m-Learning has been criticised as an under-theorised field of research, lacking in conceptual models and frameworks (Koole, Buck, Anderson, & Laj, 2018). Initial attempts to explore how Third Space Theory informs the practice of mobile learning suggest the potential for developing a framework to support this field (Schuck et al, 2017). Third Space Theory's potential for m-learning is a largely under-researched and under-theorised domain of mobile learning. Schuck et al.'s conceptual paper explores how this space might be constituted and is part of a wider study that seeks to develop a theoretical framework for thinking about MATS.

Schuck et al. (2017) had previously linked mobile learning to the concept of Third Space learning, identifying many similar features within both areas of pedagogy. Their conceptual article asserts the homogenous emphasis on hybridity and bridging boundaries, and also highlights the shared understanding of time and place as malleable constructs within both pedagogies. Drawing on three examples of mobile learning, the authors argue that mobile learning activities can be designed to foster learning in a Third Space and suggest a theoretical framework to depict mobile learning in a Third Space. A subsequent empirical study (Schuck & Maher 2018) describes how the use of mobile learning creates a new and unique Third Space in which time and place become more malleable and unlimited. Their study shows how mobile learning allows the "reconfiguration of existing spaces and the creation of new ones" in that it creates a space that traverses the informal and formal, the physical and the virtual and provides increased opportunity for collaboration with a wider network of people (Schuck & Maher 2018, p. 10). The "flexible open spaces" explored in this study highlighted the potential of mobile learning to foster Third Spaces that were more democratic as teachers' and students' roles became untethered from traditional conceptions of banker and bank (Freire, 1970). The democratic aspect of mobile learning in

Third Space is echoed in Guerra-Nunez's (2017) study of foreign born Latino students in American classrooms. The study illustrates how the use of mobile learning inherently redistributes power within classroom settings both between students and teachers but also amongst students themselves. Instances where technologies were used to create "organic Third Spaces" saw students challenge power asymmetries and engage in more "power-sharing dialogue" (Guerra-Nunez, 2017, p. 335). Reportedly this increased motivation and engagement amongst students from all backgrounds. The great potential of mobile learning to contribute to reduced hegemony and increased democracy is evident. However, it is widely recognised that these tools are being under-used and their potential to improve educational opportunities across the globe is far from being utilised (West, 2012).

Concomitantly, Burden and Kearney (2017, p. 121) herald the "virtual, network-based characteristics" afforded through the use of portable devices in educational contexts as having the potential to create new spaces that bridge both formal, informal and semi-formal learning. Burden and Kearney's work highlights the current under-use of mobile learning features that can support deeper collaborative and personalised learning experiences and exploit access to a wider range of contexts. They call for more confident and creative task designs that fully utilise the features mobile learning offer to allow learning to engage with Third Space practices. Many of the examples above use technology which is supported by the use of portable devices and has begun to highlight the features of Third Space which are arguably synonymous with the affordances of mobile learning (Schuck et al., 2017). One example is the use of mobile technology to support disengaged pupils through Third Space practices in McDougall, Readman and Wilkinson's (2018) Digital Families project. Mobile devices bridged school, community and home spaces through a series of activities aimed at researching and enhancing the digital practices of students and their families who were experiencing special educational needs (SEN) and low achievement. By engaging Hybrid Discourse, the project was able to situate the mobile affordances against not only educational objectives but also "social well-being and public good" (McDougall et al, 2018, p. 276). Through engagement with mobile technology in a Third Space, co-learning between parents and students was increased and perceptions of wider community were shifted. Schuck and Maher (2018) call for further empirical research into Third Space generated through the ubiquitous use of mobile technology and the necessary changes to curriculum, roles and practices required to fully exploit its potential for learning.

Mobile Assisted Third Spaces

The mutual constitution of mobile learning practices and Third Space is evident. The examples through the previous sections highlight a synergetic relationship between Third Space Theory, mobile pedagogy and wider sociocultural pedagogies. This section explores this relationship further by proposing the conjugation of the Third Space features identified earlier with the affordances of mobile technologies for learning.

Mobile learning offers a great deal of affordances that are specifically useful for education such as greater opportunity for collaboration or anytime anywhere access which disrupt the traditional concepts of time and space for learning. Such affordances are often underutilised (Burden & Kearney, 2017) which may be due to a resistance to the necessary disruption of the conventional use of time and space and the necessary conceptual shift of what learning is (Schuck & Maher, 2018). Another possibility may be the tendency of research in this field to focus either on the mobile device characteristics rather than focusing on the sociocultural environments they create or the movement of learning across contexts (Grant, 2019). One body of research which is grounded in the affordances using mobile devices for learning rather than the technical aspects is the mobile pedagogical framework (Kearney, Schuck, Burden & Aubusson, 2012, p. 8). Developed through a belief that to fully capitalise on the affordances of mobile learning it must be underpinned by pedagogy rather than a focus on the device or technology, the mobile pedagogical framework captures what its authors refer to as the signature pedagogy of mobile learning: the iPAC Framework (Burden & Kearney, 2017) (see Figure 15.1). The framework includes the constructs of Personalisation, Authenticity and Collaboration, along with each of their subconstructs. At the heart of the iPAC Framework are the concepts of time and space, which point heavily towards the concept of Third Space.

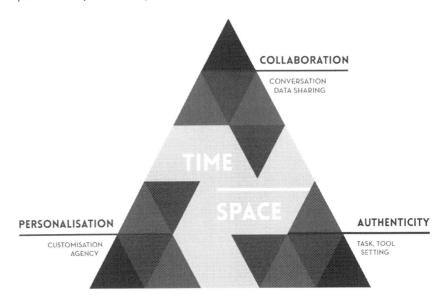

FIGURE 15.1 iPac Framework
Source: Burden & Kearney (2017, p. 3).

Drawing upon sociocultural perspectives (Burden & Kearney, 2017), the iPAC Framework is analogous with Third Space concepts in several ways. First, the central location of time/space as the epicentre of this framework emphasises the critical influence of context. The framework promotes the importance of innovative uses of the temporal and spatial dimensions of learning as being crucial to mobile learning practice. Secondly, the inclusion of personalisation takes advantage of how learning is experienced individually; learners have an increased agency over how, when and where their learning can occur. Thirdly, authentic aspects of mobile learning allow learning to happen in realistic contexts making it more transferable between the classroom space and real life spaces. Finally, the collaboration construct privileges the importance of hybrid discourses, interactions between diverse individuals and environments, which is emphasised as a key feature of mobile learning. All the features of mobile learning described are apparent in Third Space pedagogy, indicating their synergetic potential. It is therefore possible to assume an anterior model when considering MATS and that when the affordances in the iPAC Framework are mobilised that the features of Third Space will become evident. When combined Third Space Theory and mobile learning pedagogy raise confronting questions about what the future definitions and designs of learning could and should be. The following section will probe these questions by examining a recent project that supported the development of rural small-scale farmers in South Africa.

MATS in ACTION

In this final section we will explore this model of MATS in relation to the Food for Us project – a sustainable food systems mobile phone learning pilot project initiated in 2017 by a consortium of partners in South Africa (Food for Us, 2019). The project developed a transformative and innovative opportunity to address the disconnect between food wastage during agricultural production, handling and storage and poverty by developing an app that could support farmers to reduce surplus and promote their social learning (Food for Us, 2019).

The app was designed to overtly facilitate interaction between small-scale food producers and consumers in the hope of increasing sustainability through the provision of a market place where farmers could upload available produce for sale posts and notifications of future availability. This feature was initially designed with the aim of reducing food waste but opportunities for social learning were apparent and an adjunct to this original aim (Food for Us, 2019). Farmers from Western and Eastern Cape areas were targeted for use as they were from isolated rural communities considered to be largely marginalised not only in terms of their agriculture but socially. The app allowed these distinct groups to interact and brought together a diverse range of people who would not have previously engaged. Participating farmers were able to send messages and posts to other farmers with expertise in different areas of agriculture but also to make contact with businesses that could utilise their produce such as shops, market stall holders and food outlets (Food for Us, 2019). This facilitation of interaction capitalises on the mobile's potential to support collaboration and hybrid discourse. Intergenerational learning was cited as a frequent occurrence as younger and older members of the app market place supported and traded their knowledge, both of the agricultural process and markets and the mobile platform being used. Through the process of data sharing as farmers uploaded pictures of produce and interaction within the app they were able to capitalise on the hybridity of perspectives, which helped them gain a deeper understanding of the market requirements. Researchers found evidence of how farmers developed new approaches as a result and began to transform their practices (Food for Us, 2019). Through participation both researchers and participants described themselves as experiencing a process of interactive "boundary crossing learning" (Food for Us, 2019), in particular, participants reflected on the importance of relationships and the benefit of meeting (virtually) farmers from other areas.

Although researchers initiated this project and were heavily involved in its mobilisation, participants were active in generating their own networks, they personalised their experience within the app and tailored their participation to their personal needs. Through generating new connections researchers reported how farmers were able to learn more about their potential markets and view the problem of food waste from different perspectives. This was described as transformative learning for participants and strengthened their farming practices (Food for Us, 2019). The app supported a disruption of existing value chains which previously placed the small-scale rural farmers produce at the lowest end of this chain. By connecting farmers and local buyers in this way the produce was more likely to secure a higher value use (i.e. human consumption) by bypassing the prescriptive aesthetic and security standards of the larger food corporations which had previously marginalised them. In this vein the use of mobile devices to create this space went some way to facilitating a more democratic system for these farmers to engage in.

This project highlights how the use of mobile devices can by default generate Third Spaces in which, intentionally or unintentionally, learning occurs. Although some features used within the app such as the messaging and market place were actively designed by the researchers the way in which learning occurred was not always so prescribed. By using the device in this way it could be said that participants became engaged in a process of Third Space learning that has been described in previous sections. The affordances of mobile pedagogy are all utilised through this project and all six features of Third Space are evidenced. This example supports the generation of confronting questions about what the future definitions and designs of learning could and should be.

Conclusions

This chapter has described instances of Third Space Theory being applied in the field of educational technology. It highlights the potential mutual constitution of

Third Space Theory and mobile specific pedagogy. It is clear from the literature that technology is already in active use to support Third Space learning practices at various levels. The similarity in affordances of mobile technology to the requirements of Third Space learning practices has also been made explicit. It is clear that there is great potential for mobile technology to support Third Space learning practices and, even, that by default using mobile devices could generate MATS which can be capitalised on greatly by individuals and educators engaged in a process of learning. The potential of MATS to support the learning of marginalised groups is evident in the many examples described in this chapter and to raise questions about what teaching and learning could and should look like. As research and practice continue to further our understanding of MATS the closer we can get to realising the full potential of mobile learning across the globe.

References

Aaen, J., & Dalsgaard, C. (2016). Student Facebook groups as a Third Space: Between social life and schoolwork. *Learning, Media and Technology*, 41(1), 160–186.

Ai, B., & Wang, L. (2017) Re-entering my space: A narrative inquiry into teaching English as a foreign language in an imagined Third Space. *Teachers and Teaching*, 23(2), 227–240. doi: doi:10.1080/13540602.2016.1203778.

Bhabha, H. (1994). *The location of culture*. London: Routledge.

Brown, B. (2016). Lyricism, identity, and the power of lyricism as the Third Space. *Science Education*, 100(3), 437–458.

Burden, K., & Kearney, M. (2017). Investigating and critiquing teacher educators mobile learning practices . *Interactive Technology and Smart Education*, 14(2), 110–125.

Bustin, R. (2011). The living city: Third Space and the contemporary geography curriculum. *Geography*, 96, 60–68.

Chapman, K. (2016). An English geography curriculum abroad: Using 'Third Space' as an ideal type to understand similarity and difference. *Research in Comparative & International Education*, 11 (4), 357–368.

Chau, D., & Lee, C. (2017). Discursive construction of identities in a social network-educational space: Insights from an undergraduate Facebook group for a linguistics course. *Discourse, Context & Media*, 18(2), 31–39. Dyrness, A., & Hurtig, J. (2016). Migrant Third Space pedagogies: Educative practices of becoming and belonging. *Diaspora, Indigenous, and Minority Education*, 10(4), 185–188.

Evolvi, G. (2017). Hybrid Muslim identities in digital space: The Italian blog Yalla. *Social Compass*, 64(2), 220–232.

Fitts, S. (2009). Exploring Third Space in a dual-language setting: Opportunities and challenges. *Journal of Latinos and Education*, 8(2), 87–104. doi:10.1080/15348430902750668.

Flessner, R. (2009). Working toward a Third Space in the teaching of elementary mathematics. *Educational Action Research*, 17(3), 425–446. doi: doi:10.1080/09650790903093334.

Flessner, R. (2014). Revisiting reflection: Utilizing Third Spaces in teacher education. *The Educational Forum*, 78(3), 231–247.

Food for Us. (2019). Phase one report. Retrieved from http://foodforus.co.za/food-for-us-phase-one-report.

Foucault, M. (1984). *The Foucault reader*, Ed. Paul Rainbow. New York: Pantheon.

Freire, P. (1970). *Pedagogy of the oppressed*. New York: Continuum.
Giroux, H. (2005). The terror of neoliberalism: rethinking the significance of cultural politics. *College Literature*, 32(1), 1–19.
Grant, M. (2019). Difficulties in defining mobile learning: Analysis, design characteristics, and implications. *Education Technology Research & Development*, 67(3), 361–388.
Guerra-Nunez, O. (2017). The use of digital educational technology and Third Spaces with foreign-born Latinos. *Journal of Latinos and Education*, 16(4), 323–337. doi:10.1080/15348431.2016.1257426.
Gutiérrez, K. D. (2008). Developing a sociocritical literacy in the Third Space. *Reading Research Quarterly*, 43(2), 148–164. doi:doi:10.1598/RRQ.43.2.3.
Gutiérrez, K., Baquedano-Lopez, P., & Turner, M. (1997). Putting language back into language arts: When the radical middle meets the Third Space. *Language Arts*, 74(5), 368–378.
Gutiérrez, K., Baquedano-Lopez, P., & Tejada, C. (1999). Rethinking diversity: Hybridity and hybrid language practices in the Third Space. *Mind, Culture, and Activity*, 6(4), 286–303.
Howell, P. B., Sheffield, C. C., Shelton, A. L., & Vujaklija, A. R. (2017). Backchannel discussions during classroom observations: Connecting theory and practice in real time. *Middle School Journal*, 48(2), 24–30. doi:doi:10.1080/00940771.2017.1272919.
Idrus, F. (2015). Examining classroom transformational spaces using the Third Space Theory in developing students' sense of shared identity. *Theory and Practice in Language Studies*, 5(1), 28–37.
Kearney, M., Schuck, S., Burden, K., & Aubusson, P. (2012). Viewing mobile learning from a pedagogical perspective. *Research in Learning Technology*, 20(1). Retrieved from https://doi.org/10.3402/rlt.v20i0/14406.
Kearney, M., Burden, K., & Rai, T. (2015). Investigating teachers' adoption of signature mobile pedagogies. *Computers & Education*, 80(1), 48–57.
Kirkland, D. (2008). "The rose that grew from concrete": Postmodern blackness and new English education. *English Journal*, 97(5), 69–75.
Koole, M., Buck, R., Anderson, K., & Laj, D. (2018). A comparison of the uptake of two research models in mobile learning: The FRAME Model and the 3-Level Evaluation Framework, *Education Sciences*, 8(3), 114.
Kirkland, D. E. (2010). Teaching English in a sea of change: Linguistic pluralism and the new English education . *English Education*, 42(3), 293–306.
Lave, J., & Wenger, E. (1991). *Situated learning: Legitimate peripheral participation*. Cambridge: Cambridge University Press.
Lapp, D., Fisher, D., & Frey, N. (2014). Blended learning as a Third Space. *Voices from the Middle*, 22(2), 7–9.
Levy, R. (2008). 'Third Spaces' are interesting places: Applying 'Third Space theory' to nursery-aged children's constructions of themselves. *Journal of Early Childhood Literacy*, 8(1), 43–66.
Luk-Fong, P. Y. Y. (2010). Towards a hybrid conceptualization of Chinese women primary school teachers' changing femininities: A case study of Hong Kong. *Gender & Education*, 22(1), 73e86.
McDougall, J., Readman, M., & Wilkinson, P. (2018). The uses of (digital) literacy. *Learning, Media and Technology*, 43(3), 263–279. doi:10.1080/17439884.2018.1462206.
Moje, E. B., Ciechanowski, K. M., Kramer, K., Ellis, L., Carrillo, R., & Collazo, T. (2004), Working toward third space in content area literacy: An examination of

everyday funds of knowledge and discourse. *Reading Research Quarterly*, 39, 38–70. doi: doi:10.1598/RRQ.39.1.4.

Moll, L. C., Amanti, C., Neff, D., & Gonzalez, N. (1992). Funds of knowledge for teaching using a qualitative approach to connect homes and classrooms. *Theory into Practice*, 31(2), 132–141.

Organization for Economic Cooperation and Development (OECD). (2018). Preparing our youth for an inclusive and sustainable world: The OECD PISA global competence framework. Retrieved from https://www.oecd.org/education/Global-competency-for-an-inclusive-world.pdf.

Oldenburg, R. (1989). *The great good place*. Cambridge, MA: Da Capo Press.

Schuck, S., & Maher, D. (2018). Creating opportunities for untethered learning. *Technology, Pedagogy and Education*, 26(2), 473–484.

Schuck, S., Kearney, M., & Burden, K. (2017). Exploring mobile learning in the Third Space. *Technology, Pedagogy and Education*, 26(22), 121–137.

Soja, E. (1996). *Third Space, journeys to Los Angeles and other real and imagined places*. Oxford: Blackwell.

Thomas, P., Haug, S., & Enstad, M. (2016). Third Space epistemologies: Ethnicity and belonging in an 'immigrant'-dominated upper secondary school in Norway. *Improving Schools*, 19(3), 212–228.

Turner, A. M. (2016) Third Space openings at a two-way immersion elementary school in North Carolina: Lessons from parent language classes. *Bilingual Research Journal*, 39(2), 107–120. doi: doi:10.1080/15235882.2016.1167138.

Vygotsky, L. (1978) *@Mind in Society*. Cambridge, MA: Harvard University Press.

West, M. (2012). *Turning on mobile learning: Global themes*. UNESCO Working Paper Series on Mobile Learning. Retrieved from http://unesdoc.unesco.org/images/0021/002164/216451E.pdf.

Wenger, E. (1998). *Communities of practice: Learning, meaning, and identity*. Cambridge: Cambridge University Press.

Williams, J. (2013). Boundary crossing and working in the Third Space: Implications for a teacher educator's identity and practice, *Studying Teacher Education*, 9(2), 118–129. doi:10.1080/17425964.2013.808046.

CONCLUSION

Breaking Hegemonic Structures and Conventions in Looking Towards a Critical Mobile Pedagogy

John Traxler and Helen Crompton

Looking Outwards

As the world becomes ever more connected and ever more complex, even those communities at the margins are part of an evolving global context. Some of the components of this global context are the political, the technological, the ecological and the economic; these components are, however, not separate and discrete. This wider global context of learning with mobiles for people and communities who are marginal and disadvantaged consists, *inter alia*, of the global advance of digital technologies alongside the globalisation of many organisations and systems such as education, ongoing environmental degradation, periodic economic crises, political populism and the Fourth Industrial Revolution but is resisted by, for example, ideas of decolonisation, indigeneity, local community, internationalism and climate activism. We are writing in the midst of the COVID-19 pandemic early in 2020 and some analysts would see this as an extreme example of the convergence of some of these trends, specifically increasing urbanisation, promoting the faster spread of infection, environmental degradation, causing the increased mutation of diseases and the rise of populism, with its assaults on the funding of public health services and on international cooperation, and its preference for conspiracy theory over scientific fact. Other analysts may see the COVID-19 pandemic in the bigger picture as basically spontaneous or random, having only local bacteriological causes. Whichever it is may make little difference to its impact, except that the latter analysis presents humanity as nature's victim, whereas the former may hint at the need to prepare for the next pandemic and to expect it sooner rather than later.

We are seeing the rapid, though haphazard, transition to online learning across many sectors in many countries and a renewed interest in 'mobile learning' in its wake. The forms of education – and the economic resources to fund it – on the other side of the pandemic are largely unknowable, as will be the nature of the learning needed to survive and to flourish in this new world. At its margins and at its periphery will still be the people and communities addressed in this book, some of them in some respects insulated from the current crisis and its short and medium-term consequences but most of them probably suffering in the short and medium term because of their inherent exclusion and disenfranchisement. Only time will tell.

The current pandemic is predicted to have a profound impact on societies. Over and above the enormous number of fatalities, the lockdowns will have substantially reconfigured and restructured many national economies, industrial sectors and working practices whilst self-isolation, home-schooling and social distancing will have changed the patterns of social relations, though perhaps less amongst cultures and communities with fewer sophisticated technologies, less economic resources and less industrialised economies. Economic output, at least amongst cash economies, and the sense of economic well-being and security are predicted to plummet and the tax-base that funds most education systems will shrink dramatically. We are, however, seeing a major and possibly permanent transition to all sorts of digital learning in many education systems, including renewed interest in 'mobile learning' alongside an increased use of mobile technologies for all those activities that are not necessarily recognised as education. In advanced economies, different sectors are being affected differently, but in the current context, during lockdown and self-isolation, the digital economy is booming. Whether the communities discussed in this book are disconnected and insulated from these events or are the most vulnerable and exposed to them remains to be seen. Our default assumption is that communities and cultures are all different and that generalisation is impossible.

There are many accounts of, for example, the Internet of Things (IoT), artificial intelligence (AI), robotics (Smith & Anderson, 2014) and more generally the so-called Fourth Industrial Revolution (Bloem, Van Doorn, M., Duivestein, Excoffier, Maas & Van Ommeren, 2014) alongside the 'hollowing-out of the labour market' (McIntosh, 2013). However, these accounts inevitably refer to impact on the mainstream and the established rather than the marginal and the fragile. Likewise, the decline of democratic legitimacy and the rise of populism with its disdain for truth and expertise – implicitly an anti-education posture – are features of so-called advanced societies. So again, it is difficult to predict the impact on those communities on the periphery and at the bottom. Clearly there are arguments in favour of sustainable local livelihoods and resilient local cultures. Our closing objective is to plot a way forward in these uncertain times. The arguments for the place of criticality in pedagogy become ever stronger as the global contexts become more complex and subtle and as considerations of consequences, harm and hegemony become more confused.

Looking Forward

So, given that we started out with a generalised case against 'mobile learning' and we have now heard voices from different developing or disadvantaged communities, what are the pointers to the way forward?

First, we must worry about how much we, working mostly in sophisticated Western environments and mindsets, really know about the lives and aspirations of people in these communities. How authentic and trustworthy is our understanding of their lives, their needs and their aspirations? How is this understanding coloured and filtered by our own interests and conceptions? These are questions about how our knowledge of other societies, communities and cultures was acquired, and about the research tools and research techniques we used. So, we must ask ourselves, are there other research communities beyond conventional 'mobile learning' who might have tools and techniques we could adopt and adapt?

Secondly how can our collaborations and our adapted tools and techniques empower communities to articulate and express their needs and aspirations in ways which will enable us to support and work with them? How can we devise research ethics and research governance that are aligned to empowerment and meaningful collaboration?

Next, what tools and techniques coming out of informal and innovative digital learning might provide the basis for adaptation and adoption? What are the methods and formats that would enable us to explore, evaluate and assess these tools and techniques? How can we integrate or reconcile the various types of constraint and opportunity in each community, those of culture and tradition, those of technology and infrastructure, those of finance, cost and resource and those of livelihood, employment and business?

Lastly, how can communities develop, populate, manage and sustain their own informal digital learning spaces, ones that respond to the changing diversity of their needs and environment, ones that exploit the potential synergies between free and familiar digital systems and that reconcile the tension between their own traditions, language and culture and the opportunities, resources and threats from the wider outside world? Many of the ideas and resources for this work already exist in the research literature. Our claim is not so much about any claim to originality as to the need for collaboration, imagination and synthesis, hoping to bring these resources together. We should look at their potential in more detail.

Research methods

Our basic position must be, 'just because it works for *us* doesn't mean it'll work for *them*'. And perhaps, 'just because it works for some of *them* doesn't mean it'll work for the rest of *them*'. As we move forward, we will add, 'nothing about *us*, without *us*'. Here we review some approaches that could contribute to a research methods toolkit that would help researchers to move towards a better understanding of the communities discussed in this book, in the hope that better mobile pedagogies and better mobile learning spaces might emerge.

Some sources already give us a generic overview of research methods (Desai & Potter 2006) but most lack the digital or learning dimensions. Some do focus on indigenous cultures and others on the mobilities that might characterise some nomadic cultures (Büscher & Urry, 2009). Classical/conventional methods (Binns, 2006; Simonds & Christopher, 2013) in the context of indigenous communities are however problematic, and by the classical/conventional methods, we mean questionnaires, focus groups, semi-structured interviews and surveys, the defaults within the social sciences of the global North. They are problematic in the context of decolonising development studies research (Bozalek, 2011; Heleta, 2016) and might not even be appropriate within some communities in the global North. The critique raised by the sources we cite might however be transferable! The same is true of recent work on decolonising research ethics (Kruger, Ndebele & Horn, 2014). ICT-for-Development (ICT4D) (Unwin & Unwin, 2009; Heeks, 2017) can be educationally simplistic.

The Mobilities Turn

Mobilities (as described, for example, in Urry, 2007) encompass both the large-scale movements of people, objects, capital and information across the world, as well as more local processes of daily transportation, movement through public space and the travel of material things within everyday life. The *mobilities turn* draws on "contributions from anthropology, cultural studies, geography, migration studies, science and technology studies, tourism and transport studies, and sociology" (Sheller & Urry, 2006, p. 208) – but significantly not from education –

> and enables the 'social world' to be theorized as a wide array of economic, social and political practices, infrastructures and ideologies that all involve, entail or curtail various kinds of movement of people, or ideas, or information or objects. This turn brings to the fore theories, methods and exemplars of research that so far have been mostly out of sight. 'Mobilities' is about establishing a 'movement-driven' social science in which movement, potential movement and blocked movement, as well as voluntary/temporary immobilities, practices of dwelling and 'nomadic' place-making are all conceptualized as constitutive of economic, social and political relations.
>
> *(Sheller, 2014, p. 43)*

The mobilities literature already documents how various nomadic communities and individuals produce and consume knowledge and make meaning, and it documents the techniques and methods to explore these activities (Büscher &

Urry, 2009). Mobile devices themselves offer ways to collect these novel channels of learning data through sensors including a microphone, cameras, a gyroscope that determines direction, an accelerometer that provides data on speed, a magnetometer and global positioning system to provide location and compass direction and even a barometer showing atmospheric pressure (Bernacki, Crompton & Greene, 2019) and these could provide a toolkit to explore aspects of the epistemological shifts with an empiricism of mobility.

Personal Construct Theory

Personal construct theory (PCT) suggests that people develop personal constructs, essentially their own theories, about how the world works, frameworks for structuring their experiences, however mundane. People use these constructs to make sense of their observations and experiences and give order to them. The world we live in may be the same for all of us, but the way we experience it will always differ (Kelly, 1970; Horley, 2012). These personal constructs have potential commonalities within cultures and potential differences between cultures. The PCT community has developed research tools and techniques that try as much as possible to elicit ideas and information based on the individual's understanding of their world rather than questions that are derived from the questioner's conception of it, or indeed from the questioner's culture, based around the tacit norms and expectations of the questioner culture. These tools and techniques, sometimes called 'constrained', have been widely used in market research, product design and website development (and other professional and academic disciplines) because they are easy and robust to administer and analyse, with no sophisticated capacity prerequisites or significant technical or infrastructural overheads. They can be used across language and literacy barriers. For our work we intend to explore card-sorts, laddering (Rugg & McGeorge, 2005) and Q-methodology (Hunter, 2014); early relevant work has already been done (Butler, 2004; Bicksler et al., 2012). These tools offer ways to understand those cultures and communities in this book.

Soft Systems Methods

The rich pictures of Soft Systems methods have considerable potential for adaptation.

> Soft systems methodology (SSM) is an approach for tackling problematical, messy situations of all kinds. It is an action-oriented process of inquiry into problematic situations in which users learn their way from finding out about the situation, to taking action to improve it.
>
> *(Checkland & Poulter, 2010)*

They are visual, non-technical and informal.

The starting point for Soft Systems is the rich picture. A group is provided with a blank sheet of 'flip chart' paper and a set of coloured felt-tip pens, ideally of different colour. What goes into the picture, the form of diagrams, the linkages and colours are entirely up to the group. In effect it provides a tangible (albeit 2 dimensional in physical terms) space for the group to discuss, negotiate, share, and hopefully to arrive at a consensus.

(Bell & Morse, 2013 p. 331)

This has great potential in our work across cultures because,

the rich picture used in the Soft System Methodology, offers a way of global communication that far exceeds the limitations of text and speech. Simple graphics can be rapidly communicated, processed and transmitted within a large and culturally diverse constituency.

(Berg & Pooley, 2013, p. 361)

Practical 'how-to' guidance is available (Walker, Steinfort & Maqsood, 2014) derived from use in the field. Simple pictorial techniques help community members represent the interests, factions and transactions in their communities and have value in surfacing different perspectives on contentious issues. They might, for example, help expose friction between women and men in a community, or between subsistence farmers, cash crop farmers and eco-tourism activists.

Human-Computer Interaction for Development

Human-Computer Interaction (HCI) is the exploration of how people work with computers and how an improved design of keyboards, dialogue, screen layout, icons, for example, could improve these interactions. Interaction with mobiles has been a subset of HCI but seems largely untouched from the perspective of the *mobilities turn* and is still largely characterised by a psychological rather than sociological or anthropological mindset. This particular branch (Irani, 2010) of HCI (Preece, Rogers, Sharp, Benyon, Holland, & Carey, 1994) specifically addresses the problems and challenges of using digital technology amongst communities and individuals outside the digitally sophisticated global North (Merritt & Bardzell, 2011; Wyche et al., 2012). This discipline has not focused much on education. Mainstream HCI has focused on formal e-learning and conventional 'mobile learning' (Kumar & Mohite, 2018), but principally in the Global North. HCI4D (Belay, McCrickard & Besufekad, 2016) has developed a range of tools and techniques and devoted some attention to the formats for participative development and co-design.

Delphi

One technique that is extensively used in accessing opinions and views of domain experts (rather than data from research participants) is the Delphi technique (Brady, 2015). Following the Delphi methodology, open-ended questions are asked, and feedback is provided by the group of experts in a discussion with an iterative process, building a consensus. As the literature shows, there is considerable experience in using online and mobile versions and it might be to adapt a version for use in different cultures and communities, with some local 'expertise', especially as a complement to adaptations of some of the other methods we describe. Delphi can also be combined with card sorts (Paul, 2008). The format and process are simple, and resemble a structured conversation where the group of 'experts' – they could be village elders but 'expert' in the given topic – answer a simple open question, hear and consider each other's views and offer a revised answer to the group, and the process repeats until some consensus emerges, or saturation occurs.

Fairer Funding and Fairer Governance

Whilst we might have mentioned methods that would build a better understanding of the needs and aspirations of diverse, different and disparate communities and cultures, working together to build mobile learning spaces obviously requires a rigorous commitment to equity and this surfaces in how research is funded and managed. Obviously building consortia and obtaining research funding is one very important way to carry this work forward. It does however have its challenges. As we start to build consortia and look for partners amongst disadvantaged and disempowered communities, we necessarily break away from established institutions and practices, and it becomes harder to understand the environment and culture in which our potential partners work and consequently harder to create equitable relationships. The established practice across Western Europe might be – and even this is not consistent – that the funder gives the researchers' universities funding to buy the researchers' time for the contracted project. However, even for potential partners working in universities, there may be diversity in their practices; some universities may take the funding but not reduce the researchers' existing workload, some may not value research or partnerships in promotion criteria, some may not pay researchers a living wage so reimbursing that wage would be insulting.

Some external funding might reach consortium partners via some intermediary organisation, a national research council perhaps, but these may not do this promptly and completely. Also, whilst researchers across Western Europe and North America might value peer-reviewed high-impact research papers, researchers elsewhere might value overseas conferences or upgraded equipment.

If, however, the role is not an easily defined one within an established career structure or is actually partly outside the national cash or cheque economy, for example a village elder organising development workshops, then establishing the 'going-rate' for the funder is a challenge. So too might be paying loss-of-earnings honoraria for research participants who are subsistence farmers or nomadic pastoralists outside the cash economy.

Consequently, establishing an equitable consortium, with a budget that fairly distributes what each partner values most, is not easy.

This has to take place, however, within the accounting procedures of the funder, meaning audit trails, receipts, pay-slips, invoices, procurement and data management, and within the categories allowed by the funder, which might still include laptops but will not include an air-conditioned SUV.

The problem could be addressed by building an open and accessible knowledge base, where as many researchers as possible, from as diverse backgrounds as possible, can describe their motivation, their situation and their constraints. This would help anyone building a consortium understand the range of parameters in terms of values, rewards, incentives and remuneration. At the moment many such consortium builders do not know what they do not know, questions can be difficult and embarrassing to ask and there can be a temptation to settle for known partners with established practices rather than reaching out beyond academia and institutes.

Consistency and integrity call for 'decolonising' governance as well as research methods. How can equitable decisions be made across differentials of culture, distance, time-zones, language and experience? It might seem that we have travelled a long way from specific narratives of disadvantaged communities and from a dissatisfaction with 'mobile learning' as currently conceived but practical progress based on rigorous and critical positions must be the next step.

And again, we state our case that the partners we are talking about, away from the established institutions and practices, may not be living in what seem to be exotic locations, they may be communities in the industrialised global North, they may be Roma or homeless or illiterate. They are nonetheless marginal, peripheral and excluded. Heeks' (2008) *ICT4D 2.0* hints at a goal as does the Capability Approach (Kleine & Unwin, 2009), which emphasises the substantive freedoms that people have reason to value and feasibility to achieve, in talking about enabling lives that people themselves value. Our mission in this book is research methods able to find out what those lives might be and use mobile digital pedagogy to bring them about.

Innovative Mobile Digital Learning Tools and Techniques

We can pursue these ideas about research tools, and about research ethics and governance, and they will help us to understand the needs, situations and aspirations of different communities and the place occupied by digital technologies in those communities. Our next question is, how can emerging pedagogic ideas, mediated by mobiles, empower individuals and communities to address these needs, situations and aspirations? What are these ideas and what are the free and familiar digital technologies, mediated through the ubiquitous mobile portal, that might deliver them, whilst enabling a critical pedagogy? Our central concept could be called a community massive online open course (MOOC) (Traxler, 2018a), but this is just a name for the orchestration and coordination of free digital and open mobile digital tools, systems and resources that could produce learning community learning spaces; (De Waard et al., 2012). These emerging pedagogic ideas include:

- critical digital literacy, building the skills, attitudes, competences and knowledge to flourish in an increasingly digital world, and to critique the underlying forces and relations, by *taking a position,* asking, of digital resources and interactions, and of education and training, 'whose interests are being served?' (Bawden, 2008), building on critiques of largely Eurocentric conceptions of digital literacy (Traxler, 2018b);
- curation, the skill of identifying, managing, critiquing, evaluating and exploiting external digital content and communities (Mihailidis & Cohen, 2013);
- personal learning environments, encouraging and enabling learners to customise or create their own digital learning space (Dabbagh & Kitsantas, 2012) and develop a robust digital identity (Alexander, Becker, Cummins & Giesinger, 2017);
- user-generated content, learning by creating shared digital resources (Dyson, 2014), drawing on much older community worker-writer traditions (Pollard, 2012);
- game mechanics, encouraging active and critical digital learning through community review and recommendation (Lameras, Arnab, Dunwell, Stewart, Clarke & Petridis, 2017);
- flipped learning, encouraging engagement and reflection, catalysing discussion and optimising meaningful contact and community (Bishop & Verleger, 2013);
- digital badges and other forms of learning recognition and credentialing (Ostashewski & Reid, 2015);
- open learning, without any barriers, specifically open development, in the sense of 'open international development' (Reilly & Smith, 2013) adapted for learning, open source for systems and technologies (Von Hippel, 2001) and open educational resources (OER) (Butcher 2015; Atkins, Brown & Hammond, 2007) for content;
- e-moderating, the techniques for encouraging online learners to take control of their own learning and move away from a dependence on tutors and teachers (Salmon, 2003), adapted for mobile pedagogy (Brett, 2011);

- heutagogy, a pedagogy articulating the attitudes, methods and tools of self-directed learning, encouraging the locus of control to move towards the learners and the community (Blaschke, 2012).

These ideas might form a starting point for dialogue, inspiration, adaptation and integration. There are already a vast number of free or open mobile digital apps, tools and technologies that could support learning and be designed, or rather co-designed, into mobile digital community spaces in ways that would blend flexibility, ownership, responsiveness and sustainability. There are lists (Traxler, 2019) but these are merely indicative, and hopefully stimulating. Many of the tools in one category are acquiring the functionality of other categories; some are simple, some are complex, some are technical, some are obvious, some require a leap of the imagination. Any prototype community system should start with just a core system as its landing page and evolve as the community's confidence, familiarity and aspirations increase. Subsequent development would be determined by technical issues such as the tariffs, functionality, bandwidth and coverage of mobile devices, cultural issues such as the expectations and experiences of learning and of education, and contextual issues such as livelihoods, regulations, environment and infrastructure, in essence mapping out the 'design space' within which the community could make viable design decisions. How this happens is, however, a design question, a question about the collaborative and participative design and development practices that would match the culture and relationships of any given community (Rodil, Winschiers-Theophilus, Jensen & Rehm, 2012). There are accounts that feature elements of co-design and participation working with widely spread indigenous communities; they offer philosophical foundations and practical tools (Akama, Evans, Keen, McMillan, McMillan & West, 2017). There are already reviews that draw these together (David, Sabiescu & Cantoni, 2013) as well as work that supports the mobile dimension (Dyson, 2014). There are already critiques of existing design practices (Tunstall, 2013) and proposals including education amongst indigenous communities (Kam, Ramachandran, Raghavan, Chiu, Sahni & Canny, 2006). These and others all feature elements of co-design and participation working with widely spread indigenous communities; they offer philosophical foundations and practical tools (Dearden, Rizvi & Gupta, 2010). The new design processes must, however, differ from many earlier documented participative processes (David et al., 2013) in aiming to digitally engage and empower communities, rather than deliver an artefact.

The overarching objective is to explore and develop how these tools, methods and ideas can be applied within an educational, or rather a mobile digital learning, adaptation of Heeks' (2008) *ICT4D 2.0*, describing the move from an ICT4D *pro-poor,* done on their behalf, towards an ICT4D *para-poor,* alongside them, or ICT4D *per-poor,* by them, to governance and project management, and to research methods and research ethics. Heeks also uses the analogy of the long tail

(Seely Brown & Adler, 2008), the capacity of ICT to 'intelligently' and profitably respond to smaller and more diverse needs and communities, and this too is useful in how we think about governance, management and ethics, but also fundamentally how we think about learning.

Next Steps

This book finishes with a beginning, not with a summary but with a call for readers to take forward the ideas and views and to share them, try them, improve them and extend them. We must build networks and connections, of civil society, voluntary sector and community groups, some in developing countries, some at the margins of the developed countries, in order to articulate and test the emergent concepts and practices we have outlined. There should, however, be no expectation that an overarching theory, model or concept would emerge from across these communities or could be developed elsewhere, only the assumption that these various communities are at the margins of the established, the powerful and the mainstream. We would make no assumptions about the nature of learning within any specific cultural context, only that all communities constitute spaces where necessarily information and opinions are acquired, produced and shared, nor any assumptions about preferences for local or external information or the pedagogies by which communities engage with it, nor any assumptions about which digital devices, systems or technologies communities can access and afford.

In many of our contributions there is a tension between the obvious, simple and straightforward ways in which mobile technology can solve people's problems and address people's needs and the more complex, nuanced and problematised ways in which it might disempower or disadvantage them. In some respects, there may be a similar tension around (mobile) digital literacy – some of us ponder the risks of technology-mediated fake-news and post-truth in the context of hegemony and postmodernity whilst bogus transactions, child pornography and identity theft might be simpler and more important concerns for most learners and users, including those in the communities our authors describe. What becomes obvious in comparing the chapters here with the historic 'mobile learning' literature is the pragmatism of doing what works, using what's available and mixing what's necessary rather than the worries about the definitions and demarcations of the research-oriented mobile learning community towards which we hope this book provides the first steps.

References

Akama, Y., Evans, D., Keen, S., McMillan, F., McMillan, M. & West, P. (2017). Designing digital and creative scaffolds to strengthen Indigenous nations: Being Wiradjuri by practising sovereignty. *Digital Creativity*, 28(1), 58–72.

Alexander, B., Becker, S. A., Cummins, M., & Giesinger, C. H. (2017). *Digital literacy in higher education, Part II: An NMC Horizon project strategic brief* (pp. 1–37). Austin, TX: The New Media Consortium.

Atkins, D. E., Brown, J. S., & Hammond, A. L. (2007). *A review of the open educational resources (OER) movement: Achievements, challenges, and new opportunities* (pp. 1–84). Mountain View, CA: Creative Common.

Bawden, D. (2008). Origins and concepts of digital literacy. In C. Lankshear, & M. Knobel (Eds.), *Digital literacies: Concepts, policies and practices*, Vol. 30 (pp.7–32). New York, NY: Peter Lang.

Belay, E. G., McCrickard, D. S., & Besufekad, S. A. (2016). Designing mobile interaction for low-literacy. In K. Awori, & N. J. Bidwell (Eds.), *Proceedings of the First African Conference on Human Computer Interaction* (pp. 251–255). New York, NY: ACM.

Bell, S., & Morse, S. (2013). How people use rich pictures to help them think and act. *Systemic Practice and Action Research*, 26(4), 331–348.

Berg, T., & Pooley, R. (2013). Rich pictures: Collaborative communication through icons. *Systemic Practice and Action Research*, 26(4), 361–376.

Bernacki, M., Crompton, H., & Greene, J. (2019). Towards convergence of mobile and psychological theories of learning contemporary educational psychology. *Contemporary Educational Psychology* 60, 101828.

Bicksler, A., Bates, R., Burnette, R., Gill, T., Meitzner Yoder, L., Ricciardi, V., & Srigiofun, Y. (2012). Methodologies for strengthening informal indigenous vegetable seed systems in northern Thailand and Cambodia. *Acta Horticulturae*, 958, 67–74.

Binns, T. (2006). Doing fieldwork in developing countries: Planning and logistics. In V. Desai, & R. Potter (Eds.), *Doing development research* (pp. 13–24). London: Sage.

Bishop, J. L., & Verleger, M. A. (2013). The flipped classroom: A survey of the research. In *ASEE National Conference Proceedings*, 30(9), pp. 1–18.

Blaschke, L. M. (2012). Heutagogy and lifelong learning: A review of heutagogical practice and self-determined learning. *The International Review of Research in Open and Distributed Learning*, 13(1), 56–71.

Bloem, J., Van Doorn, M., Duivestein, S., Excoffier, D., Maas, R., & Van Ommeren, E. (2014). *The Fourth Industrial Revolution – things to tighten the link between IT and OT*. Groningen, Netherlands: Sogeti VINT.

Bozalek, V. (2011). Acknowledging privilege through encounters with difference: Participatory learning and action techniques for decolonising methodologies in Southern contexts. *International Journal of Social Research Methodology*, 14(6), 469–484.

Brady, S. R. (2015). Utilizing and adapting the Delphi method for use in qualitative research. *International Journal of Qualitative Methods*, 14(5), 1–6.

Brett, P. (2011). Students' experiences and engagement with SMS for learning in higher education. *Innovations in Education and Teaching International*, 48(2), 137–147.

Büscher, M. & Urry, J. (2009) Mobile methods and the empirical. *European Journal of Social Theory* 12(1), 99–116.

Butcher, N. (2015). *A basic guide to open educational resources (OER)*. Vancouver: Commonwealth of Learning.

Butler, C. (2004). Researching traditional ecological knowledge for multiple uses. *Canadian Journal of Native Education*, 28(1/2), 33–48.

Checkland, P., & Poulter, J. (2010). Soft systems methodology. In M. Reynolds, & S. Holwell (Eds.), *Systems approaches to managing change: A practical guide* (pp. 191–242). London: Springer.

Dabbagh, N., & Kitsantas, A. (2012). Personal learning environments, social media, and self-regulated learning: A natural formula for connecting formal and informal learning. *The Internet and Higher Education*, 15(1), 3–8.

David, S., Sabiescu, A. G., & Cantoni, L. (2013). Co-design with communities. A reflection on the literature. In J. Steyn, & B. van der Vyver (Eds.), *Proceedings of the 7th International Development Informatics Association Conference* (pp. 152–166). Pretoria, South Africa: IDIA.

Dearden, A., Rizvi, H. & Gupta, S. (2010). Roles and responsibilities in agile ICT for development. India HCI 2010/Interaction Design & International Development 2010 (IHCI), Mumbai, India.

Desai, V., & Potter, R. (Eds.). (2006). *Doing development research*. Newbury Park, CA: Sage.

De Waard, I., Koutropoulos, A., Hogue, R. J., Abajian, S. C., Keskin, N. Ö., Rodriguez, C. O., & Gallagher, M. S. (2012). Merging MOOC and mLearning for increased learner interactions. *International Journal of Mobile and Blended Learning*, 4(4), 34–46.

Dyson, L. E. (2014). Framing the indigenous mobile revolution. In L. E. Dyson, S. Grant, & M. Hendriks (Eds.), *Indigenous people and mobile technologies* (pp. 15–36). New York, NY: Routledge.

Heeks, R. (2008) ICT4D 2.0: The next phase of applying ICT for international development. *Computer*, 41(6), 26–33.

Heeks, R. (2017). *Information and communication technology for development (ICT4D)*. New York, NY: Routledge.

Heleta, S. 2016, Decolonisation of higher education: Dismantling epistemic violence and Eurocentrism in South Africa. *Transformation in Higher Education*, 1(1), 1–8.

Horley, J. (2012). Personal construct theory and human values. *Journal of Human Values*, 18(2), 161–171.

Hunter, W. C. (2014). Performing culture at indigenous culture parks in Taiwan: Using Q method to identify the performers' subjectivities. *Tourism Management*, 42, 294–304.

Irani, L. (2010). HCI on the move: Methods, culture, values. In E. Mynatt, D. Schoner, G. Fitzpatrick, S. Hudson, K. J. Edwards, T. Rodden (Eds.), *CHI'10 extended abstracts on human factors in computing systems* (pp. 2939–2942). New York, NY: ACM.

Kam, M., Ramachandran, D., Raghavan, A., Chiu, J., Sahni, U., & Canny, J. (2006). Practical considerations for participatory design with rural school children in underdeveloped regions: Early reflections from the field. In K.-J. Räihä, & J. Höysniemi (Eds.), *Proceedings of the 2006 Conference on Interaction Design and Children* (pp. 25–32). New York, NY: ACM.

Kelly, G. A. (1970). A brief introduction to personal construct theory. *Perspectives in Personal Construct Theory*, 1, 1–25.

Kleine, D., & Unwin, T. (2009). Technological revolution, evolution and new dependencies: What's new about ICT4D? *Third World Quarterly*, 30(5), 1045–1067.

Kruger, M., Ndebele, P. & Horn, Lyn. (2014). *Research ethics in Africa: A resource for research ethics committees*. Stellenbosch: Sun Media.

Kumar, B. A., & Mohite, P. (2018). Usability of mobile learning applications: A systematic literature review. *Journal of Computers in Education*, 5(1), 1–17.

Lameras, P., Arnab, S., Dunwell, I., Stewart, C., Clarke, S., & Petridis, P. (2017). Essential features of serious games design in higher education: Linking learning attributes to game mechanics. *British Journal of Educational Technology*, 48(4), 972–994.

McIntosh, S. (2013). Hollowing out and the future of the labour market. *BIS Research Paper Number* 134. London: Department for Business, Innovation and Skills.

Conclusion 225

Merritt, S., & Bardzell, S. (2011). Postcolonial language and culture theory for HCI4D. In D. Tan, B. Begole, W. A. Kellogg (Eds.), *CHI'11 extended abstracts on human factors in computing systems* (pp. 1675–1680). New York, NY: ACM.

Mihailidis, P. & Cohen, J. N. (2013). Exploring curation as a core competency in digital and media literacy education. *Journal of Interactive Media in Education*, (1), part 2, 1–19.

Ostashewski, N., & Reid, D. (2015). A history and frameworks of digital badges in education. In T. Reiners & L. C. Wood (Eds.), *Gamification in education and business* (pp. 187–200). Cham, Switzerland: Springer International Publishing.

Paul, C. L. (2008). A modified Delphi approach to a new card sorting methodology. *Journal of Usability Studies*, 4(1), 7–30.

Pollard, N. (2012) Occupational narratives, community publishing and worker writing groups. *Groupwork*, 20(1), 9–33.

Preece, J., Rogers, Y., Sharp, H., Benyon, D., Holland, S., & Carey, T. (1994). *Human-computer interaction*. Boston: Addison-Wesley Longman Ltd.

Reilly, K. M. A. & Smith M. L. (2013). The emergence of open development in a network society. In M. Smith & K. Reilly (Eds.), *Open development: Networked innovations in international development* (pp. 15–50). Cambridge, MA: The MIT Press.

Rodil, K., Winschiers-Theophilus, H., Jensen, K. L., & Rehm, M. (2012). Homestead creator: A tool for indigenous designers. In L. Malmborg, & T. Pederson (Eds.), *Proceedings of the 7th Nordic Conference on Human-Computer Interaction: Making sense through design* (pp. 627–630). New York, NY: ACM.

Rugg, G., & McGeorge, P. (2005). The sorting techniques: A tutorial paper on card sorts, picture sorts and item sorts. *Expert Systems*, 22(3), 94–107.

Salmon, G. (2003). *E-moderating: The key to teaching and learning online*. London: Psychology Press.

Seely Brown, J., & Adler, R. P. (2008). Open education, the long tail, and learning 2.0. *Educause Review*, 43(1), 16–20.

Sheller, M. (2014). The new mobilities paradigm for a live sociology. *Current Sociology*, 62(6), 789–811.

Sheller, M. & Urry, J. (2006) The new mobilities paradigm. *Environment and Planning*, 38, 207–226.

Simonds, V. W., & Christopher, S. (2013). Adapting Western research methods to indigenous ways of knowing. *American Journal of Public Health*, 103(12), 2185–2192.

Smith, A., & Anderson, J. (2014). *AI, robotics, and the future of jobs* (p. 6). Washington, DC: Pew Research Center.

Traxler, J. (2018a). Community MOOCs – back to basics, back to the future. In D. Jansen (Ed.), *OpenupEd Report: Latest Trends on MOOCs*. The Hague, Netherlands: EADTU.

Traxler, J. (2018b). Digital literacy: A Palestinian refugee perspective. *Research in Learning Technology*, 26, 1–21.

Traxler, J. (2019). Only connect: Indigenous digital learning. *Interaction Design & Architecture(s)*, 41, 7–23.

Tunstall, E. (2013). Decolonizing design innovation: Design anthropology, critical anthropology, and indigenous knowledge. In W. Gunn, T. Otto, & R. C. Smith (Eds.), *Design anthropology: Theory and practice* (pp. 232–250). London: Bloomsbury.

Unwin, P. T. H., & Unwin, T. (Eds.). (2009). *ICT4D: Information and communication technology for development*. Cambridge: Cambridge University Press.

Urry, J. (2007). *Mobilities*. London: Polity.

Von Hippel, E. (2001). Learning from open-source software. *MIT Sloan Management Review*, 42(4), 82–86.
Walker, D., Steinfort, P., & Maqsood, T. (2014). Stakeholder voices through rich pictures. *International Journal of Managing Projects in Business*, 7(3), 342–361.
Wyche, S. P., Oreglia, E., Ames, M. G., Hoadley, C., Johri, A., Sengers, P., & Steinfield, C. (2012). Learning from marginalized users: Reciprocity in HCI4D. In S. Poltrock, C. Simone, J. Grudin, G. Mark, & J. Riedl (Eds.), *Proceedings of the ACM 2012 Conference on Computer Supported Cooperative Work Companion* (pp. 27–28). New York, NY: ACM.

LIST OF CONTRIBUTORS

Poline Bala is an Associate Professor in the Faculty of Social Sciences, and a research fellow at the Institute of Social Informatics and Technological Innovations, University Malaysia Sarawak (UNIMAS). She obtained her PhD in 2008 from Cambridge University. Her area of interest and research includes the impact of political boundaries on the formation of cultural, political, and economic units in the border regions of Borneo. Most recently her research explores the role of technology in the social transformation of Sarawak, particularly the introduction of information communication technology (ICT) in rural areas. She is the knowledge engineer and domain specialist of the community-led massive open online courses (MOOCs) for the UNIMAS Competen-SEA project.

Jonathan T. Bartels is a teacher educator and visiting professor at Grand Valley State University, Allendale, Michigan; in his current position, he teaches courses on research methodologies, the historical and socio-cultural foundations of the American educational system, and the socio-cultural perspectives of literacies. His research focuses on the intersection of new literacies and popular technologies – particularly social media.

Matthew Bennice is a Special Education teacher with the Anchorage School District. He grew up in Bethel, Alaska and has lived in Anchorage for the past 20 years. He attended the University of Alaska Anchorage where he earned a BA in English and an MA in Teaching. He began his teaching career in the village of Nunapitchuk, Alaska.

Meaghan Brugha is an experienced researcher with particular emphasis on the use of technology in education. Alongside her work as Senior Researcher at

Jigsaw Consult, she is currently completing her PhD at the University of Cambridge with a research focus on teacher professional development and the role of technology to support classroom dialogue.

Belinda Daniels is the founder of the *nehiyawak* Language Experience (15 years) and teaches others how to teach Cree as a second language or speak Cree in various First Nations communities and urban cities. Belinda won the Outstanding Canadian Aboriginal Educator Award in 2015. Belinda is currently a doctoral candidate at the University of Saskatchewan and visiting scholar of the University of Tromso, Norway, 2019. She is an avid volunteer for her community of Saskatoon and Sturgeon Lake First Nation, SK.

Elena Deleyto La Cruz carries out her role as Commissioning Editor for Digital Learning Associates from Barcelona. A media graduate with a combined experience in language instruction, Spanish-English translation, and children's fiction publishing, she currently designs strategies for scaled English learning using media and technology. For the last two years, Elena has taken a leading role in the development of materials for English language acquisition in emergency settings.

Angela Gerrard is Senior Researcher and Project Manager for the Wales-based Pontydysgu Ltd. Working from her remote office in Pontypridd she specializes in technology for education and professional development for educators as well as media and digital literacies.

Catherine Gladwell has specialized in education and forced migration for the last 15 years. She is the Chief Executive of the education charity Refugee Support Network, and a board member at Jigsaw Consult. She has a degree from Oxford University, a master's in Education and International Development from the University of London, and is an honorary fellow at Winchester University.

Stephen Haggard is a graduate of King's College, Cambridge and the London School of Oriental and African Studies, whose career as a broadcasting executive took a turn towards learning when, in 2001, the BBC appointed him to transform its film partnership with the Open University into an online and digital-first model. He went on to work in senior roles in several e-learning organizations, including Africa's largest low-cost mobile learning provider Eneza Education, before co-founding the education content company Digital Learning Associates in 2016. As a director he sets strategy for its mobile learning business on five continents, and leads worldwide teams (including subcontractors) developing digital content.

Cheryle Herman is currently employed with the Meadow Lake Tribal Council as Superintendent of Education. She is from Treaty 8 territory and is a member of the Clearwater River Dene Nation in Saskatchewan. After her eight-year career as a First Nations and Métis Consultant with Northern Lights School Division No. 113, Cheryle has continued her work in languages as a Dene Language Consultant where she was appointed to her current position.

David Hollow is the team leader of Jigsaw Consult, an independent research organization working in the international development and humanitarian sectors. He holds a PhD in Development Geography from the University of London. David is Research Director for the Department for International Development (DFID) EdTech Hub and Chair of the Board for Justice Defenders and a trustee for Refugee Support Network.

Rebecca Kelly is a PhD student in the School of Education at the University of Hull.

Saila Kokkonen worked with Funzi projects and the Community and Ambassador Program 2016–2019. She currently works as Producer on the Funzi premium course library.

Marguerite Koole has a PhD in e-Research and Technology-Enhanced Learning from Lancaster University, UK and a Master of Education in Distance Education from Athabasca University, Canada. Dr Koole has studied French, Spanish, German, Blackfoot, Cree, Latin, Mandarin, ancient Mayan hieroglyphics, and linguistics. She has worked in online and distance education for over 15 years. During that time, she has been involved in teaching, instructional design, multimedia programming, content management, e-portfolios, and social software. Dr Koole is currently working in the area of Indigenous language revitalization and maintenance through learning technology.

Narayanan Kulathuramaiyer has served almost three decades in academia as one of the pioneer staff of Faculty of Computer Science and Information Technology (IT) at the Universiti Malaysia Sarawak (UNIMAS). He is currently the Director of the Institute of Social Informatics and Technological Innovations (ISITI) at UNIMAS. He received his PhD in Computer Science from Graz University of Technology, Austria. He is the team leader and the designer of the community-led MOOCs for the UNIMAS Competen-SEA project.

Kevin (*wâsakâyâsiw*) Lewis is a *nêhiyaw* (Plains Cree) instructor, researcher, and writer. Dr Lewis has worked with higher learning institutions within the Prairie Provinces of Manitoba, Saskatchewan, and Alberta in the areas of Cree language development and instructional methodologies. For the past 15 years, Dr Lewis has been working with community schools in promoting land and language-based education and is founder of *kâniyâsihk* Culture Camps (www.kaniyasihkculture camps.com), a non-profit organization focused on holistic community well-being and co-developer of the Land-Based Cree Immersion School *kâ-nêyâsihk mîkiwâhpa*. Dr Lewis is from Ministikwan Lake Cree Nation in Treaty 6 Territory.

Candi Miller, a writer of ethnologically-informed fiction, attempts to rethink research narratives to offer a culturally appropriate response to particular problems. She is a Senior Lecturer in Creative and Professional Writing at the University of Wolverhampton.

Dick Ng'ambi is an associate professor and a leading researcher in mobile learning in resource-constrained environments. He works at the School of Education at the University of Cape Town (UCT), South Africa. He is the Head of Educational Technology programs. He is the founder and Project Director of the Educational Technology Inquiry Lab (ETILAB). He is a rated researcher by the National Research Foundation. He holds a PhD in Information Systems from UCT, a master's degree in Computer Science from Birmingham University, and a Bachelor of Science degree in Mathematics from the University of Zambia.

Amit Pariyar is a Postdoctoral Researcher at the Institute of Social Informatics and Technological Innovations (ISITI) in Universiti Malaysia Sarawak (UNIMAS). He received his PhD in Informatics from Kyoto University, Japan. His research papers are published in the Institute of Electrical and Electronics Engineers (IEEE) and Springer in the proceedings of international conferences and journals related to culture computing, social informatics, information and knowledge management. His research interests are in the areas of Knowledge Management, Social Informatics, and ICT4D.

Aape Pohjavirta is President and Founder of Funzi, and an active entrepreneurship coach and speaker at conferences, in universities, and in entrepreneurship programs.

Miemo Penttinen is Chief Experience Officer and is responsible for all things design at Funzi and functions as the Head of Product.

Isabella Rega is Principal Academic in Digital Literacies and Education and Deputy Head of the Centre of Excellence in Media Practice at Bournemouth University. She is also Global Research Director of the Jesuit Worldwide Learning: Higher Education at the Margins.

Gill Ryan uses open learning to engage disadvantaged learners and develop pathways into higher education as part of the Access, Participation and Success team in The Open University in Scotland. She is co-host, with Gabi Witthaus, of the Refugee Learning Stories blog.

Christelle Scharff is a Professor of Computer Science at Pace University in New York. She has a PhD in Computer Science from the French Institute for Research in Computer Science and Automation (INRIA) in France. Her current research focuses on Information and Communications Technologies for Development (ICTD). She was awarded two US Fulbright scholarships to Senegal.

Sara Vannini is Lecturer at the University of Sheffield Information School. Her research is at the intersection of critical studies of technology and society, social change, and information ethics.

Ruth Wallace is the Dean of the College of Indigenous Futures, Arts and Society, and Director of the Northern Institute at Charles Darwin University.

Greg Williams is the Assistant Dean Learning Futures in the College of Indigenous Futures, Arts and Society at Charles Darwin University (CDU). He teaches in the field of Indigenous studies and Indigenous policy and coordinates the Master of Public Policy in the CDU's Northern Institute. His research interests lie in examining epistemological and pedagogical processes for intercultural learning environments.

Gabi Witthaus is a learning designer at the University of Birmingham and an independent consultant and researcher focusing on learning design, open and online learning, and pathways into and through higher education for all. Gabi blogs at www.artofelearning.org and can be found on Twitter at @twitthaus.

INDEX

African Storybook (ASB) 18
agglutinative languages: Cree, 126; Dene, 126
Alaska, study of digital literacies and literacy practices 52–53; cultural standards in curriculum, 59–60; graduation rates, 55; history of education, 56; location, 53; native ways of learning, 54–55; non-verbal gestures and cues, 55; participants, 53; technological access and use, 56–58; technological instruction and support, 58–59; western education, 55–56
Alaska Native Knowledge Network (ANKN) 55
Alliance for Affordable Internet 27–28
AM/FM radio 26–27
analytic-synthetic language continuum *126*
ARADES 66
artificial intelligence (AI) 28
asylum seekers 24, 76–78

Bead artefacts *99*
Bhabha, Homi 82
Biesele, Megan 13
bite-sizing content 30
blended learning programmes 153
Bluetooth 113
Bridges Programmes 80, 83
British Council mobile learning solution 176

BTEC 165
business process outsourcing (BPO) 169

camp-based refugees 151
cascading style sheets (CSS) 27
case study: going digital with the beads 96
Chinese handsets 69, 72
citizen developers 137
citizen development *138*
collaboration 200
Common European Framework of Reference for Languages (CEFR) 184
community-based activities 133
community-oriented learning 41–2
community technology centres (CTCs) 112–13; context and needs of, 114; CTC-owned tablets, 115; in Latin America, 119; mobile-related initiatives, 113
conferencing tools 132
Connected Learning in Crisis Consortium 152
content delivery on web 27
core learning loop 30, *31*
cost of acquisition (CAC) of learners 177
Coursera 36, 78
critical learning process 31
curriculum design 117–118
cyberbullying 116, 140
CyberCafé 65

democracy 201
democratic education: goal of, 139

Index

design thinking process 141
digital and mobile learning environments 190
digital divide 50–51; access/use inequalities, 51; case study, 52–53; cultural inequities, 52; digital inequities, 52; instruction/support inequalities, 51
digital environments, 187
Digital Equity Summit 50
Digital Learning Associates for educational projects 162, 178
digital learning environments 186, 189
digital learning resources 76
digital literacy 63, 111; curricula, 111; defined, 111; skills, 112–113
digital technologies 187
Dysgu Ponty model 40–41

e-Bario Project 98
EdTech industry 162
educational applications 199
educational institutional action 193
Educational Technology Inquiry Lab (ETILAB) 144, 148
edX platform 104
e-learning business 28–29
empathy 141
empathy-driven mobile app development process **146**
empathy-led designs 141
empathy map 141, *142*
empathy mapping tool 141
English and Development: Policy, Pedagogy and Globalization 168
English language teaching (ELT) 166
English language teaching (ELT) experts 175
entrepreneurship 32–33, 35
Erasmus+ Our Town project; 40, 42–43, 48; languages used, 44–46
Ethiopian refugee context 185
Ethiopia's Agency for Refugee and Returnee Affairs 177
exclusion 13; from digital connectivity, 18

Facebook 65, 155; free basics 28
fairer funding and fairer governance 218–19
Filming model teacher instruction *179*
First Nations Control of First Nations Education 125
First Nations Media Australia (FNMA) 192
First Nations Reserve communities 132

flexible open spaces 204
folk wisdom 18
footprint 124
Fourth Industrial Revolution (4IR) 137
Funzi Ambassadors 36
Funzi service 22–23, *24,* 29–30; audience for, 23–24; blended learning programs, 35–36; entrepreneurship course, 32–33, 35; informational and upskilling services for refugee, 33–35; key learnings, 36–37; language and tone of voice, 30; learner feedback, 31; scalability of, 24
fusional languages 126

game-inspired behavioral patterns, for pedagogy 29–30
Gartner technology hype cycle *25,* 25–26
Giddens' theory 140
Global South mobile education projects 162
Google 65
Google Docs 113
growth mindset 31–32
GSMA mobile internet skills training toolkit 65
GSM Association study 154

Human-Computer Interaction (HCI) 217
hybrid discourse 200–201
hybridity 82
hybrid/mixed-mode learning 152
Hype cycle *138*
hypertext markup language (HTML) 27

incorporating language 126
indigenous knowledge (IK) 59
indigenous language 123
informational and upskilling services for refugee 33–35
information and communications technology (ICT): literacy 159; skills 154
information literacy 111; defined, 111
information technology 18; reach of, 24–25; robust *vs* fragile, 25–26, *29*
institutional policy 192
institutional practice 191–192
intellectual property (IP) acquisition 168
interactive webinar 164
International agency support 178
International Covenant on Economic, Social and Cultural Rights 151

234 Index

International Telecommunication Union (ITU) 89
International Trade Centre and Zimba Women 35
internet penetration 27
InZone 80–81, 83
iPac Framework *206*
iPhone 27

Ju|'hoan group 11–12; children's stories, 18; keyboard for androids, 13; problem-solving based thinking, 18; tuberculosis and alcohol addiction, 12; wag, 13

Kalahari Passage 11
Kearney, Matthew 163
key performance indicator (KPI) 167
kinship groups 12
Kiron Open Higher Education 81
knowledge-making processes 190
Kolmogorov-Smirnov statistical test 182

land-based learning 128
language 123, 170
language characteristics 126; incorporating, 126; polysynthetic, 126
Language for Resilience (L4R) 177
language reclamation 124–125; great multitudes, 124; strategies and approaches to, 125
language revitalization **128**
language teachers 128
language teaching and learning: technology in 131–132; Unicode system 131
language teaching strategies **129**
learner activation 31–32
learning 22
learning cards 30
learning context 93; physical factors, 94; psychological factors, 94; social factors, 94
Learning for Development (L4D) sector 165
learning in displaced communities, motivations for 77–78
Learning Regions and Learning Cities 46–47
linguistic characteristics and writing systems 126
linguistic systems and practices 124
low-code development tools 137
low to middle income countries (LMICs) 27–28

The Machine for Making Things Easier 13–17
Massive Open Online Courses (MOOCs) 89; assumption to inclusion, 92; challenges in contextualizing, 100; community led, 96, *97*; community participation, 92, 102; cultural sensitivity, 101; design model, 101; educational paradigm, 89; gaps in, *91*; inclusive learning for participatory, *92*; Kelabit beads and cultural significance, 98; learning context, 103; module, *102*; model for inclusive learning, 91; platforms 78, 82; production of, 101; with social purpose, 96
migrants 24
mobile and digital environment, 189
mobile app builders, 149
mobile app building blocks, 144f
Mobile Assisted Third Space (MATS), 197, 202; in action, 207
mobile digital learning environments, 186
Mobile Digital Learning Tools and Techniques, 219–22
mobile digital literacy, 64; difficulties with routine uses, 69–70; effectiveness of videos, 70–1; limitations of handsets, 69; mobile phone usage patterns, 67–9; motivations in learning, 69; research methodology, 66–7; scalability of teaching, 65; security and privacy concerns, 70; toolkit, 65–6, 71–2, **72**; usability issues, 70
mobile information literacy(MIL) 111, 113; activities, 118; concepts, 111; curricular, 113, 119; defined, 111–12; digital literacy, 111; educational initiatives, 119; practices, 116; relevant topics, 119; specific curricula, 118
mobile language tools 132
mobile learning 48, 76, 89, 163; and education policy, 194; challenges in, 78–9; mode of production, 166; projects, 163; programmes, 164; for Refugee Teachers, 177
mobile learning materials: contract-based production of, 167
mobile operating system 27
mobile-predominant access 110
mobile-related learning activities 115
mobiles and computers 115
mobile technologies 110, 113–114, 191
mobile web 28
multiculturalism, 82

Index   235

Namibian Broadcasting Corporation (NBC) 18
Netflix 59
New Refugee Doctors 83
non-reflexive feedback cycle 140
Nyae Nyae Conservancy 12

Old Bridge 40
Online Program Managers (OPMs) 167
Open Access Centre 80
open educational resources (OERs) 79–81, 83
Open University in Scotland (OUiS) 80
'Opera Mini' Wikipedia 27
operating system (OS) 24

pedagogical models 187–189
Pedagogy in Process: The Letters to Guinea-Bissau 164
Personal construct theory (PCT) 216
power-sharing dialogue 205
problem-solving mindsets 139
Program for Migrant Integration 33
programme models 158
programme strengths 154

quality education 24
quick response (QR) codes 39, 41–42, 44, 48

rapid application development (RAD) platforms 137, 143
reading-writing literacy 13
Reflecting on Transitions 83
reflections, 144–145, 202
refugee camp schools, **180**
Refugee Journey Map, 33, *34*
refugee learners 151
relational empiricism 190
remote tutoring 164
research funding 18
residential schools 123
resource-constrained environments 137
robust technology 25–27; innovation in, 28–29; mobile web, 28
Rosenworcel 50
rural defined, 54; remote-rural communities, 54

Salt & Honey 11
San folktales 17
San projects 17–18
school-based programming 132
scientific consensus 11

The Season of the Researcher 18–20
self-directed neuroplasticity 31
Senge, Peter 22
smartphone-centric access 111
smart phones 19
Snapchat 59
social cohesion 22
Social Media 113
social media campaigns 35
social practice 139
solar panels 19
special educational needs (SEN) 205
storytelling 11
storytelling collaboration techniques 18
structuration theory 139–141; aim of, 139
Sub-Saharan Africa, mobile subscription rates 25
system-based policies 123

Tagish language 60
tangible factors 95
teacher training 128
Teacher Online Professional Development Initiative 175
technology 12
technology-based data collection systems 157
technology-dependent programmes 159
technology-enhanced higher education for refugees 159; background, 151; connectivity and hardware, 156; programme structure, pedagogy, and use of technology, 153; research study, 152; student and staff perspectives, 154–155
technology-enhanced learning, 157–158
Technology Trigger 27
The Great Good Place 198
The Truth and Reconciliation Commission 125
Third Space 82–83
third space: mobile assisted third spaces 205–206; and mobile learning, 204; technology supported, 203
Third Space: Journeys to Los Angeles and Other Real and Imagined Places 198
Third Space teaching/learning 199
Third Space Theory 197–199
Threading Beads 105
tone of voice 30
transferability 202
transformation 201–202
Translators Without Borders (TWB) 184
Trello *103*
Tuckett, Alan 13

UNDRIP Declaration 126
United Nations Children's Fund (UNICEF) 163, 184
United Nations Declaration on the Rights of Indigenous Peoples 125
United Nations High Commissioner for Refugees (UNHCR) 76, 151, 163, 177
Universal Declaration of Human Rights 151
user interface (UI) 24

Viber 155
visual communication 29–30

walled garden 110
WAP 27
Westbury Youth Centre (Mashup Community Development) 35
WhatsApp 65, 113, 155
Wikipedia 65
workplace study 164
writing systems 127

Xylagani Folklore Museum, 46

YGG Pont Sion Norton, Pontypridd, 45, *45*
YouTube 65

Printed in the United States
By Bookmasters